THE
BOYS
IN THE
LIGHT

ALSO BY NINA WILLNER

Forty Autumns

THE BOYS IN THE LIGHT

AN EXTRAORDINARY
WORLD WAR II STORY OF
SURVIVAL, FAITH, AND BROTHERHOOD

NINA WILLNER

DUTTON

DUTTON
An imprint of Penguin Random House LLC
1745 Broadway, New York NY 10019
penguinrandomhouse.com

Copyright © 2025 by Nina Willner

Penguin Random House values and supports copyright. Copyright fuels creativity, encourages diverse voices, promotes free speech, and creates a vibrant culture. Thank you for buying an authorized edition of this book and for complying with copyright laws by not reproducing, scanning, or distributing any part of it in any form without permission. You are supporting writers and allowing Penguin Random House to continue to publish books for every reader. Please note that no part of this book may be used or reproduced in any manner for the purpose of training artificial intelligence technologies or systems.

DUTTON and the D colophon are registered trademarks of Penguin Random House LLC.

LIBRARY OF CONGRESS CATALOGING-IN-PUBLICATION DATA
has been applied for.

ISBN 9780593471272 (hardcover)
ISBN 9780593471289 (ebook)

Printed in the United States of America

1 3 5 7 9 10 8 6 4 2

The authorized representative in the EU for product safety and compliance is Penguin Random House Ireland, Morrison Chambers, 32 Nassau Street, Dublin D02 YH68, Ireland, https://eu-contact.penguin.ie.

For Auguste and Siegfried

A person is only forgotten when his or her name is forgotten.
—The Talmud

CONTENTS

Preface   1

PART I

1. American Innocence   5
2. A German Jewish Boy   13
3. Patriots and Parasites   21
4. Rise of Hate   29
5. Promise   37
6. Kristallnacht   41
7. Blue Ribbon America   46
8. On the Run   56
9. Training   61
10. The Vineyards   67
11. New York Harbor   70
12. Transport 31   72

CONTENTS

PART II

13.	Ship to England	81
14.	Łazy	87
15.	Coming Ashore	93
16.	Auschwitz	97
17.	Baptism	108
18.	North Plant	120
19.	"*Kom Goed Thuis*"	130
20.	Thanksgiving	146
21.	Siegfried's Prophecy	159

PART III

22.	Christmas Eve	167
23.	*Butch*	176
24.	The Long March	181
25.	The Talisman	187
26.	The Tunnels	195
27.	The Prayer	201
28.	Breakout	209
29.	Angels	216
30.	"They're with Us Now"	222
31.	Big Brothers	229
32.	Unbreakable Bond	234
33.	Liberation	239
34.	The Final Goodbye	247

CONTENTS

PART IV

35. "I Want Those Days Back"	253
36. The Call	264
37. The Reunion	271
38. Postscript	278
Coda: Supper with Uncle Pepsi	281
Epilogue	283
Acknowledgments	*291*
Notes	*299*
Selected Bibliography	*347*
Index	*349*

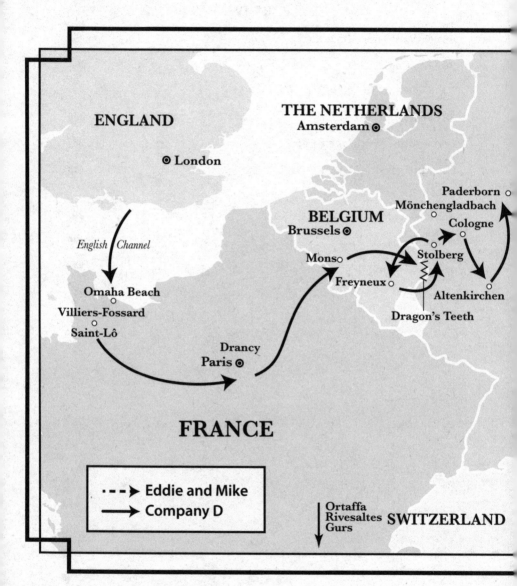

*Using the boundaries of today's European political map.

THE
BOYS
IN THE
LIGHT

PREFACE

December 2016
Waltham, Massachusetts

IN A TINY Catholic church, a large Jewish family comes in from out of town and files into a modest funeral service that will honor a local man, an Italian American, a hometown fixture who once ran the Monarch Diner on Main Street. As neighbors, friends, old customers, and the parish community crowd into the chapel, the seemingly out-of-place family fills up the entire second pew, reserved for the closest relatives. While everyone else has come to honor the life of a man they knew as Sammy, the Jewish family called him Uncle Pepsi. But he wasn't really their uncle, and his name wasn't really Pepsi.

Winter 1938
Mönchengladbach, Germany

Together they hurried over the cobblestones, leading their boy firmly by the hand as bright red, white, and black Nazi flags snapped in the wind.

At the train station, his mother bent down, pulled his coat collar up against the chill. One last time she checked to make sure the note pinned to the inside of his coat was securely fastened. It was, in essence, a plea, asking a stranger in another country to find him, take him in, and give him refuge. These were dangerous times and this was a desperate act of love.

"Don't be afraid," his mother said as she brushed his cheek with the back of her hand.

"Be a good boy," his father said. "We will find you."

Six years later
Somewhere in the forest, Saxony-Anhalt, Germany

Second by second, the escape team shifted glances at one another to get a pulse on what others were thinking. Just then, a lone British fighter was spotted in the sky, and the guards ordered their prisoners off the road so they could not be seen from the air. It was exactly the distraction they had been waiting for. Eyes locked, and their leader yelled, "Go!"

They took off, scattering in different directions, and then all hell broke loose. An explosion of machine-gun fire ripped through the ranks and raked their path; the attack dogs were released. Through a hail of bullets, two teens made a run for the water, sprinting down the grassy bank while others in their group were shot down in the melee. Desperation running through their veins, they ran so fast, they tore up the light and flung themselves into the river.

A few days later, a bow gunner peered through his periscope and shouted at the driver to stop. In the first morning rays of sunlight streaming through the trees, they jolted to a halt. The tank commander called over the radio, "Lieutenant, you better get up here. There's something you're gonna wanna see."

PART I

ONE

AMERICAN INNOCENCE

The 1930s

It always starts with innocence.

EIGHT-YEAR-OLD ELMER HOVLAND stood steadfast on the dusty plains beneath the big open skies of Kenneth, Minnesota, wheat-blond hair waving in the wind, his clear blue eyes taking on the color of the sky.

His parents, Nels and Mary, were devout Lutheran immigrants from Oppland, Norway, who, in the late 1890s, along with a million other Norwegians, left poverty and hunger in their homeland for a pioneering life on the great plains of Minnesota.

They lived at first in a sod house, then eventually settled into a simple log home they built themselves, a spartan dwelling with no electricity or modern conveniences, with an icebox to keep food cold and a wood-burning cast-iron cookstove, which helped heat the home. They drew their water from a well and had an outhouse in the backyard. It was the definition of an austere life.

Moving to a new country was difficult enough, but the Great Depression brought hard times and distress, especially in the farming sector. Despite the hardships, the Hovlands settled into their new life on Dakota tribal land platted only at the turn of the century, with towns seven miles apart, because that's as far as you could go in one day in a horse and buggy.

They set up a farm just outside Kenneth, population 118, a tranquil town one square mile in size with one crossroad, and became a part of the patchwork fabric of Scandinavian immigrant families drawn by the timber, mining, and farming industries rooted in Minnesota's barren, windswept plains, river valleys, and cold climate. In many ways it was not unlike the land they had left behind.

The Hovlands and those like them lived in relative isolation, but there was new opportunity for growth and prosperity in this land of rolling hills and fertile black soil borne of flat lake plains. The family grew corn, wheat, and barley and raised dairy cows and chickens, laboring on a land that carried its story in the winds of its dusty promise. Unable to cope with the changes and homesickness, many went back to the land of the midnight sun, but the Hovlands stayed on and built a life.

By 1930, they were living an uncomplicated existence grounded in hard work, their days marked by sobriety and an abstemious reverence for the pure and simple.

Guided by their deep Lutheran faith, a pious family who believed in the power of prayer, the Hovlands bowed their heads at every meal, prayed over their crops, knelt bedside at night, and woke up every morning asking for God's blessings on every new day.

Faith helped them weather every challenge they encountered, from the heavy black clouds of the Depression years to droughts that marred the land for a time. The family was thrifty and frugal: they made their own or did without. Nels didn't talk much, believing that the hardest truths could be spoken with the fewest words, and he instilled in his children an upstanding propriety rooted in the rectitude of his Norse ancestral lineage. He taught them that an honest day's work was a virtue, that a man had to be competent and skilled, and that he had to have a backbone to get a job done right.

Nels taught Elmer at an early age how to wield tools and build things. At twelve years old, Elmer surprised his mother with the family's first clock, which he had carved out of red pine, working over many months to master the inner workings of the intricate mechanical parts, the gear train and time hands, trying to get it to work. His mother praised his ingenuity and placed his creation up on the mantel of their log cabin, where it became the centerpiece of an otherwise unadorned home. For a family who had only ever known the time by the positioning of the sun in the sky, Elmer's clock was a luxury.

Above all else, Nels and Mary emphasized sound moral character; that one should lead with the virtues of *kos*, warmth and compassion, and *janteloven*, the self-deprecating concept that family and community, the group, was always more important than one individual standing alone; that each member was a thread woven into the tapestry of a greater good.

While Nels still read the *Norwegian News* and the family still embraced their native customs, singing old Norse songs, speaking Norwegian around the dinner table, ice fishing in the winter, and celebrating around midsummer bonfires, and Mary and the girls griddled up *lefse* during the holidays, the Hovlands embraced life in the United States and acclimated well to their new home. They even gave their children American names, making sure Elmer LeRoy and his siblings learned the words to the national anthem.

Though hard work, dust storms, and privation were harsh realities, it didn't occur to Elmer that life was difficult. A happy, humble, seemingly ordinary boy, he faced his days tilling soil and baling hay with an eager optimism.

Despite his serious affect, young Elmer was the epitome of winsome American boyhood. When he wasn't at school or helping on the farm, he could be found immersed in the simplest of bucolic childhood pleasures in the verdant playgrounds of nature: taking walks among the tall June prairie grasses and dallying through wildflower meadows in his blue cotton dungarees. His idea of a perfect afternoon was to walk barefoot down to the fishing hole, reel in a pike, skip stones across the surface of the lake, then fling himself off a rock into the cool water. He learned how to swim by jumping off a bridge into the Rock River, and for fun and frolic, he and his brother hopped railroad cars that came through Kenneth. A farm boy at heart, Elmer's playgrounds were the vast open spaces of an unsullied landscape where green cornfields met the blue sky on the horizon, and where at night one could gaze at a million stars that spanned the great Minnesota sky.

By the mid-1930s, millions of immigrants had settled across the United States, eager to become a part of mainstream America. Encouraged by President Roosevelt's welcoming words to root and assimilate, to plant and to build, they were grateful to be given an opportunity to forge a new future. They came together to support and learn from one another, to establish their communities, and to contribute to America's greater purpose and aspirations.

By the time he reached adolescence, Elmer was solidly grounded in faith, tethered to his family and to his community. While his mother swept a dusty porch as tumbleweeds rolled by and his father tinkered with farm machinery, young Elmer looked to the horizon and wondered where life would take him, certain of only one thing—that the Lord would lead the way.

AMERICAN INNOCENCE

. . .

On the other side of the country, just outside the densely populated cosmopolis of Boston, lived another boy from another immigrant family.

As streetcars and trolleys clanged, making their way past peddler pushcarts and commuter carriages, and horse-drawn carts clopped their way around vendors hawking their wares in the market district, the Custom House Tower near Boston Harbor stood watch over a bustling humanity of nearly 800,000 in a city that was home to the Revolutionary American independence movement and aptly known as the Cradle of Liberty.

On the streets, men with Brylcreemed hair wore derby bowlers in the city and boater hats on the waterfront as ladies shopped the market district. It was a city teeming with immigrant laborers toiling in shoe, garment, and rubber factories. Boston newspapers ran the scores coming out of Fenway Park and announced horse-race winners in between pages of ads for Lucky Strike and Chesterfield cigarettes. In a city where the end of Prohibition was celebrated with gusto, taprooms once again served up gin rickeys, burlesque tempted, and organized crime operated just under the surface as tommy gun–wielding gangsters hung back in the shadows between iconic American landmarks, five-and-dimes, and flophouses, all of which were mixed into new Irish and Italian immigrant neighborhoods.

Beyond the brownstones and the busy streets, in nearby Waltham, Sammy DeCola lived with his large, spirited family in a predominantly Italian Catholic area.

A few years older than Elmer, the two boys could not have been more different. Short, wiry, and scrappy, an Artful Dodger of sorts, Sammy was a street-smart, extroverted kid with a thick Boston accent who had a flat boxer's nose, wore an Italian coppola cap, and had a wisecracking, little-tough-guy attitude to match.

Like many Italian families, cooking and eating was central to the DeColas' well-being, and their lives revolved around a rich, soul-giving "food is love" *modo di vivere* way of life. Conversations were loud and animated, sometimes explosive, punctuated by whipping hand gestures and playful digs. Tempers flared and doors slammed, but they embraced the messy and the beautiful and argued as fiercely as they loved.

While Ma grew tomatoes in the backyard garden to make her homemade pasta sauce from the pera d'Abruzzo recipes handed down from her family in the "old country" in their native Civitaquana, Sammy's pa, Nicassio DeCola, was fixated on his American dream—to own an iconic single-module, stainless steel, silver barrel-roof diner that served up all-American fare like burgers, meatloaf, and apple pie. The diner, as it turned out, would be an instant success.

It was a hardscrabble life in the city for the immigrant family with five children, but the DeColas were determined to make it. They loved baseball and listening to Red Sox games on the radio. Sammy was raised with a lot of passion, rapturous laughter, and a fallback to the lighter side of life when things got tough.

Little Sammy was passionate about two things: food and Ma. She was built like a tank, boldly embracive, and unapologetically unfiltered, and she spoke little English. Ma was Sammy's whole world—he adored her, and Sammy, her youngest son, was her *bambino*. She coddled him in her beefy arms, where he nestled shamelessly in her bosom. She called him *pomodorino* (her little tomato), which sometimes landed as the butt of his father's teasing that he'd grow up to be a "*Pomomammone*," Mama's sweet little tomato boy, tauntings that didn't faze Sammy one bit. Sammy helped Ma raise tomatoes in the garden and she taught him how to harvest at peak. Warmed by a big black potbellied stove and braising smells in the kitchen, he kept her in stitches, her full-bodied belly laughs music to his ears. His second favorite sound was when Ma called, "*Andiamo! Si mangia!*" (Let's go, it's suppertime!), especially when she served his favorite spaghetti and meatballs.

Ma was the backbone of the family and her unexpected death when Sammy was eleven left him heartbroken. Inconsolable, Pa was suddenly left with five children to raise. He threw himself round the clock into work at the diner to push through his grief and provide for his family. Lost and rudderless, unsupervised Sammy acted out, at times even talking back to his father. He became a bit of a hooligan around town, an angry boy with a chip on his shoulder and a newfound propensity for finding trouble, picking fights, and skipping school. Pa found it hard to curb his youngest son's errant behavior, and with all he had to tend to, a chasm grew between father and son.

In 1933, Americans were still struggling through the Great Depression. Some 15 million, about 25 percent of the workforce, couldn't find jobs, and those who could were scraping by on an average of 40 percent less pay. With more Americans than ever before facing hard times, there were long lines at soup kitchens as a nation came to a standstill.

In Kenneth, Minnesota, in addition to the farm, the ever-frugal Nels had scraped together enough to buy a modest inn, a small grocery, and an animal-feed grain elevator, and all that helped bring in income until the market crashed and they lost their businesses, though the farm harvest helped sustain them through the toughest times.

In Waltham, Pa did his best to keep his diner on Main Street afloat, but when things went south and he couldn't pay his employees, he pulled in his older sons and wrangled in a rebellious thirteen-year-old Sammy, saying, "We're not giving up. People still gotta eat."

Despite the collapse of the nation's economy, somehow the two families persevered.

By the time they reached their teenage years, as sober and rooted as Elmer was, Sammy was a bit of a lost soul. The boys didn't know each other and had little in common, but their paths as young men would one day cross.

While young Elmer helped his family on the farm, and Sammy bused tables at the diner, like millions of other young boys growing into American teenagers, along the way they learned the ethos of Americana: duty to family, community, God, and country. They pledged allegiance to the Stars and Stripes and idolized their baseball heroes, Babe Ruth and Joe DiMaggio.

TWO

A GERMAN JEWISH BOY

ACROSS THE OCEAN, in Mönchengladbach (MG), near Cologne, in northwestern Germany, life was just starting to blossom for Eddie Willner, a cherubic little eight-year-old boy with a mop of curly black hair and jet-black eyes. An only child in a thriving middle-class Jewish family of many cousins, aunts and uncles, great-uncles, and grandparents, everyone either lived across the cobblestone street, down the road, or in surrounding boroughs around the city, an old urban municipality that dated back to the tenth century that had grown around a Benedictine monastery named Monks Gladbach for the Archbishop of Cologne and the monk Sandrad of Trier who settled the town on the Gladbach River.

Eddie's family had lived in and around the city for seven generations. As European Jewish families tended to be, the Willner clan was close-knit and communal. They came together in some form or another nearly every day to celebrate life, to share in their joys and their problems, to confer with or advise one another in their work while sitting in the garden, in the parlor, or around the dinner table, chattering in German and in Yiddish.

In Mönchengladbach, a flourishing midsize European commercial center for the textile industry, Jews were doctors and lawyers, some owned clothing factories and weaving mills, but the vast majority were, like the Willners, middle-class merchants, tradesmen, and livestock dealers.

Jews first appeared in MG in the 1300s. In the mid-1800s, German law gave Jews full legal rights as citizens, and by the 1930s, the city's nearly 1,400 Jews—about 1 percent of the total population—had become a part of the fabric of everyday life, experiencing little systematic antisemitism and, in the main, enjoying harmonious relationships with their Christian neighbors.

In other words, Mönchengladbach's Jews were fully German.

It was a town where everyone knew each other in their local districts, where grocers, barbers, and pharmacists knew everyone's name and the baker would open the cookie jar to let Eddie take a marzipan *Plätzchen* and wave it off, letting him pay next time or not at all if he was short a few pfennigs.

The Willners, a religiously moderate, solidly middle-class family, were fully assimilated into the broader German community. While some kept kosher, the Willners did not, nor did they wear yarmulkes or tallit prayer shawls. Originally drawn to the city for its progressive, liberal openness toward Jews, the Willners were proud Germans by nationality, had German first names, and were Jews by religion and cultural identity. Their allegiance was, first and foremost, to their country, not to their Judaism.

Jews in MG lived throughout the city, both in Jewish neighborhoods and interspersed among the Christian population. Eddie and his parents, Siegfried and Auguste, lived on Weiherstrasse, a tidy, sloping street in a lush green part of the old city at the base of the St. Vitus Basilica, a Roman Catholic church. They lived on the second floor of a two-story dwelling that they shared with their best friends, a Catholic family, who lived downstairs on the first floor and operated a butcher shop out of the front part of their house.

The Willner flat was decorated with paintings depicting modern European life—a French garden scene, a landscape of the snow-covered German Alps. A silver family menorah stood in the window of their apartment. At sundown on Shabbat, Eddie's mother lit the Shabbat candles, they said the kiddush and hamotzi blessings over the wine and bread, then together, hand in hand with his grandfather Opa Josef, Eddie and his family walked to the synagogue, a stately edifice of exquisite Moorish architecture decorated inside with interlaced wooden arches and intricately carved pews, Opa carrying his treasured purple velvet family siddur in which he had handwritten in Hebrew thanking God for the *bentsch* (blessings) of his family's "good fortune." At the synagogue, they came together to welcome the day of rest with the temple community, where everyone smiled and embraced or shook hands, wishing one another a *gut Shabbes*.

At Christmas, Eddie's father, Siegfried, dressed up in a red robe and white beard to play Santa Claus (*Weihnachtsmann*) for their Catholic neighbor Fritz's kids, and on Hanukkah, Fritz dressed up as the Hanukkah Man (*Chanukka Mann*), donning Siegfried's yarmulke and the same white beard, to the great delight of little Eddie. It was all in good fun, searing indelibly happy childhood memories in Eddie's mind, and all done in the spirit of genuine respect for cultural diversity, Christians and Jews together embracing the old Bible adage and the first rule of human decency, *Liebe deinen Nächsten wie Dich selbst*. Love your neighbor as you would yourself.

Eddie attended a local German public grade school, where he was well liked among his classmates, Christians and Jews alike. On weekends they palled around, went to the cinema to see Laurel and Hardy and Charlie Chaplin films, or played soccer in the park. Like every other boy in the city, Eddie dreamed of one day playing on the hometown club team, Borussia Mönchengladbach, a topflight contender in the regional professional league and the pride of the city. To the envy of some of his friends, Eddie was even good enough to be invited to join the junior club soccer team.

Siegfried was a World War I veteran, a lean handsome man who, even fifteen years after the end of the war, still kept his close-cropped hair and carried himself with the bearing of a soldier. A German patriot, Siegfried was a war hero who had been awarded one of the country's highest military honors, the *Ehrenkreuz für Frontkämpfer*, the Iron Cross for valor and bravery, for his four years of distinguished service fighting on both the Eastern and Western Fronts, from the Battle of Vilnius to French Flanders and Cambrai. A proud German citizen who felt strongly that a man should serve his country, he had volunteered as a horse-mounted forward observer whose job it was to sneak up on enemy lines and pinpoint their positions so they could be targeted by German artillery. It had been a dangerous and risky job (he once had a horse shot out from under him), and he came out of it a role model around town as an example of courage and selfless devotion to Germany.

After the war, Siegfried found work as a regional sales representative for a silk-tie company. He met Eddie's mother when he came home from the war and went to find and thank the young girl who had sent him letters and a box of home-baked cookies, which had lifted his spirits while he was on the Russian front. While he didn't take to the baker, he fell in love with her younger sister.

Eddie's mother, Auguste—or Gustel, as she was called by family and friends—was a light in her family, a soulful doe-eyed beauty with an aquiline profile and a wavy French bob angled fashionably downward at the chin; in all her strength and femininity, she resembled a cross between a Mucha *femme nouvelle* and Chagall's Bella. A bon vivant with an infectious laugh, she was a lively counterbalance to Siegfried's reserve.

She laughed at Siegfried's jokes and moved through the world with an airy grace unbound by life's burdens. Auguste was Eddie's soft place. He loved how she would brush his cheek with the back of her hand, settle him into bed with old Yiddish fables, Aesopian in nature, that were filled with humor and teachings about life, often ending with a moral lesson. Then she would tuck him in with his favorite soft blue downy *Bettdecke* (comforter), and he would drift off to sleep thinking all was good and right with the world.

Auguste adored her curly-headed boy and doted on her black-and-white cat, Mimi, whom she called Mimiche. Piano was her passion. She performed at weddings and at community events. At home, music filled the apartment, her practice sessions more like small recitals. Neighbors delighted in hearing her play; passersby would stop on the street just to listen for a while, then stroll on feeling that their lives had been touched for just a moment by something magical.

Auguste brought people together. On weekends, she hosted parties for family, friends, and neighbors, always a healthy mix of Jews and Christians. She was a good cook and wrote her own recipes in German, French, and Dutch, which she kept in an overstuffed green notebook. She made echt Jewish comfort food like Eddie's favorite latkes, challah, and rugelach just as expertly as she made German rouladen, French petit fours, and Dutch *banketstaaf,* party foods that she served on bone china plates as guests sipped wine in crystal glasses that had been in the family for generations.

Eddie was an active child with a cheeky sense of humor that especially amused his grandfather Opa Josef, a retired widower and former cattle dealer with a perfect snowy-white gentleman's mustache that curled upward when he smiled, who wore a suit with a pocket watch and always had a coin or a sweet in his pocket for his *kleinen Süßen*, his sweet little boy.

To Opa Josef, little Eddie was a *Goldkind*, a golden child, who could do no wrong, and he was endlessly entertained by Eddie's antics, especially by his silly faces and voices when he impersonated his teachers or his uncles. While Siegfried was determined to shape his only son to be an upstanding young man and good citizen, Opa Josef encouraged his puckish side, calling his ability to make others laugh a "gift."

"*Mit dem Talent*," Opa Josef would say, "*wird er weit kommen.*" He has a talent that will take him far.

Happy-go-lucky and a bit of a class clown, Eddie was often the center of attention in school, providing levity to what he saw as an otherwise dry and monotonous day. He was, typically, the only one of his friends to follow through on a dare, pulling stunts others wouldn't think of doing. He had a lot of moxie, which got him into plenty of trouble.

He once ate a bug on a dare. Another time he released a frog in the classroom. Sometimes he even played practical jokes on his teacher, such as when he hid the chalk, which left his friends bowled over with laughter as the teacher searched high and low for it. His pranks kept his friends in stitches but got Eddie pulled by the ear into the headmaster's office on more than one occasion.

Such stories delighted Opa Josef, but Siegfried was not amused by his son's shenanigans in the least. Siegfried wanted his son to be a leader, not a class clown. *Härte, Mut und Tapferkeit*—toughness, courage and fortitude—were strong Prussian virtues. *Ungezogenheit*—naughtiness—was not.

Siegfried only grew more concerned by his son's immature behavior, and it all came to a head one day when he caught Eddie hunched over the windowsill of their second-floor apartment, giggling and throwing water-filled balloons that burst on unsuspecting passersby down below. As was typical of stern, Prussian parental discipline of the day, Eddie felt the sting of his father's hand, and that incident marked the last time Siegfried let his boy get away with anything.

Siegfried had his work cut out for him. He now made Eddie stand at attention when he spoke to his father. At the dinner table, before Eddie was allowed to eat, Siegfried inspected the boy's fingernails, and he was made to sit ramrod straight, holding books under each arm to learn proper posture. Siegfried demanded impeccable manners, that Eddie keep his room spotless, and that he show respect to his elders. When Siegfried struck for any infraction, he demanded that Eddie not cower and whimper but take it like a man, to be tough and show some courage. Eddie chafed at the iron discipline, but Siegfried was adamant about raising a son with strong character. Now, at the dinner table, Siegfried kept a switch hanging from a nail within easy reach as a constant reminder to Eddie to behave.

Despite Opa Josef's pleas to let the boy just be a child, Siegfried became even stricter with Eddie, spanking him when he was out of line, threatening an even bigger spanking if he was called in even one more time to speak with the headmaster.

While Eddie still preferred to hide behind his mother's skirts, Siegfried began to pull him away for hikes in the forest, made the boy join him in his daily calisthenics, and work in the yard. When Eddie complained that he was tired or that his father was walking too fast, Siegfried kept him out longer. When Eddie begged to go home, Siegfried simply led him on another lap around the forest trail. Siegfried was persistent with his boy, stern but loving, patient and steadfast, knowing from experience that life would one day test his mettle, and it was Siegfried's greatest hope that, when that day came, his boy would be ready for it.

As it would turn out, Siegfried's timing to teach his boy the importance of self-discipline was fortuitous, as the winds of change were already blowing throughout Germany, and Eddie would need to summon an inner fortitude for the extraordinary, harrowing journey that lay ahead.

While little Eddie didn't yet know it, it would be this harsh and systematic discipline imposed by his father that would become the cornerstone of his survival.

Over the next year Eddie tried hard to conquer his immaturity and curb his mischievous behavior. That Rosh Hashanah, he penned a letter in his best cursive to his father:

"For the new year I wish you a lot of good luck. I shall ask God that he will keep you in good health. I shall always be a good boy. I shall work very hard at school so that you will have much joy. Many kisses, your grateful son."

THREE

PATRIOTS AND PARASITES

They were indoctrinated into a belief system which fanaticized them and appealed to their emotions, not their critical thinking.
—John Steiner, Holocaust survivor

As AMERICANS WERE finding ways to cope with the Great Depression, in Europe, debt-laden Germany had still not recovered from the economic collapse that followed World War I and was doubly devastated by the onset of the global economic downturn that rippled out from the crash of the U.S. stock market.

The defeat of Germany during the war and the debilitating terms imposed by the Versailles Treaty of 1919 had left Germany under a mountain of debt and forced to cede big chunks of territory. The loss left a nation out of work, reeling with a shattered national identity and teetering on the brink of becoming a failed state. A decade later, the feeling of hopelessness had still not lifted, and Germans were looking for any way up and out of their despair. Germany needed a savior.

Adolf Hitler, a fascist leader of the once fringe Nazi Party, emerged, claiming to be the answer to Germany's prayers. A former army corporal, a loner, a drifter, and perpetual underachiever, he had gained increasing popularity for his scathing radical right-wing nationalist preachings and raucous beer-hall oratory that incited hate-mongering and scapegoating.

A gaunt-faced man with side-swiped jet-black hair, a black toothbrush mustache, and penetrating blue eyes, Hitler wore a perpetually combative scowl. He was hardly the image of Prussian power and might. Despite his many shortcomings and failures, he was driven by an immense ego. Ridiculed for much of his political career as a fringe extremist, he was an almost comical character, an outlier who espoused crazy ideas based on conspiracy theories. Many found him full of bluster, but some also admired his ability to say what others dared not say aloud.

He slammed Germany's surrender in World War I and ridiculed the terms of the Versailles Treaty, calling those who had signed it traitors. Lashing out at the idea that Germans could ever be a defeated people, he vowed simply to tear up the treaty and reclaim land that had been surrendered to the victors. Scoffing at terms that limited Berlin's future military power, he brazenly announced that, to the contrary, the country would rearm with such profound magnitude that Germany would never be humiliated again. He assured ever-growing crowds that they had suffered a terrible injustice at the hands of a weak, leftist, and ineffectual fledgling parliamentary democracy that had undermined traditional German values. With near religious zealotry, he called on the German people to lift their heads high again, vowing to restore the nation to global prominence in a *Tausendjähriges Reich*—a thousand-year empire—that would become the envy of the world. The new Germany, he said, would rise up like a phoenix out of the ashes and surge to heights the world had never before seen and, as it did so, restore the dignity of a people to its proper place of greatness. It was a reassuring message to Germans that they deserved so much better than their looming postwar indignation.

Hitler branded himself a lone genius, promoting himself as the righteous defender of the voiceless little guy, which appealed to the disenfranchised working class and the down-and-out, and he asked them to put their faith in the power of his new visionary brand of leadership. Reinforcing over and over again the message that they had been victimized, he told them that he and he alone could right the wrongs they had suffered.

Moreover, he promised to avenge those treacherous inner forces he claimed had stuck a knife in Germany's back during World War I: the Jews. A conspiracy of Jews, he railed, had, throughout history, exploited the German people for their own greedy purposes. It was an extremist, racist ideology that squarely pointed the finger at one minority for all of Germany's failings.

Hitler claimed Germany would have won the war if more Jews had fought. It was a baseless accusation. In fact, census figures showed Jews fought at a slightly higher rate than the general population: of some 100,000 Jews who served Germany during the war, 80,000 served in combat, 35,000 were decorated, and 12,000 were killed. In the Willner family alone, Siegfried, his brothers, and his cousins all served. On Auguste's side, all eight male cousins in one family had fought on the front line. Nevertheless, the Nazis spun their narrative that one of the main reasons Germany lost the war was because Jews had shirked their duty to fight and had profited while others took their places. It was a twisted propaganda ploy to blame Germany's defeat on a group that made up less than 1 percent of Germany's total population. It was a brazen lie, but to Hitler and the Nazis, truth did not matter.

Hitler's message was clear: Help me rid the country of Jews and I will deliver to you what you want, what you need, what you deserve, and together we will make Germany great again.

Obsessed with racial purity, Hitler insisted that the German people were a superior race that had to fight against contamination by inferior bloodlines, which would ultimately result in Germany's demise. Nordic people topped the racial hierarchy, according to Hitler, while Jews were at the bottom and posed an existential threat to the very survival of the entire German gene pool. Jews, he said, were fixated on global financial domination and wanted to control the banks and the media. At the same time they were controlling capital markets, they were communists, responsible for the creation of Bolshevism. It was illogical, but Hitler twisted the narrative to make it all seem plausible, and Germans sponged it up, even if things sounded absurd and made no common sense. And so Hitler ramped up his smear campaign, and Jews became the scapegoat for all of Germany's ills, past and present.

Hitler had always been open about his radical beliefs, publicly using inflammatory hate speech right from the start. From his earliest rallies in the Nazi Party in the early 1920s, he called for the rise of the Aryan race to destroy the Jews, arguing that the aim of the government "must unshakably be the removal of the Jews altogether." In 1921, Hitler founded the Nazi *Sturmabteilung*—the SA, or storm troopers—a band of alt-right thugs who assaulted and pummeled Jews and party foes in the streets, proudly rallying to the slogan "We'll beat our way to the top."

Hitler was heavily influenced by like-minded thinkers and eugenicists on the topic of Aryan supremacy. The American automaker Henry Ford, a virulent antisemite, was a Hitler favorite. Ford's scathing racist diatribe, *The International Jew: The World's Foremost Problem*, was translated into German and widely distributed. Hitler had a portrait of Ford in his office and allegedly told an American reporter: "I regard Ford as my inspiration."

In 1924, Hitler was convicted of treason for inciting an armed revolt to overthrow the government. While in prison, he wrote *Mein Kampf* (*My Struggle*), a hate-filled manifesto that spelled out his extreme racist ideology and battle against the Jewish plot to rule the world, writing "the Jew... is a [poison] to the bloodstream" and "contaminates everything he touches, overthrows all that is noble, good and pure," adding "the personification of the devil as the symbol of all evil assumes the living shape of the Jew."

Hitler even contested the part of the New Testament that said Jesus was Jewish and offered his own interpretation that, on the contrary, Jesus was an Aryan warrior, a combatant against Jews, and thus a role model for the Nazis. In *Mein Kampf,* Hitler made a case for genocide, reviling Jews as vermin that needed to be "exterminated." And so, by the 1930s, it was clear who Hitler was and what he stood for.

Despite originating on the political fringe, economic collapse and a series of weak governments propelled the Nazi Party into the mainstream and opened the door to extremism and political violence. Seizing their chance, the Nazi Party stormed into people's lives. In 1928, they received only 2.6 percent of the vote in a national election, but just four years later, by 1932, Hitler had found his following when that number jumped to nearly 40 percent and the Nazis became Germany's largest political party. With an unemployment rate hovering around 30 percent, the Nazi movement attracted droves of unemployed, disaffected young men eager to hear Hitler's message of salvation. Not long thereafter, Nazi Party membership exploded to almost 3 million and was growing so fast that they had to freeze new membership applications because they couldn't process them fast enough. As their numbers grew, so did the Nazi capacity for destruction. Now buoyed with great confidence, they became even more violent, targeting political foes and Jews as they descended on cities and towns, shouting, *"Deutschland erwache!"*—"Germany wake up!"

. . .

The Nazis campaigned relentlessly, exploiting people's fears, prejudices, and hopes for their future as a nation became what Peter Hayes in his book *Why?* called a "witches' brew of self-pity, entitlement, and aggression." Hitler seduced his supporters with conspiracy theories, misinformation, and lies, which stoked anxiety about an international Jewish conspiracy at every turn. He stirred up chaos and confusion, blaming storm trooper street fights on communist provocateurs and liberal democratic forces. Gaslighting a nation, he created an atmosphere of intimidation and said shocking things over and over again, which, over time, dulled people's capacity to know where the red line was. He attacked the press and called his political opponents traitors and enemies of the state. Conversely, he called his loyal supporters "patriots" and praised them as the only true Germans. It was the first time many, especially the disenfranchised, had been called special, important, and worthy. They felt emboldened to find new meaning in their lives, found a sense of community, and rallied to Hitler's side.

With the Nazis now holding the largest number of seats in the parliament, Germany's aristocratic right-wing political elite thought they could capitalize on the Nazis' popularity. As a result of backroom dealings and convinced they could control the young forty-three-year-old political upstart, who they believed was not a political threat, Hitler was made chancellor. But they had woefully underestimated him. Instead of being easily manipulated, Hitler made a power grab. A month later, a suspicious fire destroyed the Reichstag, the parliament building, which Hitler blamed on his rivals, the communists, giving the Nazis a pretext to seize total control of the government. In the blink of an eye, the once fringe political outsider who many thought was crazy became the leader of Germany.

The swastika, a far-right-wing symbol, replaced the German flag as democracy was snuffed out and fascism ignited the country.

Hitler turned Germany into a one-party junta, silenced and even murdered political opponents, and jailed others without charges. The Nazis weaponized the court system; Hitler inserted his own judges and created the Gestapo, the secret police. New decrees gave Germany's new leader ultimate power to make his own laws without parliamentary approval. He took control of the media and the message, and the free press came to an end. The SA held book burnings, with citizens stepping up to hurl now-censored literary works into massive bonfires and, in so doing, casting off their free will and critical thinking.

Germany's new chancellor insisted on being referred to as the Führer, the Leader. Every home and every public place had to prominently display Hitler's portrait. *Mein Kampf* became a national bestseller and sales roared to over a million copies. An entire nation was taught a mandatory new salute, arm stretched palm down, while simultaneously shouting with conviction, *"Heil Hitler!"*—"Hail Hitler!" Before long, the greeting became a normal part of everyday life and anyone who did not render the salute immediately when it was expected found themselves on the wrong side of the Nazis.

Hitler demanded a pledge of 100 percent loyalty, and Germans learned to obey without question. Military and civil servants swore an oath not to serve the country or the constitution but to serve the man himself.

Antisemitism surged into overdrive as, almost overnight, new measures peeled away the rights of Jews, with Hitler simultaneously gauging the public's reaction to it all. The first wave of legislation ousted Jews from government jobs, removed Jewish doctors from state hospitals and Jewish lawyers from federal courts, curbed Jewish attendance at universities, and ejected Jewish actors from the stage.

Realizing that most Germans did not share their virulent antisemitic views, Hitler and the Nazis let the constant drip of their message seep into the German psyche, then took a wait-and-see approach before completely ratcheting up repression.

An us-versus-them mentality took root and hate beçame mainstream. Posters and pamphlets declared, "All men are not created equal." Newspapers depicted the Jew as a grotesque character with a misshapen face and a large, crooked nose, emphasizing that Jews were genetically different from the rest of the population; caricatures of Jews were captioned with words like "filthy" or "a diseased lot," racial slurs meant to galvanize a nation to join in the hate. Words like "vermin" and "parasites" became commonplace, eroding people's respect for their Jewish neighbors, who were now being seen as a plague infesting German society, which made it easier to see them being hurt. *Der Stürmer (The Attacker)* was an alt-right newspaper whose sole purpose was to infect German minds with antisemitism. The paper sold everywhere and was prominently displayed in public glass cases set up specifically for mass reading, with every edition's front-page banner splashed in boldface type: *"Die Juden sind unser Ungluck"*—"The Jews Are Our Misfortune."

FOUR

RISE OF HATE

At Eddie's German school, the new curriculum worshipped Hitler, who stared down at students from his portrait on the wall. Children jumped up and snapped to deliver the Nazi salute each time the teacher walked into and out of the room. When Hitler came on the radio, lessons were halted and the pupils were made to stand at attention as he delivered his chilling messages about Germans uniting to rid the country of Jews, every hateful speech causing Eddie's classmates to look him over.

One day Eddie and his classmates were led to the main train station because the Führer was passing through Mönchengladbach. In a sea of thousands of adoring citizens, the schoolchildren were ushered to the front of the excited crowd. The train approached, slowed, and when it came to a stop, a loudspeaker boomed, *"Achtung!"* Onlookers snapped the Nazi salute and the crowd erupted in unison, *"Sieg heil! Sieg heil! Sieg heil!"* which echoed throughout the station. Little Eddie saw Hitler through the window, his pale face, black side-swept hair, and mustache. He looked back at the crowd, dismissively returning a halfhearted salute, his all-powerful deific hubris on full public display.

Hitler was strangely magnetic and kept pulling in followers. His rallies were shock theater that throbbed with the fervor of a religious revival. He often spoke with a wild look in his eyes, thrusting his fists up to the heavens as if, through a thunderbolt, he was absorbing direction directly from the Almighty himself. At times he barked his words like a rabid dog but would then recede to whispers in an otherworldly, meditative state. For many it was so dramatic, so hypnotic, it was hard to look away. His rally-goers traveled long distances and often waited for hours to see him. He typically arrived late, after the crowd had been whipped into a frenzy in anticipation, then entered to a coliseum of rapturous cheers. At the podium, he would stand in silence for a full minute or more, in a carefully choreographed strategy to ramp up the suspense to a fever pitch so that when he finally did speak, the audience was in a state of ecstasy. It was bizarre, but it worked. People became drunk on his performances and his cult of personality rocketed. For many, the onetime social outcast and oddball now seemed to speak directly to their souls.

He spoke in illusory truths, relentlessly repeating the same lies, and many came to believe him even if they knew logically his speeches were filled with deception. In *Mein Kampf* he had written: in order for propaganda to reach the masses, it should be simple and consist of slogans repeated over and over again, "as long as it takes for the dumbest member of the audience to get an idea of what they mean."

Hitler claimed to be a messiah who had been called to lead the Aryan world. "Providence," he said, "had ordained that I should be the greatest liberator of humanity." He declared that it was not he but God himself who had dictated what should be done with the Jews: "I am convinced that I am . . . not a Christian if I do not . . . wage war against the Jews" and "Hence today I believe that I am acting in accordance with the will of the Almighty Creator: by defending myself against the Jew, I am fighting for the work of the Lord." Nazism was a Christian movement, he proclaimed, and it was one's Christian duty to help him fight the Jews. Though his twisted message had nothing to do with the teachings of Christ, many who called themselves devout allowed themselves to be drawn into his web.

Hitler delivered on some of his promises to the German people, getting them back to work, embarking on vast new public works, and infrastructure projects like the German autobahn system, and he began rebuilding Germany's military and rearming the nation. He put affordable consumer goods into the hands of ordinary Germans, which left people feeling like their lives were taking a turn for the better, like a cheap home radio that brought music and culture into their homes but, at the same time, conveniently, allowed Hitler the perfect tool to blast nightly propaganda into every family's living room. In return for delivering on some of his promises, people traded in their freedoms to buy into his warped ideology.

Nazi films glorified Hitler and demonized the Jew. The film *Jud Süß* (*The Jew Named Zuse*) was a huge box office hit, even winning the top award at fascist Mussolini's Venice Film Festival. The main character was a shifty-eyed, goblin-like villain with a hooked nose and whiny voice who committed heinous crimes including rape. In the end, Zuse is executed, leaving the audience feeling that justice had been served, and some left the theater better understanding the need for eliminating Jews from Germany. The film got neighbors talking.

The sudden onset of mass hatred against Jews came as a shock to the Willners in progressive-minded MG and to many Jews across the country. Throughout Germany's history, there had been periodic upsurges of antisemitic persecution and violence, and there had always been Germans whose prejudices simmered just below the surface, but, by 1870, Jews had been granted full legal rights as citizens and prejudice had gone into decline, except among the reactionary, extreme right. For the next sixty years, Jews assimilated, blending into the fabric of everyday German life and succeeding in business, sciences, and the arts. It was alarming to see how easily ordinary Germans seemed willing, almost overnight, to trade in their belief systems and sign on to Hitler's hate-filled ideology of race warfare.

Neighbors and colleagues began to distance themselves from the Willners. Siegfried's old war buddies began to detach from the man they had respected and called a friend. Opa Josef's tailor and grocer began to disassociate themselves from their Jewish customers. Germans boycotted Jewish businesses, then altogether turned away, telling them simply, "I'm afraid we can't do business anymore." Auguste's secular neighborhood parties were suddenly a thing of the past. Fritz, the Catholic neighbor, and his family didn't turn away but worried that, in time, their association with their Jewish friends could come back to haunt them.

Eddie's world spiraled. Now his classmates were reading books like *Der Giftpilz* (*The Poisonous Mushroom*), a story about a mother and young boy collecting mushrooms in the forest. She points out the differences between good mushrooms and deadly ones, saying: "Just as a single poisonous mushroom can kill a whole family, so a solitary Jew can destroy a whole village, a whole city, even an entire people [*Volk*]."

Eddie was excluded from their games. *Juden Raus!* (Jews, Get Out!) was a board game requiring players to roll dice and advance brightly colored figures around a village, along the way capturing dunce-capped Jews and removing them from the board. Whoever kicked six Jews out of the village was hailed the winner.

The superiority of the Aryan race was drilled into the nation's youth. At school, teachers showed up in Nazi uniform, boys came to school wearing Hitler Youth and girls Bund Mädel League uniforms. To keep in good favor, teachers had to prove what fine Nazis they were. Those who did not play the game were sacked, while younger, newly indoctrinated ones took their place. Even the littlest students were spoon-fed pro-Hitler propaganda. Kindergartners learned how to draw the swastika and memorize the jingle "Our Führer is Adolf Hitler. He is a great soldier and tireless worker. He delivered Germany from misery. Now everyone has work, bread, and joy. Our Führer loves children and animals."

New curricula immersed students in the study of Aryan superiority, where they learned to recognize "worthy" and "unworthy" races, their textbooks explaining, "Jews have different noses, ears, lips, chins than Germans" and "They walk differently, they have flat feet, and their arms are longer." In another: "The animal world can be classified into two groups: Nordic men and lower animals." Girls with blond plaits and "handsome Aryan boys" became model youth over darker, curly-headed Jewish children like Eddie.

One day, Eddie's teacher walked into the classroom, the class jumped to their feet, shooting out their arms in salute. The teacher told Eddie and the other Jewish pupils to lower their arms and sit down. Now Jews were no longer even allowed the "privilege" of honoring the Führer. Soon after that, the Jewish children were made to sit in a separate section from their classmates. It was an isolating turning point. From then on, if the teacher posed a question to the class, he no longer called on Eddie, even if he was the only one with his hand in the air.

Eddie had never been bullied, but now his classmates began to see him through a different lens. He became confused when the same pals who had joined in his pranks now bullied him in the schoolyard. One day, one of his closest friends, a boy he had shared a school bench with for years, called him a "dirty Jew" in front of their teacher, who did nothing about it. Eddie was heartbroken when none of his friends spoke up in his defense. Then his classmates quit talking to him altogether.

Phase I of Hitler's plan had been a resounding success. He had carefully watched to see how the great majority of Germans who had not been fervent antisemites would respond to increasing aggression toward Jews, and when hatred and hostility took root in the general population and no longer shocked or even offended Germans—when there was no significant reaction in the international community, and when Hitler realized that no one was going to stand up for the Jews—he got his green light to ramp things up even further.

In 1935, Hitler took things to the next level when he implemented the Nuremberg Laws stripping Jews of their citizenship, whereby they lost all rights to be protected by the police and the court system. Further Nazi laws would seize Jewish assets and freeze bank accounts and access to safe-deposit boxes. No longer could Jews retrieve their own money from their banks. They could no longer serve in the military, and mixed marriages were forbidden and annulled.

In the streets, while Germans held their heads up high, the Willners had to take off their hats, bow to non-Jews, and move aside on the sidewalk to let them pass. As Germans engaged in the usual cordialities with one another just as they always had, Jews were humiliated, made to walk a gauntlet of teasers and tormentors to be bullied and beaten up. Such abuses were by now encouraged and even considered patriotic. They proved to the Nazis a German's willingness to do his loyal duty against Jews, which set him up nicely to join and move up the ranks of the Nazi Party.

The regime gave every newly married German couple a copy of *Mein Kampf*, "a wedding gift from the Führer," to start their new lives together "in love and promise for the future." The Nazi salute became so commonplace, even department store clerks greeted customers with the salute and *"Heil Hitler*, how may I help you?"

A curfew was imposed on Jews. They could no longer use public transportation, restaurants and shops posted signs saying "Jews Forbidden," and they were barred from theaters and swimming pools. Now not only could Eddie no longer get a cookie from the bakers; he wasn't even allowed near the bakery. He could no longer play in the park because Jews were no longer allowed entry. Much to Eddie's heartbreak, he was kicked off his beloved soccer team, and his friends never came around again. Mönchengladbach's Jews stopped going to temple for fear of being beaten. Siegfried lost his job with the silk-tie company and was politely asked to no longer show up at his veterans' meetings. Clients stopped livestock trading with Eddie's uncles, Opa Josef could no longer get a haircut at the barber, and people stopped inviting Auguste to play piano recitals at community events. Then Eddie was kicked out of his school altogether.

In just a few short years, one of the world's most accomplished and culturally advanced societies, the home of such renowned luminaries as Bach, Beethoven, Kant, and Goethe, had plunged into a full-blown dictatorship. Fanning the flames of economic and political discontent and stoking religious hate and xenophobia, Hitler managed to turn Germany's belief system on its head. Few stood in his way as the moral bedrock of a once-principled nation crumbled and a new regime based on extremist right-wing thinking replaced it.

Suddenly patriots were no longer Iron Cross winners who had fought courageously and sacrificed for Germany, but any white Aryan who blindly followed Hitler's lead.

They bowed to Hitler's perverted ideology, finding ways to rationalize what they saw with their own eyes, rejecting what they knew in their heads and in their hearts, trusting a distorted reality to guide them. *Don't believe the truth*, he told them. *Don't believe what you see and what you know to be true. Believe only what I tell you.* A lie said over and over again to them became fact.

By and large, Germans followed Hitler, handing their futures and the fate of a nation over to a madman who, just a few years earlier, was the butt of jokes. Seduced by his prodigious power, his meteoric rise, and his promises to usher in a glorious national rebirth, they bought into the apotheosis that held him up like a god. They believed he was devoted to them, and in return they became devoted to him.

Hitler had lit a spark for racial extremism, hate had metastasized, and now that Germans had either bought into Hitler's lunacy or were willing to look the other way, it all augured disaster for the Jews of Europe.

FIVE

PROMISE

By the mid-1930s, the impacts of FDR's New Deal reforms were starting to kick in and the economy showed signs of life. There was still plenty of hardship and many Americans were still out of work, but things were improving and government programs like the Works Progress Administration were putting Americans back to work on construction projects across the country building schools, hospitals, parks, roads, and airports, including Washington National (now called Reagan National) and New York's LaGuardia. The monthly WPA wage of $42 wasn't much, but it was enough to put food on many American tables.

Despite the tough times, there were plenty of distractions to keep people's minds off their troubles. A daring young aviator named Howard Hughes set a new airspeed record of 354.4 mph in his Hughes H-1 Racer plane; Parker Brothers introduced a "real estate game" called Monopoly; Amelia Earhart became the first person to successfully fly solo (two thousand miles) from Hawaii to California; and the first can of beer, Krueger's Cream Ale, was sold in Richmond, Virginia.

To learn what Americans had on their minds, a new scientific polling method started gauging how Americans thought about their future. Gallup's 1936 survey showed that, despite the trauma the country had just been through, the majority of Americans were optimistic, thought the government was doing a good job trying to navigate a way out of the crisis, and were unified behind the president and his programs.

In Kenneth, Elmer got only average marks in school, but his classmates were drawn to him for his cool and his infectious self-assurance. He was confident and stoic—some said it was a Norwegian thing—facing everything with composure. He didn't talk much, but when he did, his words mattered and people listened.

At the heart of it, Elmer was just a simple farm boy and a problem solver; he did things without being told what to do, which caught the eye of the neighbors, who praised Nels and Mary for the fine job they'd done raising *that boy* and could they borrow him for this task or that, to which his parents proudly lent him out.

With so many Americans down-and-out across the country, it was only natural that some turned to a life of crime, which saw a spike in the number of bank robberies. In 1934, the FBI was given the job of protecting banks and, within a year, managed to take down several notorious criminals, many who had achieved celebrity-like status, including John Dillinger, Bonnie and Clyde, Baby Face Nelson, and Charles "Pretty Boy" Floyd. Rumor had it that Bonnie and Clyde had even robbed a bank a year earlier in nearby Okabena, just forty miles away from Kenneth.

At thirteen years old, Elmer found work at a local pool hall. So reliable was he that his boss gave him a loaded handgun and bags of money with instructions to run the daily earnings over to the bank.

In Waltham, Sammy remained devastated at the loss of Ma. He missed everything about her—her larger-than-life presence, her "sweet voice," her hearty, all-consuming embraces—and he remained angry at the world for taking her from him too soon. Pa suffered in silence but paid tribute to his dear wife the best way he knew how when he put her on the menu, introducing "Ma's Meatballs," the only Italian dish he offered alongside otherwise strictly American fare.

Pa rode Sammy hard at the diner and he often missed school to work the counters and the booths, sometimes pulling double shifts. In what little downtime he had, he kept up Ma's gravesite, pruning, spreading loam, and adorning it with flowers. He escaped stressful shifts at the diner by tuning in to baseball on the radio, following stars like Lou Gehrig and Hank Greenberg, and he would never forget when Babe Ruth hit the last of his 714 home runs while playing for the Boston Braves.

In 1936, Germany was given the honor of hosting the Olympic Games and, with it, was handed a propaganda gold mine to showcase Germany's rise under Nazism. Hitler intended to use the Games as a worldwide stage to demonstrate German racial purity and Aryan superiority, but his plans were foiled when Black American track-and-field great Jesse Owens stole the show, winning four gold medals and becoming the star of the Berlin Games.

Owens's victories were an embarrassment for Hitler, but the Games were important for another reason. The Nazis had made it no secret that Jewish athletes were not welcome to participate. Although there was initially talk by some countries of a boycott, nearly all acquiesced and sent athletes to compete. In the wake of Germany's dehumanizing Nuremberg Race Laws, put into effect less than a year earlier, the U.S. and other Western democracies had lost a perfect chance to stand up to Hitler.

For Hitler, the Olympic Games had been a litmus test. When there was no international outcry for his escalating aggression against

Germany's Jews, Hitler knew the world was not going to stand in his way, which gave him the go-ahead for the next stage of his plan.

For the Jews of Germany, including Siegfried and Auguste, listening to Nazi radio broadcasts of the Olympic Games must have caused despair as they wondered if anyone cared about their plight.

SIX

KRISTALLNACHT

IN GERMANY, THINGS were bad, but many Jews hoped they would be able to weather the storm, not imagining things could possibly get any worse. Others held their breath, waiting to see which way things would go, what exactly Hitler would do next.

Then, overnight, it all blew up.

Kristallnacht, the Night of Broken Glass, on November 9, 1938, hit like an explosion that shattered throughout Germany, terrorizing Jewish communities. Under swastika banners, Nazi storm troopers marched across cobblestones into cities and towns across Germany. In a matter of just hours, scores of Jews were killed and tens of thousands of Jewish men were arrested.

In Mönchengladbach, SA thugs, Hitler Youth, and rampaging mobs of vandals smashed storefront glass, plundered and defaced Jewish-owned shops with the Star of David, now a symbol of hatred of the Jews, and violently attacked any Jew within sight. Some forty men were rounded up and disappeared into the bowels of Gestapo headquarters. Siegfried's status as a decorated World War I Iron Cross veteran seemed to protect him from arrest for the time being, but it didn't stop the Gestapo from starting a file on him. He was being watched.

Throughout Germany, thousands of synagogues, Jewish businesses, and cemeteries were destroyed. Police stood by as the violence raged. Firemen were present not to protect Jewish buildings from burning but to ensure that the flames did not spread to adjacent Aryan-owned property.

Storm troopers descended on the Mönchengladbach synagogue. They extinguished the holy eternal light, ripped out the Torah scrolls, and stripped the parchment from the rollers. They smashed wooden pews, ran off with the treasures of the temple, and torched the building. In the basement, Eddie and the city's Jewish children were huddled together, hidden in a makeshift classroom set up after they had been expelled from public German schools. Teachers rushed to get the children out before the fire reached the basement and engulfed them. Eddie and his classmates sat on a berm across the street, watching in disbelief as their synagogue went up in flames. When a local firefighter tried to douse the inferno, a storm trooper appeared and sliced the hose. The mayor showed up on the scene, pleading with the mob to stop. "This must cease immediately!" He was hauled away and, not long thereafter, replaced by a hard-line Nazi.

At the rabbi's house, furniture, including a piano, was thrown out the window and smashed on the sidewalk below.

Throughout Germany, Jews were forced to relocate. Eddie and his parents were evicted from the duplex they had shared with Fritz for ten years and ordered to move across town to Humboldtstrasse 28, a newly designated Jewish-only section of town near the train station, where the Nazis were cramming four Jewish families into single-family apartments.

Opa Josef was removed from the stately three-story brick home he had lived in all his adult life and forced to move into an *Altersheim* senior citizens' home, where, packed beyond capacity along with the rest of the region's Jewish elderly, they entered via a salon where Hitler's portrait hung on the wall, his virulent gaze boring down on them.

Days after Kristallnacht, Hermann Göring, a senior Nazi official, fined the German Jewish community one billion marks for the damages that the Nazis themselves had inflicted on Jewish communities across the country. Three days after that, he warned of a "final reckoning with the Jews."

The pogrom of November 9, 1938, sparked a desperate, mad scramble for Jews to get out of the country, resulting in tens of thousands immediately applying for visas to leave Germany. Wealthier Jews, especially those who already held passports, could pay their way out to safety, but families of lesser means, or those who could no longer retrieve money from their banks, were trapped. Without Nazi approval to leave or money to pay for their travel, many were out of luck and could not escape. Their bank accounts frozen, some could no longer even buy food. In MG, Auguste tried to sell the family furniture and her jewelry, until that path to raise money for passage out was cut short by a new law that required Jews to turn in their jewelry to Nazi authorities.

Siegfried tried desperately to find ways for the family to escape, writing feverishly to international aid organizations around the world, including to the United States, asking for help. The U.S. Association of Jewish War Veterans responded, "We stand ready to help you," but there was only so much they could offer. They could neither fund his trip out nor sponsor his emigration.

Throngs of frightened Jews sought refuge wherever they could. Ships sailed for Cuba, Palestine, Africa, to the Americas, even to

Shanghai. Their biggest challenge was finding a port willing to accept them. The German passenger ship MS *St. Louis* sailed from Hamburg, Germany, to Havana, Cuba, carrying 937 refugees, almost all Jewish. The Cuban government refused to allow the ship to dock, so they sailed on. The United States and Canada also turned the ship away, so the vessel was forced to make its way back to Germany, and the passengers were left to face the consequences of that failure.

Like many others, Siegfried and Auguste waited anxiously for their passports to be approved. Knowing that any illegal attempt to flee could result in the family's immediate arrest and imprisonment, Siegfried found himself in a hopeless dilemma. Because he was still on the rolls as a reserve German soldier, the Nazis refused to let him leave, a paradox because Jews could no longer even serve in the military. It was a devastating irony. His proud service in World War I was now an obstacle to his family's ability to escape. Meanwhile, the Gestapo continued to build their case against Siegfried.

Then one day in early December, less than one month after Kristallnacht, Eddie's passport miraculously arrived. Siegfried reacted to the news that his son could leave Germany with such elation, he "looked like he might have a heart attack." Siegfried and Auguste had not received their papers, and so in that moment they made a gut-wrenching decision: no matter what, they had to get their boy out.

So, in a desperate act of love, just two days later, they put twelve-year-old Eddie on a train bound for Brussels, Belgium, with a note pinned to his coat asking for him to be picked up and cared for by anyone willing to take him in. They packed some clothes in a small suitcase and put in a silver kiddush cup for good luck. It was his first time traveling alone. Siegfried and Auguste were terribly worried but had to put their faith in the kindness of strangers they hoped would come to the rescue of a Jewish child and offer their son safe harbor.

KRISTALLNACHT

. . .

Together they walked hand in hand, their grip on their boy firm and protective as they moved up the cobblestone street toward the train station. As Nazi flags snapped menacingly in the wind on that cold December morning, they moved quickly, trying to avoid attention as they bypassed Jewish shops destroyed on Kristallnacht. At the train station, Eddie's mother bent down, adjusted his coat collar up around his face, and pulled the flaps of his woolen cap over his ears. He looked up at her with his big black eyes. She smiled, but he saw that her expression was pensive.

"Don't be afraid," his mother said, fighting back tears as she stroked his cheek with the back of her hand.

"Be a good boy," said his father. "We will find you."

As the train rolled out of the station, Siegfried and Auguste were distraught to see their only child disappear into the unknown. Eddie settled in somewhere between believing his parents would find him and wondering if he would ever see them again.

SEVEN

BLUE RIBBON AMERICA

Our strength is our unity.
—FDR, State of the Union "Four Freedoms Speech," January 6, 1941

By 1939, THE worst economic disaster in American history had lifted and America's future was looking up. Millions who had lost their jobs were finding work again, and most bankruptcies and home and farm foreclosures were in the rearview mirror. Dreams that had been dashed by the uncertainty of the future seemed to, once again, hold promise.

The Great Depression had tested the resilience of Americans, but none more so than new immigrant families, who had tried to start fledgling farms and businesses against the backdrop of universal financial calamity. Somehow the Hovlands survived with their farm, and the DeColas with their diner. They didn't give up and they didn't lose faith, and Elmer's and Sammy's families and millions of others were starting to get back on their feet.

It was a time of national promise in America, of new optimism and of clarity. FDR's New Deal had been a smashing success. It had gotten Americans working, put money in their wallets, and allowed people to save again, to buy a new car or even a house.

It was a golden age of innovation; new industries and technologies were taking off. The modern American auto industry rocketed. The engine of progress strung electricity across America and brought indoor plumbing to most households, which allowed Americans to enjoy a better life. By the end of the decade, America was transforming, powered by a citizenry inspired to dream big in a land of unlimited opportunities.

Nothing illustrated this new era of promise more than the 1939 World's Fair in Queens, New York. Under the banner "Dawn of a New Day," America rolled out a series of inventions to propel a growing modern middle class: an ultramodern kitchen featuring the automatic dishwasher, the electric typewriter, the fax machine, the first computer game, and the first live television broadcast of a U.S. president. Westinghouse even featured a cigarette-smoking robot, "Elektro the Moto-Man"; General Motors' Highways and Horizons pavilion, entitled Futurama, rolled out the company's vision for a car-centric future for American suburbia set in a clover-leafed highway cityscape. IBM exhibited a Teletype machine equipped with a cathode-ray tube that relayed concurrent televisual messages between the New York Fair and the Golden Gate International Exposition in San Francisco.

Despite the fair's overarching message of international progress and global goodwill, the celebration was partially eclipsed by Germany's invasion of Poland and its ongoing occupation of Austria and Czechoslovakia. Fascism was sweeping across Europe. And while Hitler had closed the aperture on ethnic diversity, reviling any threat to Aryan purity, American prosperity was powered by its multicultural melting-pot mentality, with FDR exhorting his listeners, "Remember, remember always, that all of us, you and I especially, are descended from immigrants," declaring, "We are a nation of many nationalities, many races, many religions bound together by a single unity, the unity of freedom and equality," and reminding Americans of their common bonds and that "our strength is our unity."

Sports, music, and the arts saw a transformation that shaped a distinctly new American style. Baseball superstars continued to achieve the impossible on the field, Billie Holiday's silky jazz vocals seduced the soul, and Dixieland great Louis "Satchmo" Armstrong trumpeted out new rhythms and boogie-woogie beats that got a nation on its feet.

It was an awakening in a merging of musical genres: old-time spiritual revivals, gospel, and ragtime mixed with country and western and immigrant sounds blending in a unique fusion of cultures and energies all celebrating a common ambition. American Jewish composers Aaron Copland and George Gershwin hit the scene, writing songs about the unlimited promise of America, like Gershwin's *Rhapsody in Blue*, a composition he described as "a musical kaleidoscope of America, of our vast melting pot, of our unduplicated national pep, of our metropolitan madness."

Where just ten years before, movies were black-and-white and silent, now Hollywood produced Technicolor motion pictures like *Gone With the Wind* and *The Wizard of Oz*, filling theaters across America. The Glenn Miller Orchestra played big band swing on the radio and Jimmie Rodgers yodeled about cowboys and heartbreak. The freewheeling acrobatic moves of the jitterbug replaced more conservative ballroom waltzes, and Shirley Temple came dancing into America's heart.

A promising future beckoned teenagers like Elmer and Sammy, who were riding in on the dawn of a new era of national solidarity and goodwill, where neighbors and church volunteers pitched in to lend a hand to those in need—Americans doing good, helping one another to "make it"; where gangs of pals who might have fought a time or two shook hands and forgot about it, disagreements handled in the spirit of healthy competition and winning. Americans had cultivated an ethos of respect, teamwork, and playing to win. The highlight of the summer in many towns was the county fair, where folks looked forward to competing and also to witnessing each other's victories, looking on with pride to celebrate the one who raised the prized pig, the prettiest heifer, or baked the tastiest pie.

It was a simple time when decency mattered, when everyone knew their neighbor, nothing came as a handout, and if you wanted something, you worked for it or traded for it; where religion meant guidance toward good, and a nation held dear that hard work and family, well-behaved children, reliable neighbors, and church be placed above all else; where baseball games hard-fought on the sandlots of America ended in hand-shaking and pats on the back in a civil good-natured conclusion with the losing side tipping their hats to the winner.

"We look for a younger generation," FDR said in a speech to the Daughters of the American Revolution, "that is going to be more American than we are. We are doing the best that we can, and yet we can do better than that, we can do more than that by inculcating in the boys and girls of this country today some of the underlying fundamentals, the reasons that impelled our Revolutionary ancestors to throw off a fascist yoke."

It was an era of blue ribbon American spirit.

Babe Ruth inspired, saying things like "You just can't beat a person who never gives up" and "Never let the fear of striking out get in your way," which helped build the character of youth all over the country and made them proud to be American. A new comic book hero, Superman, arrived on the scene, captivating young boys' imagination that America was a place where good would always win out over evil.

It was not all rosy in America, however.

Despite the progress, the 1930s had a darker side. America's Black citizens remained oppressed and forced to live in a strictly segregated, often violent society that used a series of arbitrary "Jim Crow" laws to limit their freedoms and keep them down. Other groups like the Chinese community were also often the target of racial stereotyping and widespread discrimination. The German American Bund, a vocal pro-Nazi right-wing movement, even as late as 1939 managed to pack Madison Square Garden to the rafters for a rally to listen to xenophobic, antisemitic pro-Hitler rantings. Under a 150-foot-tall floor-to-ceiling banner adorned with the image of America's first president surrounded by swastikas, the twenty thousand attendees began the evening reciting the Pledge of Allegiance while delivering the Nazi salute. The opening speech went on to proclaim that Nazism is what the Founding Fathers would have supported and that George Washington was "America's first fascist." International celebrity aviator Charles Lindbergh, who openly espoused pro-Nazi, anti-Jewish sentiment, championed the "America First" movement, which intended to keep the U.S. out of the war in Europe. Great Britain took in ten thousand Jewish children from Europe, but although First Lady Eleanor Roosevelt ardently backed the bill to do the same in the United States, the American Legion and even the Daughters of the American Revolution strongly opposed the immigration of the same number of Jewish children to the U.S.

The United States was far from perfect, with plenty of work still to be done. Yet as imperfect as it was, America was moving in the right direction, and the forces of racial and ethnic small-mindedness would soon find themselves on the wrong side of history.

In dusty Kenneth, Nels listened to FDR's fireside chats about tensions ramping up in Europe, becoming especially concerned when news broke that German troops had invaded his native Norway. With Hitler's conquests expanding across Europe, it was getting harder and harder for FDR to maintain U.S. neutrality, and by then, in his radio addresses to the nation, he was asking Americans to keep an open mind about entering the war.

Kenneth was so remote that Elmer had to go all the way to Luverne for high school. As dry, parched summers gave way to frigid Minnesota winters, Elmer learned from Nels the spirit of *friluftsliv*, the Norwegian notion of embracing the cold, "a gift," Nels said, "to those who can stand it." It was a chance, Mary reminded her children, to turn the miserable into the magical, and so, alienating winters were broken up by snowball fights with his brothers as they made the three-mile, one-way walk to the bus stop that took them to school in Luverne.

Young Elmer LeRoy grew up tall and sturdy as a red pine. A strapping blond seventeen-year-old with broad shoulders and a sure-footed disposition, he had hallmark Nordic features, hinting to the forbearance of his Viking ancestors.

As a teenager, he faced life head-on and went out on a limb to take part in activities that did not come naturally to him. In fact, he seemed to be driven to do things out of his comfort zone, like the time he auditioned for a high school play and landed the lead. It was a leap for the naturally laconic boy who didn't care to be the center of attention. There seemed to be nothing he wouldn't do or try, especially if it intimidated him and meant he could be part of a community or a group. He was a member of 4-H and played high school football. He loved music, so he taught himself how to play several instruments, then pulled together a high school band that played swing at local venues, where the most they ever made for a gig was $3, which they split five ways. They once even made it on South Dakota radio.

His high school newspaper lauded him:

THE BOYS IN THE LIGHT

When Elmer Hovland plays his horn,
You'd swear he had talent the day he was born

Isolation in remote Kenneth was remedied by self-starting endeavors, so, in addition to helping Nels sow and harvest crops, Elmer helped his father build log homes and brooder chicken stoves, porcelain incubators that kept baby chicks warm. He had a natural proclivity for mechanics, saved his money and bought a Model T—then, while his friends waited excitedly for their first ride through town, he spent a few weeks taking it apart "just for the fun of it" so he could see how it worked before reassembling it, finally telling the boys to jump in.

Elmer followed his own star. His lack of interest in being in the spotlight drew his classmates to him even more. He was friends with everyone. If someone was being ignored, he found a way to include them. His senior class yearbook quote was "I never met a person I didn't like."

As a young man, he continued to be guided by scripture, living modestly and benevolently, taking to heart the words from Mary's Bible: "Remove all sin from my imperfect heart, and keep me humble and trusting in thy grace."

While the humble and soft-spoken Elmer shied away from attention, when all was said and done, anyone who knew him believed that, whatever the world might have in store for Elmer Hovland, he would always be a good man in a storm.

After high school, some of his friends went off to college, but Elmer chose to remain in Kenneth to help run the farm and restart the family businesses. A young man, his friends agreed, who would no doubt go on to become a valued community leader in Kenneth, Elmer was a rising star in their humble little tumbleweed town.

. . .

In Waltham, Massachusetts, Sammy hustled round the clock at the diner. Every day, he donned his crisp white shirt, red waist apron, and envelope hat. Days, nights, weekends, and holidays, too, whenever Pa needed him, he was there.

At the diner, the pace was frenetic, but Pa taught Sammy that, no matter what, "You gotta take care of people." In between pouring coffee and wiping down the counter, Sammy learned how to take time to chat up the customers, Pa telling him, "You don't shoo anyone out at closing time."

Naturally gregarious, Sammy took to the "business of people," where he interacted with everyone, from the cop on the beat, to the businessmen who came through, to the young lovers who stopped in to share a root beer float. Listening to town gossip—who was angry, what families were falling out with others, who had money problems, who had romantic liaisons or even the occasional impropriety—he learned how to cajole and console, to listen and to advise. He was quick to give an extra slice of pie to someone he knew was down on his luck or take an IOU from a customer who was short on his bill, to all of which Pa would scold, "Aw, Jeezus, Sammy, you're gonna run me dry."

Sammy would linger for too many extra minutes, dreamy-eyed over the giggly girls he knew from high school, until his father got fed up, yelling at him, "Aw, c'mon, Sammy. We got tables!"

He hustled the breakfast shift, the in-betweens, and the busy lunch crowd, seating people in vinyl booths or on swivel stools, bringing menus, darting between customers at the counter and moving from table to table, taking orders, serving coffee, ringing up checks, and bringing change. He was always on the move.

He worked the floor until Pa ordered him into the kitchen to work the short-order-cook line when they were shorthanded, serving up made-to-order sandwiches, this one without pickles, that one with two, burgers, eggs sunny-side up or over easy, bacon, pancakes, pies, all the while Pa yelling in the kitchen that things were moving too slow.

While Sammy knew his father needed him to help run the business, Pa's demands became too much for him. He became restless and started to resent Pa for holding him back. It all became overwhelming for Sammy, who was antsy to break out and chart his own path. Increasingly butting heads with his father, the tension reached a boiling point when Sammy's older brothers went off to start up a second family diner and Pa put even more weight on his youngest son's shoulders when he told Sammy that one day he would be "takin' over the business."

Feeling like the walls were closing in on him, Sammy started to resent having to be bound to Pa's American dream for the rest of his life. He yearned for some kind of adventure beyond the Monarch Diner.

Elmer graduated high school on time, and Sammy graduated one year later than his classmates, having lost too much time busing tables and frying up food.

Elmer went to work at an assembly plant making farm equipment, then soon got a promotion to testing. Sammy continued to work round the clock at a job he had grown to detest.

The two boys typified millions of teens who were coming of age in a new era of optimism in America. Americans had faith in their futures and in their president, who continued to pledge, "I hope the United States will keep out of this war."

But all that changed on December 7, 1941.

Sammy was cleaning up after the Sunday lunch crowd, listening to the radio, when a flash news bulletin interrupted his ball game. The Japanese had attacked at Pearl Harbor and FDR announced that America was going to war.

Exactly one month later, Sammy happily threw in his apron and quit the diner, and Private DeCola raised his right hand and took the oath to serve his country.

For Elmer the war came at a bad time. At twenty-one, he had just met a "pretty girl" and wanted to be with her all the time.

EIGHT

ON THE RUN

On a cold, overcast December day, the train from Mönchengladbach pulled into the station in Brussels. Young Eddie stepped down into a dizzying crowd of travelers moving every which way, running to catch their connections, porters pushing luggage carts, Belgians greeting their arrivals. For Eddie, it was all a bit overwhelming until he was quietly scooped up by a Joint Distribution Committee aid worker waiting to assist Jewish refugees escaping the Nazis, and he was whisked away.

From Berlin, Hitler spoke openly about the annihilation of the Jews of Europe. At first, he had called Jews vermin and parasites, then a cancer. Now they were *"Untermensch,"* subhuman. Not only had Jews lost the privilege of being German; now they did not even belong to the human race. To further racially profile Germany's Jews, Hitler mandated that all Jewish men be identified by the name "Israel" and women "Sara" in their official documents, and passports were stamped with a large letter *J*. Jewish businesses were "Aryanized" as Jewish families fled, were arrested, or went missing.

With their boy hopefully safe in Belgium, Siegfried and Auguste were still trapped in Germany. A couple of months later, Siegfried's name came up on the police list to be arrested. Astoundingly, at around the same time the Gestapo prepared to apprehend him, Siegfried's and Auguste's passports finally arrived, and they took off.

That night, they ran a few of their belongings to Fritz for safekeeping. Under the cover of darkness, breaking curfew and violating strict rules forbidding Jews to mingle with Christians, they came to Fritz's apartment and handed over a bundle of their family treasures: the silver family menorah, Siegfried's Iron Cross, Auguste's green notebook with her prized recipes, her favorite heirloom silver cake tongs, a few family photos, and Opa Josef's purple velvet inlaid copper-and-ivory-covered family siddur prayer book, in which Opa himself had written in his own hand in Hebrew: "God, please watch over my children."

"Keep these things for us," Siegfried said. "We'll be back to get them when all this blows over."

The Willners knew they could not trust just anyone, but the one constant they could rely on was Fritz and his family, who they believed would never betray them.

The families embraced and promised to see one another again, and then Siegfried and Auguste went on the run.

Like the slow creaking of a heavy iron prison door, the window of opportunity for Jews to get out of Germany was closing. The Jews now fully under siege, the Nazis moved in to find them wherever they were hiding, a phalanx of steel-helmeted storm troopers marching in force with clacking hobnailed jackboots, each footstep landing like a warning shot on the cobblestones as they marched in unison in a thunderous *tromp-tromp-tromp* that echoed throughout Germany, as they banged on doors, pushed their way in, and dragged people out.

As a cold morass of servitude settled over Germany, Hitler's ranting polemics on the radio readied the German people for an all-out attack on Europe. As proud Germans sang the national anthem, "*Deutschland, Deutschland über alles, über alles in der Welt,*" millions of arms thrust outward in militant salute, roaring echoes filled the sky: "*Heil Hitler!*" Siegfried and Auguste raced to Belgium to find their boy.

As the Willners fled the country, the Nazis came into their apartment and seized everything: Auguste's prized china, crystal glasses, paintings, furniture, beds and linens, even Eddie's blue down *Bettdecke* (comforter). They took Auguste's piano. In a farce to portray everything by the letter of the law, "in accordance with rules and regulations," they meticulously catalogued every single possession down to the exact number of tiny silver teaspoons. Their clothing was gathered up and distributed to German families, the rest of their belongings auctioned off to the highest bidder, with proceeds going right into Nazi coffers.

In the *Altersheim* senior home, Opa Josef and some forty other elderly Jews were made to sit for a group portrait in the rose garden before they were loaded onto trains and transferred to a place called Theresienstadt.

The next few months would be marked by fear and chaos for the Willners as they did everything they could to stay one step ahead of the Nazis.

They found Eddie in Schaerbeek, Belgium, an upscale neighborhood of Brussels. To their great relief, he had been taken in and well cared for by the Leeks, an upper-middle-class Flemish Jewish couple who dressed Eddie immaculately and had enrolled him in the most prestigious middle school in the city, the École Moyenne de l'État, the Royal School for Boys, where he picked up the French and Flemish Dutch languages remarkably quickly. At school, he spoke French; at home, he spoke Dutch. As it turned out, it was perfect timing for

ON THE RUN

Siegfried and Auguste's arrival. For a year, the Belgian couple had paid for the Grand Rabbi of Brussels to teach Eddie parts of the Torah in Hebrew to prepare him for his bar mitzvah in one month's time, in a grand ceremony that would bring out the Brussels Jewish community to usher him from thirteen-year-old boy to Jewish manhood.

Siegfried and Auguste must have been elated to find their son thriving. Eddie was anxious to show his father how well he had done. He was getting good grades. He seemed to have matured, embracing a newfound sense of personal discipline. Siegfried was indeed proud of his son and grateful to the Leek family for taking such good care of him.

But the bar mitzvah was not to be. On May 10, 1940, just one week before he was set to read from the Torah, the Nazis stormed into Belgium, and Eddie and his parents went on the run again, this time across the border to northern France. When the Nazis marched into France, the family fled south, hoping to somehow get across the Pyrenees Mountains and on into neutral Spain, but they were caught and imprisoned. In an arduous cycle of being transferred from one facility to another, they spent over a year in and out of various French internment camps at Gurs and Saint-Cyprien, where food was scarce and conditions were, at best, tolerable.

Eddie and his father landed in the Rivesaltes internment camp men's section located on the French coast, where they were separated from Auguste. There, Eddie made friends with a gendarme guard, who seemed to appreciate his joie de vivre and his command of the French language. Through long, lingering days, they fell into a rhythm, the gendarme chatting with adolescent Eddie as a way to pass the time. With little food in the camp, Eddie became listless, so the guard threw him a piece of bread once in a while. Over time, French guard and German boy prisoner made a connection, when, one day, the gendarme stood near the fence and told Eddie he should get out. Incredulous at what he was suggesting, Eddie hesitated, when the guard whispered to him, "*Au revoir. Bonne chance*," before turning away and allowing Siegfried and Eddie to dig a hole in the sand, slip under the barbed wire, and disappear into the night.

NINE

TRAINING

WITH THE WRECKAGE of the U.S. Navy's Pacific Fleet in Honolulu still smoldering following Japan's sneak attack, Hitler declared war on America. That same day, President Roosevelt urged Congress to respond in kind, warning that "never before has there been a greater challenge to life, liberty and civilization." By now, Hitler had conquered most of Europe, expanding his reach from the Arctic Circle all the way to the deserts of North Africa. In the east, he had double-crossed his former conspirator Stalin and had attacked the Soviet Union. German forces had powered through Belarus and Ukraine and were deep inside Russia. Nothing seemed to be able to stop the Nazis. Great Britain, led by its dogged prime minister, Winston Churchill, who had stood alone to repel the Nazi onslaught, was now joined by the U.S. and aided by Canada and its other Commonwealth nations.

In the United States, the declaration of war galvanized the nation as a tremendous swell of patriotism spread, which led young Americans to line up in droves at recruitment stations, waiting to enlist. Bright red, white, and blue recruitment posters sprang up throughout the country urging Americans to join the war effort. The image of a finger-pointing Uncle Sam beckoning, "I WANT <u>YOU</u> for the U.S. ARMY" was ubiquitous, appearing in every main square and every neighborhood in every town. Streamers with patriotic messages went up in post offices, train stations, shop windows, and at the cinema.

At the same time, in Germany, fourteen-year-old Eddie's former classmates, now teenagers, were members of the Hitler Youth, pledging blind allegiance to the Führer, and would soon be of age to serve in the German military.

Thrilled to bust out of the diner and chart a new path for himself, Private Sammy DeCola jumped at the chance to start a new chapter. Within hours of enlisting, he found himself on a military base, standing in a huge aviation hangar along with hundreds of other wide-eyed, anxious boys, many of whom had never ventured far from their small towns or neighborhoods, all looking at each other and "waiting for our orders."

An excited Sammy broke the ice. "I'm ready to go but I need a map cuz I'm not exactly sure where Germany is!" Which left the other recruits chuckling, albeit nervously.

The same scene played out across America as throngs descended on recruitment stations that stayed open twenty-four hours a day as young men clambered to join the Army and the Army Air Corps or the Navy and Marines. Boys as young as fifteen tried to convince their parents to let them go. Some dropped out of high school to join the ranks, wanting to go fight for their country rather than take the time to graduate. Others, sixteen and seventeen years old, lied their way in. Often brothers would sign up together. It was a massive answer to the call to arms.

Women dropped what they were doing to join the Nurse Corps, the WACs, the WAVES, and the WASPs as pilots, electricians, mechanics, and code breakers, and to serve in intelligence. Despite prejudices and the closed doors they were experiencing at home, Blacks, Japanese Nisei, and Native Americans formed up to help the cause in any way they could and would go on to show extraordinary valor in the war that lay ahead of them.

For twenty-one-year-old Elmer, there could not have been a worse time to go to war. While working at the assembly plant, he had just met the girl of his dreams. Harriet in Accounting was a smart, savvy, strawberry blonde, whom Elmer called "a fancy thing from the city." From the moment he laid eyes on her, Elmer was a goner. He wanted to be with her all the time. He arranged his work schedule so he could walk her home, and they took drives up to Sioux Falls in his Model T. Despite a budding rivalry with a boy named Hendrickson, Elmer was determined to win Harriet over.

"She was a nice girl," he would say, then, breaking into a Cheshire cat smile, would add, "And I was persistent." So he stayed home as long as he could. The day he got his draft notice, he proposed to Harriet and she said yes.

"I didn't know if she had settled on me," he would later say, "but I sure had settled on her."

Throughout America, young men worked the lines and the fields until they were called up, then their wives, girlfriends, sisters, and sometimes mothers rolled up their sleeves, stepped in, and took their places, often at hazardous jobs, in factories, in shipyards, and on assembly lines, and volunteered for war-related organizations, all in addition to managing their households. Their contributions, while filling the void, would challenge the notion that women were not suited for certain jobs and would forevermore change the narrative of how America viewed females in the male-dominated workplace.

Almost overnight, America converted 90 percent of her industrial production to the war effort. The plan required buy-in from all

Americans to build up what President Roosevelt called the "Arsenal of Democracy." New factories sprang up all over and existing ones transformed. General Motors went from making cars to making tanks, airplane engines, guns, and trucks, and Chrysler to making aircraft fuselages. At its plant in Ypsilanti, Michigan, the Ford Motor Company churned out B-24 Liberator long-range bombers. The average Ford car had some 15,000 parts, but the B-24 had almost half a million parts plus 300,000 rivets. Production went into overdrive, which eventually saw one B-24 coming off the assembly line every sixty-three minutes. Shop and factory owners found ways to contribute, like the Artistic Furniture Manufacturing Company in Cincinnati, Ohio, a small family-run business whose Jewish owner, Ben Mandel, promptly switched from making upholstered living room furniture to sewing parachutes.

The Stars and Stripes flew everywhere. Americans braced for rationing and helped to raise money for defense. They bought war bonds to invest in America and started massive recycling efforts, saving aluminum foil and tin cans, scrap metal, rubber, even kitchen grease. The American Fat Salvage Committee urged housewives to save all the excess fat rendered from cooking and donate it to the army to help produce explosives.

At basic training in-processing, new recruits were given army physicals, which checked everything from their eyesight to the arches of their feet. Questionnaires and proficiency tests aimed to match their skills and aptitude with their roles in war. If they grew up hunting and were already good shots, or were athletic or high school football players, for example, they became infantry or artillerymen. Auto mechanics were made heavy-vehicle maintenance repairmen, bus drivers became half-track drivers, and welders became combat engineers.

TRAINING

Then it was Sammy's turn.

"Step right up, son. What can *you* do?" asked a sergeant.

"I can cook."

"Good," said the sergeant. "You're gonna be a cook."

Handing Sammy his paperwork, he said, "Whip up some good chow for those boys."

Private Elmer Hovland was made a tanker and went off to Fort Sill, Oklahoma, on a troop train for basic training. All soldiers went through basic training, learning close-order drill, military courtesies, and how to take orders from officers and sergeants. They learned how to assemble and disassemble weapons, plant anti-tank mines, set booby traps, fling hand grenades, but, above all, said one soldier, "we learned to kill or be killed."

Elmer went on to learn about medium tanks, how to load, target, and fire the main gun, how to drive and maneuver, and how to bail out of them. He scored high on his math and mechanical aptitude tests. Drill sergeants noticed his steady affect and the fact that his peers were drawn to him. He performed well on all tasks, and while it was an open secret among recruits "don't volunteer for anything," Elmer answered nearly all of his instructor's calls of "I need a volunteer" with a Minnesota-accented "Yep, sure, Sergeant, I'll do it." The drill instructors noticed a leadership quality in Elmer and flagged his file.

He was called before a selection board, where a captain asked him, of all things, if he'd really taken apart a Model T and put it back together again. When he replied that he had, the captain told him he was going to be an officer. Having only ever seen himself as just one of the guys, Elmer retorted, "But I don't want to be an officer."

"Well, son," the captain said, "you don't have a choice. Congratulations, you're going to be an armor officer."

Unlike other young men who were destined for officer ranks, Elmer had no college education and, in fact, possessed a mediocre high school academic record. On paper, his work background in Kenneth, farming and building brooder chicken stoves, lacked the typical qualifications for such a responsible role. Nonetheless, armed with his orders, he went off to officer candidate school, where he was commissioned, and a reluctant Second Lieutenant Hovland officially became a leader of men.

The next months were spent getting the boys in fighting shape.

After training, Elmer and Sammy were both assigned to D Company of the 32nd Armored Regiment, 3rd Armored "Spearhead" Division, which would be called upon to lead the fight on the front lines of battle. A brand-new unit, it would soon be assigned the M4 Sherman, a brand-new tank right off the assembly line.

Soldiers were issued a duffel bag full of combat gear, uniforms, helmets, dog tags, and small pocket prayer book. They were inoculated against tetanus and typhoid and sat through films on venereal disease. A dashing photo was taken of each of them in dress uniform. They signed their wills, a colonel barked a "Give 'em hell" speech, and they were off to war.

TEN

THE VINEYARDS

AFTER FINDING AUGUSTE, who had been in hiding nearby, Eddie and his parents took off, running farther south into the French countryside at Languedoc, hoping to flee somehow over the Pyrenees and into Spain. On a balmy summer day, the family finally reached the township of Elne. At the Canton de la Plaine d'Illibéris, a majestic landscape lay before them. To the south they could see the snow-capped Pyrenees in the distance, but they were still too far away to reach them, and, anyway, with daunting peaks of 3,500 feet, it would be impossible to navigate the treacherous terrain of rocky boulders on their own. With little money to hire a guide, they continued on, searching for someplace where they hoped they could lie low until they could figure out how to get over the mountains.

Located on the edge of the arrondissement of Perpignan, Ortaffa was a pretty, provincial winemaking village just off the coast of the Mediterranean. With a fresh coastal breeze blowing in off the glittering Balearic Sea, they made their way past stucco farmhouses and fertile fields with lush green grasses that swayed in the breeze. They entered the village and walked up a narrow maze of winding arcaded streets passing salmon-colored villas with flower boxes with terracotta "monk and nun" roof tiles set sharp against a clear azure sky, until they came to a stone church, where they found a Catholic priest.

He greeted the family kindly, shaking Siegfried's hand. After hearing their predicament, he ushered them to the back of the church, where the Jewish family stood beneath a crucifix of Jesus on the cross. The priest called for the mayor, a man named Ros, and summoned his friend, Monsieur Thubert, a schoolteacher, who both came at once. With concerned looks, the three discussed the matter. Then, at clear risk to their own lives, they came up with a plan to hide the Willners. The mayor immediately arranged for false identification papers to be drawn up. Meanwhile the priest would shelter them in the rectory and the teacher would help blend them into the community. A local farmer gave them jobs in the vineyards as their cover and to help them make money to get to Spain. Together, in secret, the villagers of Ortaffa would conceal the family within the local viticulture community.

Eddie and his parents remained in Ortaffa for months, hiding in plain sight. While Siegfried worked on a harvesting crew, Eddie stomped barefoot, macerating grapes that would become Languedoc-Roussillon wine. To the delight of the community, Auguste played small piano concerts whenever she could in small repayment for their safe harbor.

While Siegfried felt grateful that he had landed temporarily in sympathetic hands, he realized time was not on their side and that they would have to flee over the mountains before the first snowfall.

Eddie developed broad shoulders from carrying heavy buckets of grapes, and he thrived working alongside French day laborers, who gave him his first glass of wine. Despite the uncertainty, it was a beautiful time for the family. Eddie felt emboldened, like it was him and his parents against the world.

The whole arrangement worked well until one day the French Nazi-collaborating Vichy police showed up. A raid had discovered the family's falsified papers. Someone had tipped off the authorities and the family was arrested.

It was a stunning betrayal. After two years on the run, they were shattered to find themselves back in the clutches of the Nazis. They had been double-crossed by someone they thought they could trust, though they did not know which of the villagers had outed them.

Suddenly, Siegfried realized that his options to protect his family had evaporated. They had come so close to escaping, but their luck had run out.

A crushing silence hung in the air as the family was led away, then put on a train bound for Paris, where Vichy police were gathering Jews from all over France, putting them in cattle cars, and telling them they were going back to Germany "to work."

ELEVEN

NEW YORK HARBOR

ELMER MARRIED HARRIET and spent his last precious moments with his new bride. Almost every young man of fighting age in Kenneth and Luverne had already shipped out. Of the twenty-one male graduates of Elmer's high school class, twenty went into the military; only one boy with a heart condition reluctantly stayed behind as his classmates marched off to war.

In New York Harbor, tens of thousands of new recruits of the 3rd Armored Division boarded sub-bareboat charters and various vessels, including huge British ocean liners like the Cunard Line's RMS *Aquitania*, a sister ship of the *Lusitania*. With her spacious chandeliered dining rooms, ornate lounges, and spiral staircases, the luxury passenger carrier once called the "Ship Beautiful," a nine-hundred-footer with ten decks, had been painted battleship gray and repurposed into a troop transport, which was now crammed to capacity with American GIs. That September, some sixteen thousand 3rd Armored Division troops would board dozens of ships for the crossing to England.

On the dock, Sammy said goodbye to Pa, who had accompanied him this far. Although his relationship with his father was still strained, Pa kissed him on both cheeks, looked him in the eye, and told him, "*Rendimi orgoglioso*" ("Make me proud").

Melancholy lingered as, one by one, soldiers' names were called and they filed up the gangplank, many looking back to wave just once more to their loved ones and the cheering crowd. As they descended into the hold of the ship, the sky rained confetti as men doffed their hats and women waved handkerchiefs. In the belly of the ship, bunks were stacked from floor to ceiling, and the boys settled in for the weeklong journey.

Ships cast off into the sunset as smoke billowed from the *Aquitania*'s four funnels; a myriad of sea vessels left their berths and slid forth toward the Atlantic, passing the Statue of Liberty, who held her torch high. Lady Liberty—who, over the years, had welcomed millions of new immigrants to her shores—now bid Godspeed to America's boys as they sailed off to Europe. Liberty became smaller and smaller behind them until she could no longer be seen.

With their whole lives ahead of them, just when life should have been filled with adventure, charms of new loves, and lessons of the workaday world, hundreds of thousands of lives were sidetracked. America, which, just a few short years before, was steadfastly isolationist and against entering the brewing conflict, was now sending an entire generation of its youth back to Europe to fight another war. Sammy and the boys of D Company were on their way to England from where they would launch to France to take part in the invasion of Europe.

TWELVE

TRANSPORT 31

It all happened so fast. The ghetto. The deportation. The sealed cattle car.

—Elie Wiesel

I wanted to look big and strong like a man.

—Eddie Willner

Throughout France, Vichy collaborators were capturing Jews and handing them over to their Nazi masters. In Drancy, a northeastern suburb of Paris, the Nazis set up a transit camp to process tens of thousands of European Jews who had been arrested while living or hiding out in France.

Corralled into the overcrowded camp, Eddie and his parents waited until it was announced that they were going back to Germany to be resettled and to work.

With France's national rail company, SNCF, working in full cooperation to transport the Jews, on September 11, 1942, Vichy police loaded passengers, including Eddie and his parents, with valises in

TRANSPORT 31

hand and bundles on their backs, into Transport 31. One hundred people were crammed into each of ten cattle cars including 171 children, like Eddie, under the age of seventeen. On the train with the Willners was one little blond-haired, blue-eyed Jewish girl, nine-year-old Anny Yolande Horowitz. The doors were slammed shut, the latch was bolted, and the train was on its way.

Telex XXVb-162 was sent to Adolf Eichmann and Rudolf Höss, commandant of a place called Auschwitz, reporting that Transport 31, filled with "1,000 Jews," was in transit.

Packed to the breaking point, the cars were crammed to standing room only as the deportees rode in near darkness, their bodies pressing tightly into each other. Other than a small slit in the door, there was no ventilation, making it hard to breathe. There was no food and only one pail to serve as a toilet for a hundred people.

The passengers were utterly bewildered. Some were deep in thought, some wept, some prayed. Some just stared vacantly. Mothers tried to comfort their children: "Don't cry. I am here with you. I'm going to protect you. I have always protected you and I'm not going to stop now."

Despite his fears, Eddie looked up to his parents for reassurance. Locked in a tight huddle, he felt secure with his parents by his side. Against the despair in the cattle car, to him they radiated strength and calm. They were a strong, close family. They had been through things before. They would manage, Eddie thought, as long as they could remain together. Siegfried turned to them.

"If we get separated," he said, "we'll meet up in Brussels when all this is over."

Hopes for a short journey to Germany faded. After three agonizing days and nearly one thousand miles spent in the suffocating boxcar, during which several died from the trauma, the train suddenly lurched to a halt. They had finally arrived at their destination. This was not Germany but Kosel, in Nazi-occupied Poland.

The doors slid open, fresh air rushed in, and blinding daylight seared across the faces of the masses inside. Chaos erupted as armed SS guards shouted over barking German shepherds. "All males between the ages of sixteen and fifty, *out*! Women, children, and the elderly remain on the train!"

"*Raus! Raus! Schnell!*" ("Get out! Move faster!"), the guards yelled as dazed men and boys spilled out onto the station platform, the guards hitting them with rifle butts and rubber truncheons as they descended amid the chaos and commotion, snarling dogs on tight leashes lunging and nipping at the passengers, all of it intended to shock and disorient.

In the cattle car, Siegfried turned to Eddie, who had just turned sixteen one month earlier. Eddie clung to his mother until she gave him a push to go with his father—a mother's instinct, perhaps, sensing he would be safer in this group of able-bodied men being ordered off the train. As they jumped down, Siegfried turned once again to Auguste and said, "We'll meet in Brussels." Eddie looked up at his mother, wondering when he would see her again. He gave her one final look before moving away with the group.

"*Raus! Schnell!*"

Frightened men and boys assembled on the platform, the Nazis shoving and whacking them into submission and forming them up into rows.

An SS guard strode through, carefully inspecting each man and boy from head to toe, making his selections, ordering them to move to the right of the platform or to the left. The stronger-looking ones were sent to the right.

Eddie's and Siegfried's physiques had been strengthened by months working in the vineyards. At forty-eight, Siegfried had barely missed the cutoff age of fifty. He was one of the oldest in this group, but he looked sturdier than many. He stood at attention, his posture pulled up to his full height like the disciplined military man he was, shoulders back, eyes straight ahead, looking strong and competent.

His military bearing must have impressed.

"To the right."

Now it was Eddie's turn. Just sixteen, he was rather small for his age and looked younger. The SS guard looked him over, this young boy mimicking his father, chest out, shoulders back, chin up, a boy soldier wanting to look big and strong. As Siegfried had, Eddie stared straight ahead, waiting for judgment.

"To the right."

In the blink of an eye, Eddie's childhood was over, and in that moment he was forced to become a man.

The doors on the train were slammed shut and re-bolted. On the platform, some three hundred men and boys stood in stunned silence, forced to look straight ahead as the train carrying their loved ones rocked forward, then rolled slowly down the tracks and on into the distance.

An hour later, the train again came to a halt. The doors slid open, and Auguste, little Anny Horowitz, and the remaining nearly seven hundred other passengers were ordered out. Women and girls climbed down with their belongings, helping the young ones and the elderly to descend. Once on the platform, carrying their parcels, they were led down the tracks.

At the *Judenrampe*, the Jewish disembarking platform, the remaining men were separated from the women and children. Then, just as the guards had done on the train platform in Kosel, the SS looked over each person and made their decisions:

"To the right. To the left."

From Transport 31, seventy-eight women were selected and sent to the right. The rest, including Auguste and little Anny Horowitz, were sent to the left.

That group was quietly guided farther into the camp. Along the way, the SS told the nervous arrivals they had nothing to fear. After their long, arduous journey, it was a reassuring thing to hear, and they hoped the days ahead would be better than the distress they had endured for three days in the cattle cars.

As they walked, they were told they had been chosen for "special treatment." In a carefully orchestrated plan to keep them pacified and unaware, they were given instructions that may have calmed them: "You are going to work. We *want* you to work. We want you to be healthy. We need people with skills."

In the main building, they were directed, "Leave your luggage, you will come back to get it later. Be sure to tell the registrar your occupation and your skills so that you can be properly placed for work." But before they could begin work, they were told, they needed to take a shower.

Led to an undressing hallway, they disrobed themselves and their children, relieved to be cleaning themselves after days if not weeks without bathing. They were instructed to tie their shoelaces together, hang their clothing on hooks, and remember the numbers so they could easily retrieve their things when they had finished washing. Signs with slogans written in German, French, and other languages hung about the room: "Take a shower. Clean is good."

With seemingly nothing to fear, they entered the "washroom." Unbeknownst to them, however, it wasn't a shower at all. It was all an illusion, a carefully designed deception to keep them unsuspecting. The SS were on a timetable and they couldn't risk having a panic or mass hysteria on their hands.

TRANSPORT 31

Nazi guards stood by, monitoring the line, as naked Jewish women, young and old, some no doubt pregnant, went into the concrete building holding their babies and clutching their children's hands. Once they were inside, the room was shut and hermetically sealed. Then pellets of Zyklon B, a powerful cyanide-based pesticide, were dropped in through a small opening. Instead of water washing over them, the pellets began to vaporize into a poisonous gas that slowly permeated throughout the chamber. Inhaling the toxic fumes, the women and children began choking and suffocating, which was followed by desperate cries for air and screams of unbearable agony. Several minutes went by before eventually everything went silent.

And just like that, Auguste Willner, age forty-two, a woman in the prime of her life, full of passion and joy, with dreams of watching her son grow up—and little Anny Horowitz, only nine, became two of more than 1 million human beings who would systematically be murdered, at six thousand lives a day, in the gas chambers of Auschwitz-Birkenau's extermination factory in Hitler's Final Solution to the Jewish problem.

When all was quiet, a cleanup crew came through, hauled out the bodies, and prepared the death chamber for the next group. They took the clothing down from the hooks, gathered up the suitcases, shoes, eyeglasses, dolls, and toys, and dumped them in collection bins that had already piled high.

And so the so-called Aryan super race descended to the depths of complete and utter depravity. Hitler's cult followed him right into the abyss to perpetuate one of the most horrific atrocities and the largest genocide ever to be carried out by human hand in an elaborately calculated scheme to wipe the Jews of Europe off the face of the earth.

PART II

THIRTEEN

SHIP TO ENGLAND

Americanism is a matter of the mind and heart; Americanism is not, and never was, a matter of race or ancestry.

—Franklin Delano Roosevelt

THE VOYAGE TO England was equal parts exciting and daunting for the boys of D Company. Sailing onward, German U-boats, on the hunt, lurked below the surface, looking to sink Allied troop and cargo transports that were on their way to Europe.

In the junior enlisted quarters, the young privates and corporals of D Company, 32nd Armored Regiment, 3rd Armored Division, spent time trying to manage seasickness, walking the corridors, lingering in bunks stacked five high, looking over photographs, reading and rereading letters, alone in their thoughts, and contemplating the uncertainty of what lay ahead.

In addition to those who had already trained together, fresh faces now joined their ranks. They tried to make friends, eighteen-, nineteen-, twenty-year-olds, many just out of high school. They were farmers, coal miners, steel factory and sawmill workers—a cross section of America that mingled first-generation Americans and immigrants and native-born sons of blue bloods, boys who hailed from the industrial north to the rural heartland, all united in one singular task.

From good families and broken homes, the impoverished and the well-to-do, boys from all walks of life and all ethnic backgrounds, from California's fertile Central Valley to the cornfields of Iowa, from Texas cattle country to the spongy swamps of Georgia, boys from every corner of America were thrust together. Young men from families long rooted in America with names like Claude Young, Tom Church, and Prescott Smith were going to war alongside immigrant and first generations like Elmer, Sammy, Laddie Devecka, and Sal Pugliese. High school graduates and high school dropouts were now bow gunners, loaders, drivers, tank commanders, kitchen crew, and half-track drivers, all wearing the same triangle-shaped 3rd Armored Division "Spearhead" patch.

They were as green as any new soldier could be, young men whose greatest achievements so far had been scoring a home run, working that first job, getting a kiss from a high school sweetheart.

For most, it was the first time they were away from home and for nearly all the first time on a ship. Many were nervous; some were excited and ready to go, like the soldier who wrote home, "I was almost shocked when I read a paper in which it was stated that German soldiers were deserting. I worry night and day that the war will be over before I get there."

Sammy was happy to let his former life go and saw it all as a big adventure. On the ship, he passed the time playing pinochle and getting to know the boys of D Company whom he would be feeding.

Sensing their apprehension, he inserted himself into their conversations.

"Hey, boys," he interrupted, "I can't wait to get over there and meet those French girls."

He joked about sending out a raiding party to go find the officers' quarters to confiscate the champagne they "must be" hoarding somewhere on the ship; and he entertained them with a steady stream of mostly off-color jokes that made everyone chuckle and, in some cases, blush.

Sammy was older than most. A bit more grizzled and life-experienced, one of the recruits chided that, at twenty-four, Sammy was the "old man" among them.

"Well," he quipped in reply, "I can be a big brother to ya, and I can be a dad to ya, but I can't be a wife to you boys, so don't ask me!" Right out of the gate, he was magnetic and reassuring, instantly drawing in those who were looking to take the edge off their nerves.

Sammy met Private Fred Headrick from Chattanooga, a tall, ruggedly handsome redhead with a disarming boy-next-door smile and a charming aw-shucks manner. He had an exaggerated Tennessee accent, his speech slow and one of rising endings, his broad grin a reflection of his only half-serious nature.

A high school dropout and hosiery mill worker, unlike the others, Fred seemed unfazed about what awaited them in Europe. He oozed southern charm, even now when he snickered at Sammy and said with a long, slow drawl, "DeCola? Zat your real name? I'm gon' call you Pepsi," and broke out in a big ear-to-ear grin. The name stuck. After that day, Private Sammy DeCola became known as just "Pepsi."

It didn't take long for the boys to get the hang of it, and the silly GI monikers rolled off their tongues, nicknaming each other for some physical attribute or a ridiculous twist on their name. Hulking six-foot-five Carl Smith became "Big Smith," which meant that five-foot-four Sam Smith, naturally, became "Little Smith." Scanlon, an Irish kid from Scranton with a prominent nose, became "Bugle Scanlon." The Jewish kid from New York became "Brooklyn." Hard-to-pronounce last names were replaced with easy-to-remember sophomoric names that cracked them all up, leaving some laughing until their sides split. Smieja, a first generation from Poland, became "Smeegee." Pete Falatovich, a slender, lanky kid, became "Fats." The Greek guy whose name no one could pronounce became "George the Greek." Hank Herz spoke a little German, so they named him "Heinie Herz." They called the Native American guy "Chief."

Fred, naturally, became Redhead Fred. Having just turned eighteen, Private James Vance was one of the youngest among them. A cotton farmer's son from Chickasaw, Mississippi, a bright-eyed boy with an angelic face, downy pink cheeks, and unusually long eyelashes, he was a shy kid who just wanted to fit in with the older guys when, much to his chagrin, someone named him "Baby Face." It was a name that would stick with him for the rest of the war.

They assembled on and around Pepsi's bunk over endless games of cards and craps.

When interest waned, Pepsi turned their attention to baseball, where he got a lively debate rolling about which was the better team, the Red Sox, the Yankees, or the Dodgers, and who was the better hitter, Joe DiMaggio, Babe Ruth, or Lou Gehrig. As the ship steamed its way across the Atlantic, Pepsi's disarming humor brought the boys of Company D closer together before they had even arrived in England.

Despite the German submarine threat, D Company made it across the Atlantic without incident.

The division arrived in southwestern England and spent the next ten months training on England's Salisbury Plain and preparing to launch to Europe.

SHIP TO ENGLAND

Elmer completed armor officer training at Fort Knox, Kentucky. In Kenneth, on final home leave, he kissed goodbye his beautiful Harriet, who was newly pregnant, lingering until he had to let her go. Pained to leave his new wife and unborn child behind, he made his way to New York City.

In the officer's cabin of his ship, coming to terms with his new role, brand-new second lieutenant Elmer Hovland was immersed in thought as he thumbed through his army-issued pocket catechism, trying to find a passage that provided solace.

"Lord, we pray thee . . . to strengthen and protect the soldiers of our country. Support them in battle. Keep them safe, endue them with courage." His thoughts constantly shifted back and forth between Harriet and the mission that lay ahead. By the end of the voyage, his catechism was already dog-eared and well broken in.

In England, the battalion's lieutenants came together. A few were West Pointers or other military academy graduates. The rest had college degrees or at least some advanced education under their belts. Elmer, whose formal education ended with high school, was the anomaly. Before long, some were strutting around, peacocking and posturing, swag on full display as they boasted about past accomplishments, working to establish their places in the pecking order among the young officers of the battalion. Elmer observed it all, unimpressed. The quiet Minnesota farm boy, who didn't have a degree, was a newcomer to the army and to the officer corps, had no long-term military career aspirations, and didn't even want to be an officer in the first place, didn't want any part of it. He soon caught the eye of another lieutenant, who didn't ask him about his education and didn't seem to care about his pedigree. It didn't seem to bother Second

Lieutenant Charles Myers in the least that Elmer was not a college man.

Lieutenant Myers, from York, Pennsylvania, was movie star handsome. A square-jawed all-star athlete and graduate from Gettysburg College, Myers had a honey-blond burr crew cut, a solid neck, and the muscular build of a welterweight. He had lettered in almost every sport, from football to basketball to tennis, in both high school and in college. An academic scholar at Gettysburg, he was a member of the Scabbard and Blade military society and an Alpha Tau Omega fraternity brother.

In England, as the two newly minted lieutenants, Elmer and Myers, prepared themselves to lead young troops on the front lines of battle, the enlisted men trained to perfect their tactics. Redhead Fred and Baby Face Vance, as it would turn out, would become as close as brothers, serving shoulder to shoulder in Lieutenant Myers's tank. Meanwhile, Pepsi would be serving up hot chow, always delivered with a side dish of levity and lightheartedness.

FOURTEEN

ŁAZY

The law changes, conscience doesn't.

—Sophie Scholl

HITLER'S TWISTED CAMPAIGN to enshrine a blond-haired, blue-eyed, Nordic-looking Aryan master race was in full swing. At the same time, the Nazis cast their net wider to weed out anyone at odds with the regime and anyone challenging their notion of a pure, cleansed society. Caught up in that net were Roma, gay people, Jehovah's Witnesses, and even the disabled, who were deemed to be nothing more than a financial drain on society. Such "burdensome individuals" who undermined the illusion of Aryan perfection had no place in Hitler's new Germany, and so they, too, were swept off the streets and into Nazi death camps.

By 1942, almost no one dared stand up to the totalitarian state anymore. Twenty-one-year-old University of Munich student Sophie Scholl of the *Weiße Rose* (White Rose) resistance group begged her fellow citizens to rise up to confront the Nazis, distributing pamphlets that read "Our current 'state' is the dictatorship of evil. . . . I ask you, if you know that, then why don't you act? Why do you tolerate these rulers gradually robbing you, in public and in private, of one right after another, until one day nothing, absolutely nothing, remains but the machinery of the state, under the command of criminals and drunkards?"

Sophie was arrested, tried, and convicted. In her defense, she said, "Somebody, after all . . . had to make a start. What we wrote and said is also believed by many others. They just don't dare express themselves as we did."

In February 1943, in Stadelheim Prison in Munich, Sophie and her brother were gruesomely guillotined for the crime of treason to the Nazi state.

In her last words, the defiant young fighter faced her executioners and said: "How can we expect righteousness to prevail when there is hardly anyone willing to give himself up individually to a righteous cause? Such a fine sunny day, and I have to go, but what does my death matter, if through us thousands of people are awakened and stirred to action?"

As Jews and others were systematically exterminated, the "fortunate ones" like Eddie and Siegfried were landing in slave-labor camps cropping up throughout Germany, Poland, and other conquered states.

The Łazy (pronounced Wah-zih) outpost, just thirty miles from Auschwitz in the Silesian Voivodeship, was a small camp located in the middle of a rural Polish village dotted with wooden cottages. A crude, makeshift work camp run by the Schmelt organization, it was overseen mostly by old and wounded Wehrmacht soldiers and some local auxiliary units assigned to manage a workforce of several hundred Jewish prisoners.

Still wearing the clothing they had arrived in from France weeks earlier, a six-pointed Star of David patch was sewn on their jackets, and Eddie and Siegfried were set to hard labor, repairing railroad tracks damaged by Russian bombs or working on road gangs to expand the main highway from Katowice to Berlin. It was difficult work for those unaccustomed to heavy manual labor, but Siegfried swung his pickax like a coal miner, setting the example for Eddie that, to make it, they would have to be seen as providing value as the strongest and hardest workers.

A few months in, a new kid arrived in the camp. Maurits "Mike" Swaab was a chubby fifteen-year-old Dutch Jewish kid with tousled brown hair that swept across his big brown eyes who hailed from a working-class family from Amsterdam's Jewish Quarter and lived just a short ten-minute walk across the canals from Anne Frank's house. Mike's family had already been murdered in other camps, so he arrived in Łazy an orphan, traumatized and terrified, constantly looking over his shoulder in anticipation of the next threat. His spirits crushed, he desperately needed someone to cling to. The sight of Eddie, a boy like him who could speak some Dutch, who had the protection of his father, a man who looked competent and trustworthy, was just the security Mike needed. The two boys were instantly drawn to one another, and Siegfried took Mike under his wing.

The Polish winter was colder than what they were used to, but they managed the best they could by layering all their clothing. Billeted in an old wooden bunkhouse with some heat and the occasional warm running water, they washed once a week and ate prison rations of soup with turnips and potatoes and a piece of bread with an occasional pat of margarine.

Everyone missed home-cooked meals, especially Mike, who had been raised on a diet rich in Dutch cheese and butter. He looked on longingly, drooling, when local civilian workers enjoyed large pieces of crusty bread dripping with jam or honey or smothered in cheese, or smoky-smelling sausages, right in front of the salivating inmates.

The Wehrmacht guards had little tolerance for inept or loitering workers and the occasional rifle butt blow to a prisoner's back kept him focused. The first time Eddie was beaten was when one of the local Polish *Hilfstruppen* guards, a man he and Mike called "the Schmuck" behind his back, ordered the inmates to move some bricks. Speaking broken German with a heavy Polish accent, the guard butchered the German language so comically that Eddie burst out laughing. That was a big mistake, an insult to the guard, who was trying his best to impress his German bosses. He struck Eddie with such force it almost knocked him out. Lessons came fast at Łazy.

Siegfried knew he had to ensure Eddie didn't step out of line again, so when Eddie ran to his father seeking comfort, Siegfried smacked his son instead. Knowing the guards had killed for less, Siegfried drilled home the point that, while Eddie had been fortunate this time, any further misstep could lead to his death.

The beating from the guard had been a tough lesson, but the slap from Siegfried stung even more. Mike watched it all and understood Siegfried's intent. There was no time to waste. The sooner the boys learned the tough lessons of camp life, the better.

That night in the bunkhouse, Siegfried put the boys through some paces, coaching them to stand at full attention with military respect when being addressed by a guard, and even teaching them how to take a blow without flinching. Certain guards were prone to be more lenient with inmates they perceived to be brave or hardworking. To fight off hunger pangs, the boys would need to cope with less food than their bodies craved. Before long, the two young teens started to get the hang of the finer points of navigating a forced-labor colony.

ŁAZY

After six months, the Łazy project was shut down and the prisoners were transferred to nearby Ottmuth, where they worked on construction projects, excavating and laying concrete foundations for new buildings. Eddie and Mike often finished earlier than the others, sometimes earning a cigarette as a reward, which they traded with other prisoners for bread. Before long, they realized that if they worked well together, they could improve their chances of making it through the day. They carried on this way until Mike was pulled off the construction site to work indoors on the assembly line in the nearby Bata shoe factory, making boots for German troops, and was threatened with a beating if he did not meet his quota of two hundred heels a day.

While Bata, a civilian Czech shoe company, had been appropriated by the Nazis and the owners run off, many industrialists, including some of Germany's largest, most well-known companies, took full advantage of Jewish slave labor and saw profits soar. In fact, slave labor would be used throughout Germany by companies like I. G. Farben, which manufactured Zyklon B gas pellets for use in the gas chambers, Daimler-Benz, Porsche/Volkswagen, BMW, Dr. Oetker food company, and Siemens. IBM's German affiliate allegedly even provided the punch card technology that would be used to identify and keep a running tally of the number of Jews arrested and ultimately murdered by the Nazis. Some of Germany's industrialists even became auxiliary officers in the SS.

A year and a half into their imprisonment, Siegfried had a beard, Eddie's thick black curls were unruly, and Mike's hair fell to his shoulders. Their clothing was now frayed and threadbare and the soles of their shoes were worn.

The boys grew close that challenging first year. Despite their differences, they found that their strengths complemented each other. Eddie had been raised with German order and discipline and thought through things logically; Mike had blue-collar street smarts and moved through life sensing things. Eddie was wired for optimism; Mike, edgy and distrusting, could easily spot a dangerous situation. Eddie understood the German character and the German language; Mike did not, so he stayed glued to Eddie. In time, they realized, they not only liked each other; they needed each other.

Siegfried encouraged the boys to grow closer; he saw that they seemed to balance one another. He became a surrogate father to Mike and tried to get all three of them on the same work details as often as possible so that he could watch over the boys, guide them, and protect them.

At Ottmuth, the guards yelled constantly at the prisoners to work harder and faster, threatening them to shape up or they would be shipped out to other camps that they promised were far worse. Then one day the group of several hundred inmates was assembled and 188 names were read off from a list, Siegfried's, Eddie's, and Mike's among them. They were pulled out of the group and put on a transport that, unbeknownst to them, was headed for Auschwitz.

FIFTEEN

COMING ASHORE

Soldiers, Sailors and Airmen,
  You are about to embark upon the greatest crusade.
  The hopes and prayers of liberty loving people everywhere march with you.
     —General Dwight D. Eisenhower's speech,
       "The Eyes of the World Are Upon You," June 5, 1944

Oh, Kitty, the best part about the invasion is that I have the feeling that friends are on the way.
     —Anne Frank, diary entry, June 6, 1944 (D-Day)

IN LATE 1943, President Roosevelt appointed General Dwight D. Eisenhower to serve as the Supreme Allied Commander and lead the invasion of Europe. His directive from the Combined Chiefs of Staff read "You will enter the continent of Europe and in conjunction with other Allied nations, undertake operations aimed at the heart of Germany and the destruction of her armed forces...."

Training ended in England and Company D and the 3rd Armored Division would soon set sail for France.

On June 6, 1944, D-Day, as dawn broke, the largest combined invasion force ever assembled descended on the beaches of France's picturesque Normandy coastline.

It would be a day of chaos and hellfire. In anticipation of a possible Allied attack, some 50,000 German troops were well dug in on a fifty-mile stretch of French coastline on beaches the Allies had codenamed Sword, Gold, Juno, Omaha, and Utah. In the most ambitious sea and airborne operation ever undertaken, more than 10,000 ships ferried in 156,000 Allied troops that, in addition to the Americans, included British, Canadian, Australian, Free French commandos, and others. As hundreds of bombers, fighters, and reconnaissance planes filled the sky, some 23,000 paratroopers dropped behind enemy lines to attack from the rear. When the Allies rushed the beaches, waiting German machine guns assaulted them, mowing down wave after wave of troops coming ashore until the tide turned a bloody red. When the sun set on that day, some 9,000 Allied troops lay dead or wounded.

Overwhelmed by the huge numbers landing on Normandy's shores, by the end of the day the Germans were in retreat, and by the third week in June, Eisenhower's invasion force had secured the beachhead and the sea-lanes and commanded the skies. Despite their initial success, however, they would soon face a deadly and determined enemy not far inland.

Those first troops sacrificed greatly to pave the way for the next wave of landing craft to hit the beaches. Now, with the Allied foothold secure, it was the 3rd Armored Division's turn to go ashore.

By June 24, the beachhead was a beehive of Allied activity and an open throughway for thousands more to pour in, bringing in a steady stream of cargo and equipment, causing traffic jams in the man-made port that saw jeeps, bulldozers, and war machinery of all kinds coming ashore. It was a sight to behold. What had been a sleepy French coastline just three weeks earlier had been miraculously transformed into the busiest port in the world.

Steaming across the English Channel, D Company prepared to enter northern France at Omaha Beach.

The channel was filled with landing craft and vessels sliding forth through the sea. Under gray skies, the ocean swelled as ships carrying thousands of 3rd Armored Division troops made their way southward, sailing across mostly calm waters that belied the storm that lay ahead. On the corridor to war, troops were quiet, and they were scared. There was a lot of silent reflection. Pepsi was nervous for himself but even more for the boys who would be fighting on the front line.

They were excited and nervous, and despite the connections they had made since the first days of training, they would soon be tested. Still very much separate individuals, they would have to learn to become a team in war and to learn to trust one another with their lives. A somber mood left each man looking at his neighbor and thinking, *I wonder how many of us will make it back home alive.*

Despite their apprehension, the hundred-mile Channel crossing was mostly uneventful. The tankers got a chance to get some fresh air on deck before going into the bellies of their landing craft to climb inside their tanks. Helmets on, they waited.

Elmer looked one last time at his combat prayer book and found comfort in Isaiah: "In quietness and trust is your strength."

In the wake of D-Day, Omaha Beach was a panorama of destruction. The fighting had moved inland, but the invasion had left the beach a graveyard littered with sharp, twisted metal and derelict vehicles. Mangled destruction lay half-submerged and rusting in the brine. Company D landing craft moved up to the shoreline; the outer doors were opened and the ramps lowered; and as waves slapped the hull, 3rd Armored Division tanks spilled out, pushed through the shallow tide, and rolled onto dry land.

While many were anxious about what lay ahead, by the time they finally reached French soil, some were eager to take on the fight, like the tanker who disembarked, yelling at the top of his lungs, "Look out, Hitler. Here we come!"

SIXTEEN

AUSCHWITZ

Monsters exist, but they are too few in number to be truly dangerous. More dangerous are the common men, the functionaries ready to believe and to act without asking questions.

—Primo Levi

I became a person without a name, known only by my number.

—Edward Gastfriend, Holocaust survivor

AT AROUND THE same time the boys of Company D were coming ashore, Eddie, Mike, and Siegfried were entering through the gates of Auschwitz.

One hundred eighty-eight Jewish men and boys were transported from Ottmuth westward through the Upper Silesian countryside through the Ehrenforst to Blachownia Śląska. On approach, warning signs with black skulls pointed the way to a compound hidden deep in the woods.

At the entrance to the camp, the Wehrmacht handed over their prisoners to sharp, highly regimented gray-uniformed Nazi SS guards.

Up above, iron lettering spelled out an ominous message to the new arrivals: *"Arbeit Macht Frei"* ("Work Makes You Free"). Eddie, Mike, and Siegfried had no idea what to expect but sensed that work probably didn't make you free and, in fact, nothing about this eerie, unsettling place could be trusted. Rumor had it that Auschwitz was killing people.

The compound, laid out over ten acres, about the size of ten city blocks, was surrounded by a concrete wall that stood fourteen feet high—high enough to conceal from the outside the barbarity that was going on inside the camp. A double coil of barbed razor wire spanned the entire top of the wall and a high-powered electrified fence provided a second layer of security. Armed guards in concrete watchtowers monitored as the new inmates shuffled in. At night, searchlights panned the camp, ensuring no one escaped. Down below, the SS patrolled with German shepherds.

Eddie and Mike were scared and looked to Siegfried for reassurance. Siegfried was sure they had been selected for work and his comportment gave the boys confidence.

"Form up and drop your things!" an SS guard shouted in German.

As the new prisoners filed in, they were also met by Karl Demerer, the *Judenältester*, or Jewish camp elder, a middle-aged, professorial-looking man, a prisoner himself, who had been appointed by the SS to enforce order and discipline among the inmates.

"Form up and drop your things," Demerer simultaneously translated the guard's words into Yiddish, the lingua franca of Jews filing in from all over Europe, for those who might not understand German.

As the Jewish camp elder, it was Demerer's job to act as middleman between the SS staff and the camp's four thousand Jewish prisoners. He spoke a refined German and appeared to rule the inside of the camp with an iron hand, which had earned the confidence of the SS. But while Demerer feigned loyalty to his Nazi masters, it was clear to the inmates whose side he was on, and to them he was a godsend. He knew how to walk the thin line, appearing harsh when the SS were watching, but out of eyesight, with a concerned and fatherly eye, he constantly found ways to aid fellow Jews in his charge and did everything in his power to extend the lives of inmates. While the SS counted on Demerer to do their bidding, he lied back to them when he could, swindling and cajoling in order to protect the prisoners.

Speaking to the Jews in a language the Nazis did not understand, Yiddish gave Demerer the opportunity to communicate with the new arrivals in a kind of code. Mirroring most of the guard's words, even mimicking his plodding cadence, while giving the impression he was translating every word verbatim, Demerer instead issued a slightly different set of instructions.

"*Alle Sachen hier hinlegen*. Drop your belongings . . ." the SS man droned. "Leave all your things here . . . watches . . . jewelry . . . money."

"Drop your belongings . . ." Demerer droned simultaneously in Yiddish. "לאו מעות *Lav moes*. Leave *most* of your things here . . . watches . . . jewelry . . . money. *Lav moes*." That phrase was an encoded message the elder Jew knew the Yiddish speakers would work out in their own heads. *Leave most of your valuables, but don't give up everything*, he was saying as he walked the ranks. *Keep a few things hidden*. And so the new inmates produced most but not all of their cherished possessions, which were collected by guards.

If prisoners thought themselves lucky to be able to hold on to one or two of their most prized possessions, they were soon disappointed, because later Demerer would quietly confiscate the valuables they had hidden, using them when needed to barter with the guards for necessities for the prisoners—a gold brooch or a wedding ring in exchange for a pair of shoes for a man who had none, a silver spoon for an aspirin for a fevered inmate, perhaps a diamond to bargain for a prisoner's life.

It was a dangerous underground backroom racket that took advantage of corrupt SS guards who pocketed the prisoners' last treasured possessions instead of turning them over to the Nazi coffers. In trying to keep as many inmates alive as possible, Demerer constantly lived on a knife's edge.

"Follow the line," the SS man ordered.

Bewildered and uneasy, Eddie, Siegfried, and Mike moved in orderly single-file fashion. They arrived at an intake building where, one at a time, they stood before a prison functionary who sat behind a desk and quickly processed the newcomers, filling out paperwork and *Häftling* (prisoner) registration cards.

"*Familienname?*" ("Last name?") "Willner." "Mendelbaum." "Widerman."

"*Vorname?*" ("First name?") "Siegfried." "Max." "Jakov."

"Country?" "*Deutschland.*" "*France.*" "*Nederland.*"

"What is your profession?"

"*Kaufmann*" ("Merchant"). "*Boulanger*" ("Baker"). "*Arts*" ("Doctor"). "Shoemaker" . . . "Lawyer" . . . "Welder" . . . all swiftly moving through to be in-processed.

When Eddie and Mike stepped in front of the registrar, it was clear they were just boys, so he didn't ask their profession and simply wrote, *Schüler*, student.

From there, they were herded to the next station and ordered to remove their clothing and file into a shower. By now they had heard rumors of the shower gassings at Auschwitz. Word had spread that if you were going in, you weren't coming out alive. Some panicked and tried to run out and were beaten and pushed back in. Alarmed, Eddie and Mike looked up at Siegfried, who was steadfast. He had sized up the situation and was still certain they had been selected for labor. Prison functionaries pushed them in.

AUSCHWITZ

When the faucetheads started spraying water, they collectively exhaled; it was in fact a shower. They had indeed been selected for work, to be slave laborers at Auschwitz III, subcamp Blechhammer, the largest Jewish forced-labor concentration camp in the Auschwitz system.

Next, their heads were shorn, prison barbers roughly plowing clippers at dazzling speed over the inmates' heads, Eddie losing his long black locks to a shaved head he didn't recognize, his curls spiraling to the floor. Sheared to the skin, he ran his hand over his bald pate. It was a feeling he had never known, having even been born with a full head of hair. He looked over at Mike, who, his long wavy hair gone, stared back at him. They barely recognized each other.

Then they were whisked to the delousing station and forced into a big tub, where a green carbolic liquid burned their skin. In a kind of baptism by fumigation, the attendant pushed their heads down into the vat and held them for a second to be sure they were completely submerged, when they were finally ordered out.

At clothing distribution, with dizzying speed and no attention to proper sizing, they were each tossed a uniform of blue-and-white-striped cotton canvas shirt and pants, clogs with cloth uppers and wooden soles, no socks, and a striped cap. With things moving so fast, some were left with a uniform that didn't fit or two left shoes.

Eddie and Mike were given shirts and pants too large to fit their adolescent frames. Apparently, the system had not prepared for small prisoners in this camp, since most young people in Auschwitz were going right into the gas chambers.

Moving on, Eddie, Mike, and Siegfried were issued patches that identified the nature of their crimes: a yellow triangle for "Jew" and a red triangle for "political prisoner" cross-intersected to form a Star of David and sewn on the left breasts of their uniforms.

THE BOYS IN THE LIGHT

Six tattooists sat side-by-side at stations in the next room, their equipment laid out on tables.

One by one the prisoners were hurriedly called forth to roll up their sleeves.

"Left arm out!" called the tattooist, a prisoner himself. He took Eddie's forearm in his hand and held it down. A metal stamp with needles punctured his skin. It hurt and his arm bled. The tattooist wiped the blood and rubbed green ink into the wound, and Eddie was dismissed to move on.

That tattoo marked a new beginning. Stripped of his name and identity, Eddie Willner became prisoner #A-5662, branded like cattle, a nameless, innominate piece of property. Mike became #A-5636. Fifty-two prisoners behind Eddie stood a French Jewish teenager, Robert Widerman. (He would later become actor Robert Clary, who would play Corporal "Frenchie" LeBeau in the American 1960s hit TV series *Hogan's Heroes*.) Some two thousand men and boys behind them, fifteen-year-old Romanian Jew Elie Wiesel became prisoner #A-7713.

Where up to 90 percent of those who arrived at Auschwitz were murdered immediately, these were the lucky ones who had been chosen to live, but they would stay alive only as long as they remained useful to the SS.

Moving farther into the Blechhammer *Judenlager* (Jewish camp), the new arrivals looked out over the gray expanse of a foreboding, dystopian compound. Even a bright spring day could not mask the atmosphere of abject evil in this camp. Everything about this place felt wrong.

On the grounds, in addition to some twenty-five wooden barracks, the camp included a kitchen, an infirmary, and a bathhouse. A kitchen certainly meant warm food, didn't it? the boys thought; an infirmary meant medical care; a bathhouse, clean, warm water.

AUSCHWITZ

Inside the barracks, a grotty odor hit them as they looked upon an overcrowded mass of humanity. In an oppressively claustrophobic scene, some two hundred ghostlike figures crammed together in a sea of shaved heads in striped uniforms, pallid faces with hollow eyes stared back at the new arrivals.

Confined in the cramped quarters, they milled about, all wearing the same Star of David patches—a melting pot of Jews from all over Europe: rich Jews from Berlin, poor ones from Polish shtetls: the educated and the illiterate; the religious and the nonpracticing; lawyers and doctors, teachers, tradesmen, tailors—all mashed together, indistinguishable from one another, including the venerable Orthodox rabbi who once had a beard and sidelocks, wore a *spodik* religious hat and tallit prayer shawl, had been deprived of wearing the vestiges of his sacred identity, and now possessed nothing more than a bald head and a striped uniform and looked no different than the rest.

At nightfall, the swarm of inmates pushed past one another, jockeying for a spot in the three-tiered wooden bunks that looked more like warehouse shelving than beds. Packing three or four into one bunk on a filthy mattress filled with straw, Eddie, Mike, and Siegfried wedged in together among other inmates, where one could lie on his side but not on his back for lack of space.

At 9 p.m. sharp, the single light bulb hanging down from a cable went out, and a *kapo*, a prisoner whose job it was to enforce SS rules, shouted, "Silence!"

Amid groans and whispers, Eddie, Mike, and Siegfried settled in among overlapping bodies, trying to get comfortable, with one man's feet on another's head, neck, or chest, and trying to get a bit of a shared ragged blanket.

The next morning, at four o'clock, well before dawn, they were awakened by a piercing whistle and a *kapo* shouting, "*Alles raus!*" They jumped to find their clogs and rushed to clean the barracks, re-scattering the straw, and cleaning floors. After a quick inspection, another whistle signaled a mad dash to the "bathhouse." In a wild stampede, it was helter-skelter as thousands of prisoners descended on washbasins or ran to get to wooden planks set over a long trench that served as an open latrine, a reeking facility with no privacy and no cleaning materials. Eddie and Mike watched as the mass of prisoners pushed their way in, leaving many unable to get anywhere near the trench or to cold water trickling from rusted spouts. When the next whistle sounded, everyone broke away and ran in a frenzied dash in order to make it in time for *Brotzeit*, bread distribution lineup, *kapo*s all the while yelling, "Hurry up! Move faster!" as everything moved in absurd, chaotic double time.

The clamor continued, Eddie, Mike, and Siegfried following on the heels of the others who lined up to get a tin cup of tasteless ersatz coffee ladled from a vat hauled in by two prisoners, guards striking inmates to keep order. Each prisoner was given a three-inch square of coarse bread that tasted like sawdust, which they devoured before the final whistle blew for formation.

"Fall in!" boomed a loudspeaker, and a swarm of men and boys rushed to claim their place on a vast open lot, running in and stopping short to line up in rows of ten with required military precision six inches apart from one another. This was the *Appellplatz*, the roll call square.

"*Achtung!*" the loudspeaker barked, causing an echo as four thousand bodies clapped to attention in unison. Prisoners stood frozen in total silence, eyes locked on the back of the head of the man in front of them, and waited. It was forbidden to talk, to fidget, to look around, or to move even an inch. Here a man could be shot for being late, for not remaining still during roll call, even for lowering his gaze.

Blechhammer was worlds apart from Łazy and Ottmuth rudimentary operations. Where Wehrmacht and locals ran work-gang

AUSCHWITZ

operations in the rural outposts of Polish villages, by contrast, Auschwitz subcamp Blechhammer was a highly militarized supermax prison run by Hitler's elite SS with two hundred handpicked guards specially trained in terror and brutality.

The 7th SS *Totenkopf Wach* Death's Head Battalion wore the frightening skull-and-crossbones insignia in the centers of their high-bridged service caps and black twin lightning bolts on the collars of their field-gray uniforms. They strutted around in jackboots carrying swagger sticks, rubber truncheons, and revolvers.

Most Blechhammer guards were not common draftees but Germans who had been specially vetted to serve Hitler's ideology of extreme racial persecution. Many were sadists, and Jews were their target. Auschwitz was a coveted assignment among these men, Hitler's so-called great patriots. Eager to carry out the Führer's dirty work, they were largely true believers, schooled in racial hatred, and had hardened their hearts to human suffering.

Camp commandant SS Hauptsturmführer (Captain) Otto Brossmann, fifty-five years old, an avowed Nazi patriot, a former schoolteacher and high school principal, had overall responsibility for the camp's operations, security, and prisoner work performance, and he vowed to make his Führer proud.

His thirty-six-year-old deputy and underling, SS Untersturmführer Kurt Klipp, carried a leather whip. A former carpenter's apprentice from Cologne with an emotionless affect, Klipp was something of a Nazi prodigy. Having already served with distinction at the Auschwitz-Birkenau killing center and as head of the crematorium at Flossenbürg, he was ambitious and had his eye on one day taking over command of the prized Blechhammer camp.

A host of other Nazis stood about: SS guard Karl Francioh, a thirty-one-year-old Silesian coal miner, and Ansgar Pichen, age thirty, a former butcher shop employee, both of whom worked in the kitchen and brutalized the inmates, earning themselves the nickname "the Goons" among the prisoners.

As cruel as these men were, one of the worst was a guard the inmates called Tom Mix. That name struck fear in the form of double holstered pistols and a chilling warning from other prisoners to avoid him at all costs. He killed at whim, they said. *"Nicht Augen fallen lassen,"* said one prisoner. ("Don't let your eyes fall on him.")

The *Appellplatz*, Eddie, Mike, and Siegfried would learn, was the center of the concentration camp universe. Formation began every morning with "the count," a meticulous, sometimes hours-long exercise conducted several times a day to ensure every single prisoner on the docket was accounted for.

Then came the twice daily *Selektion*, the selection.

Demerer, the *Judenältester*, walked up and down the rows, warning everyone to stand up tall and "look healthy."

The SS guards scoured the ranks, inspecting each inmate, every man, every boy, from head to toe, searching for the slightest sign of weakness: a sunken chest, an exhausted appearance, signs of illness or injury, a wound, or a bandaged arm.

One guard stopped before an inmate and turned to face him. The thin, sallow man nervously but swiftly removed his cap and yelled his number as rules dictated, and, as rules also dictated, did not make eye contact. With a flick of the guard's forefinger, the man was removed from the formation, and the guard moved on.

It was as simple as that. In an instant, you were judged fit for labor or unfit, the unfit sent straight to the gas chambers at nearby Auschwitz-Birkenau. Every selection was a high-stakes, life-or-death gambit that kept inmates in a constant state of panic.

Rules were made clear. Prisoners would be shot or whipped for any number of infractions: for insubordination; for congregating, which would be seen as agitators scheming to incite rebellion; for acts of sabotage; for any disruption whatsoever to SS operations. The list went on.

Eddie felt like he had landed in a nightmare. In all his teenage rebellion, he thought immediately of planning an escape, until the rule was read for those who tried to run. If one somehow managed to escape over the high-voltage barbed-wire fencing and fourteen-foot wall, amid snipers and dog patrols, he would be hunted until found, brought back, and executed along with ten of his friends. That was the ultimate deterrent. Eddie couldn't bear the thought of being responsible for the deaths of his father and Mike.

At the next whistle, Kurt Klipp ordered the inmates to form up. As Tom Mix and other guards whacked prisoners, Eddie, Mike, and Siegfried fell into column formation. Armed guards with dogs took up both sides of the column and, at 5 a.m., four thousand men and boys marched out of the Blechhammer *Judenlager* Jewish camp.

SEVENTEEN

BAPTISM

Just one day in combat and you could tell we weren't ready.
—Private Stuart Thayer, loader, Company D

BY THE END of June 1944, the boys of Company D, along with scores of other fresh-faced 3rd Armored Division troops, had come ashore in their tanks, rolling up onto the beaches of Normandy and into the French countryside for what would be an almost yearlong, thousand-mile trek across Europe.

Despite their nerves, they felt reassured they were going to war with the best equipment Uncle Sam could provide. They felt confident in their tanks, in their training, and in their leaders. Given the mission to be the iron fist that would spearhead the attack across France and into Germany, some thought it would all be over in a matter of weeks. But, of course, that's not what happened.

Company D's baptism of fire came in the bocage hedgerows of Villiers-Fossard, just twenty miles inland, where they suffered their first casualties when they found themselves confronted by a strange alien landscape: walls of thick in-line trees eight feet high with

BAPTISM

gnarled, above-earth roots—a maze of tangled hedges that had been part of the terrain for centuries, separating one farmer's field from another. It was like nothing they had ever seen before, and certainly not during training in Louisiana or on the Salisbury Plain. Unable to breach the hedgerows, they were forced to drive in single file down narrow country roads, making them sitting ducks while the enemy sat in hiding, simply picking them off one by one.

Company D was driving in a convoy when they were blasted off the road in a series of thunderous explosions that sent tankers bolting from their hatches and spilling out onto the ground below. Some drivers threw their gears into reverse, trying to retreat, only to find themselves blocked by the tanks behind, some of which were ablaze. It was a hellish surprise that, in just minutes, shattered their confidence.

"Those bastards were tough. They'd been at it for five years. They knew what the hell they were doing," said one crewman.

"It was total confusion. Everyone knew their jobs when they came ashore, but no one had done it in such noise and confusion, and that's when it all fell apart."

It came as a shock to the crews to realize that their tanks were not invincible but, in fact, were veritable death traps. In training they had been assured their Shermans were capable of standing up to anything in the German arsenal, but any certainty they had going in was shredded in an instant.

Easily igniting on impact, German shells seared through the Sherman like a hot knife through butter, sending molten metal spalling, exploding into flames and killing those inside or seeing panicked crews scramble out to safety. Tankers had practiced bailing but never imagined they would be jumping from their hatches in their first minutes of combat, further traumatized upon hearing their first anguished screams of "Medic!"

THE BOYS IN THE LIGHT

Nineteen-year-old Private Claude Young, a country boy from Missouri, was the first in their company to be killed in combat. It was a loss that struck the company hard in more ways than one. Just months earlier, during training, Young, a likable boy-next-door kind of kid, had been given the honor of holding the Company D crest in the unit's official photo, where he had been seated front row center, surrounded by the company's 140 soldiers.

Days later, they came head-to-head for the first time with the might of the German Panzer. The Panzers were superior to the Shermans in almost every way. They were much heavier, had thicker armor and a more powerful gun, and they were deadly accurate. While Sherman rounds bounced off the Panzers, German rounds sheared through the Shermans' armor with ease, often igniting stowed ammo inside, causing a huge explosion. Before long, the Sherman was earning nicknames like the "mechanized coffin" and the "burning grave." In order to knock out a German tank, the Sherman had to get within six hundred yards and hit it on the side. But the German tank could knock out a Sherman at two thousand yards from any angle.

It was a disastrous introduction to war that struck fear into the hearts of many who were mere teenagers, some too young to even shave. In one tank, the crew was brought to a halt when their loader froze, which threw the entire crew's lives in jeopardy. When the crew yelled at him to "Load 'em!" he just stared blankly back. Not long after that, the same soldier crawled into a fetal position, but his tank commander, speaking to him in firm, measured tones, calmed the terrified boy, reminding him that all of their lives depended on him.

"You can't let us down, buddy. C'mon now, we're all in this together."

In another tank, after a high-explosive round had creased their turret, the gunner bailed, then broke down sobbing, "I can't do it. I can't get back in that tank. I'm through."

BAPTISM

While some crew members had talked big at first, bragging that they were going to "club the Krauts, get it over with and be home in three weeks," now they were traumatized by the reality of war, that any man could be here one minute and gone the next.

Just three weeks in, the division had already lost a staggering eighty-three tanks, over a third of their total strength.

Changes needed to be made and fast, so the troops got to work. They came up with combat hacks to try to better their odds. To give themselves more protection, they lashed logs to the sides of their tanks and stacked sandbags on the front glacis, holding them in place with chicken wire or with anything they could find. One team even installed a heavy wooden door and ran the main gun through the hole meant for the door handle. It looked ridiculous, like little kids hiding in a fort, but in their minds at least it offered the crew some modicum of reassurance.

A sergeant named Culin in another unit came up with an ingenious idea to take on the hedgerows. Steel parts were scavenged from German anti-tank obstacles found on the beaches of Normandy in the aftermath of the invasion and welded to the fronts of their Shermans to form giant fork-like hedge-chopper blades that bore into the dirt, chewing through roots and stumps. That simple invention was typical of the American soldier's ability to improvise. Throughout that first month, Yankee ingenuity and adaptability would alter the course of their initial entry to war and give the Americans a fighting chance.

"It was lucky," one tanker would say, "that cowboy mentality was part of our cultural heritage."

Next, they had to find ways to improve their tactics. As the terrain opened up, they realized that one small advantage in the Sherman's favor was that it was lighter, faster, and more maneuverable. If crews could take advantage of speed and quicker turret rotation and get close enough to hit the Panzer on its side, where the armor was thinner, they might stand half a chance. If they got lucky, they could get two shots off before the German Panzer crew was able to hand-crank their turret to face them. It would require quick thinking, teamwork, and cool heads. Company D would have to be more aggressive and quicker to get off the first round, so they put that play into action on the battlefield and spent every spare second practicing and perfecting it.

Just twenty miles in, the Americans got stuck at Saint-Lô. For the first thirty days, it had been slow going; sometimes they moved just a few yards a day. In some cases it came down to infantry soldiers fighting the Germans in hand-to-hand combat, but with hard lessons learned about fighting a fanatical and experienced enemy, navigating the hedgerows, and improving tactics—and with the tankers starting to gel with their crews—in the end, the American tanks, aided by a devastating aerial bombardment, punched through German lines. After a month of fighting and with more than ten thousand Americans killed, wounded, or missing, the breakout at Saint-Lô was a turning point. Suddenly the tables had turned and the Americans were on the offense, fighting their way toward Paris.

That first month saw a steady stream of evacuated wounded and dead and an influx of replacements. With so many new faces, the company resembled little of the original unit that had come ashore just weeks earlier. Captain Jack Downey, the well-liked company commander who had led the unit through years of training and preparation, was seriously wounded within the first few weeks of battle, badly scorched when his tank exploded. A near-clean slate of officers replaced the first string that had arrived in France.

Lieutenant McDowell, the only platoon leader left standing, was promoted to captain and made acting commander.

Elmer served at first as battalion maintenance officer. He was

BAPTISM

alarmed at how many knocked-out tanks were being towed back for repair. He and his teams worked feverishly around the clock, the bright arcs of welding torches glowing well into the night and on into the early-morning hours. Crews called the tank mechanics miracle workers due to their superhuman efforts to bring almost totally destroyed tanks back to life and return them to the front in record time.

When yet another brand-new platoon leader was wounded in action, Elmer was pulled in to take his place on the front line. He reported to McDowell who, as commander, was responsible for 140 tankers and support personnel and sixteen tanks. As platoon leader, Elmer was responsible for five of those tanks, with five men to a tank, for a total of twenty-five. He took his place alongside Lieutenant Myers's platoon.

From the start Captain McDowell seemed unsteady and slow to act, so the platoon leaders and their sergeants banded together to find ways to improve the company, trying to get the upper hand over the deadly Panzers, all while keeping their crews from flipping out.

Buttoned up inside their tanks, Elmer, Myers, Fred, Vance, and the crews of Company D rolled across the French countryside, Pepsi and his field kitchen trailing a few miles behind.

That summer, a new division commander who had played a critical role in the success of the breakout at Saint-Lô was handpicked to breathe new life into the division. Major General Maurice Rose, who began his career as a sixteen-year-old private, came in with a reputation of letting nothing stand in his way. Rose was the son and grandson of Polish rabbis whose family had immigrated to America from Warsaw. An ambitious and daring officer, General Rose called for aggressive, think-outside-the-box leadership. A proven combat leader who commanded from the front, Rose impressed on his fighters that the future belonged to those who were bold and audacious and wanted it more.

Conversely, Captain McDowell had a habit of making himself scarce. When he did show up on the front line, he would order the company to move out, take the lead for around half a showcase mile, then call one of his platoon leaders to take over for him. Elmer, Myers, and the third platoon leader traded off, each taking the reins for a few miles at a time, while McDowell spent more and more time in a safer position in the rear. This placed all the burden on the platoon leaders, something that did not go unnoticed by the company's senior sergeants.

In McDowell's absence, occasionally Elmer decided not to wait for orders but felt the need to step in for the good of the group. As their commander slipped into the background, Elmer leaned forward, roping Myers in at every turn.

Before long, the senior sergeants noticed that the young twenty-two-year-old Lieutenant Hovland had a natural ability to lead. He took the initiative and had a knack for bringing the men together. He seemed to be able to unify the group with vastly different backgrounds. Myers, they observed, was not afraid to move his tank up to the front of the column and take point on the battlefield. It was a winning combination, and the sergeants kept their eyes on the two young lieutenants.

Fighting from village to village through the summer of '44, in Lieutenant Myers's tank, Fred saw the war through his periscope as Vance manned the main gun inside a cramped cabin. They bumped over muddy roads and gutters that reached blistering temperatures, making their tank feel like a steel boiler, and they were tossed about as they bounced along the French countryside and fell into and came out of ditches and raced across fields, all while the enemy was trying to blow them up.

Baby Face Vance, the bookish introvert, and Redhead Fred, the easygoing country bumpkin, bonded. Fred had already earned a rep-

BAPTISM

utation for remarkable calm in the face of battle, so Vance started taking his cues from Fred, who, though he was a high school dropout, seemed to Vance to be imminently wise. Five years older than Vance, Fred seemed to have a lot more life under his belt; he had a wife and a child and a sage way about him. Nothing seemed to ruffle Fred, who talked in a twangy, southern cadence and took things on the chin with a smile and a what're-you-gonna-do-about-it kind of shrug. Fred looked out for Vance and called him "Jimmy" or "kid." Vance was glad to have a friend whom he could look up to and felt he could learn a lot from Fred's levelheaded tutelage.

From Le Desert to Orval, from Mortain to Mayenne, from dairy country to provincial villages across northern France, they moved down roads and up through hillocks and ravines in their veritable death-trap tanks, taking on fierce and determined enemy resistance. As part of the 3rd Armored Division's iron fist, Company D crossed the Seine to help secure the southern flank, and in late August, Paris was liberated.

Then, in early September, the division dashed northward into Belgium.

Liberating towns and villages along the way, the French and then the Belgians came out to cheer them with "*Vive l'Amérique!*" pressing flowers, wine, champagne, and cognac into the arms of the tankers as they came through, bottles that went right into the belly of the tanks for "safekeeping." Pepsi basked in all the attention, did a lot of hand-shaking and backslapping, and didn't turn down kisses, the most sought-after gift bestowed by grateful mademoiselles. There was always a blubbering father holding his child high in the air to see the Great Liberators. In one town, Vance saw a pretty girl in a window. She looked at him, smiled, and waved. He blushed and waved back. He would spend the next weeks thinking a lot about her, only later admitting to himself that she was waving at all the American soldiers, but, at that moment, in a blissful daydream, Vance was sure he saw her smiling only at him.

At Mons, the division cut off the Germans and captured more than ten thousand prisoners. By Liège, the Americans had their sights set on crossing into Germany.

Once every couple of weeks, when the company was pulled offline for rest and refit, Pepsi and the mess crew jumped into action, firing up their range stoves and bringing the kitchen alive to make fresh bread, steaming meatloaf or pork roast, green beans, and mashed potatoes, all served with lots of good-natured ribbing and tension-easing banter.

Tankers on the move ate mostly boxed rations, dry field "ten-in-one" packaged meals with canned franks and beans; Spam, which Pepsi called "ham that didn't pass its physical"; tasteless dried bits of something called "cheese spread" that tasted nothing like cheese, which they ate with cardboard-tasting crackers called biscuits; or potted meat, which Pepsi made light of: "What's ya' pleasure—pork loaf surprise or mystery meat?" It made for enough calories to fuel a man but was nothing compared to when Captain McDowell gave Pepsi and the mess crew the thumbs-up to give the boys some good hot chow.

On those days, tankers got to the kitchen as early as they could, waiting for Pepsi's mess line to open. Cooking, serving, pointing here and there, he moved the boys through the chow line, chatting them up, jabbering and joking and engaging every soldier, calling, "Come an' get it!" "Mama's got suppah ready," throwing in the occasional "*Mangiamo*, let's eat!" or "Yoah' gonna love these homemade biscuits."

He ran his kitchen like Pa ran the diner; to him, each soldier was a customer. He'd bob about, showing up everywhere as they ate, like he was checking up on them—"You okay, fellas? What do you

BAPTISM

need?"—inserting himself into conversations, making guys feel like it was all going to be okay with a slap on the back or a wisecrack meant to make them chuckle, just like Pa had taught him: "You feed the body, but you also feed the soul."

He took his responsibility seriously, knowing it wasn't just about the piping-hot food; it was emotional nourishment as well, a time for the boys to be together and decompress, get something off their chests. They found in him a sympathetic ear, his words like a balm for whatever worried them. He was particularly consoling to those weighed down by battle, appreciating the burden they carried, and made light of his own role in comparison. "Hey, you guys do all the heavy lifting. I just carry the spatula!"

Part diner, part vaudeville, both cook and combat psychologist, Pepsi became the heartbeat of the company. Raw and magnetic, he made no apologies for his expletives, snarky wisecracks, or his spicy Boston vernacular.

"He had more energy than all of us put together," Fred would say, "and he cared about everybody."

More and more, in McDowell's absence, Elmer stepped up to take charge of the company, staying up nights talking with the platoon sergeants about how the company could improve their tactics and overcome their vulnerabilities. Myers, who had come to admire General Rose for his forward-leaning leadership, continued to volunteer his tank and crew with Fred and Vance inside to scout ahead of the company to make sure the platoon was not driving into a trap.

The Minnesota farm boy and the Pennsylvania college grad became fast friends who felt increasingly responsible for the survival and successes of the entire unit. Despite their ongoing concerns, the sergeants could see that morale and confidence were improving under Elmer and Myers, who were setting a new course for the company.

THE BOYS IN THE LIGHT

Crews began to feel a sense of "specialness" in being a part of Company D. Living inside cramped tanks, crouching in foxholes, through smoke breaks and boxed dinners, young tankers began to feel tethered to a group of boys just like them who faced the same fears and witnessed the same devastating scenes, and they found comfort in leaning on each other.

Despite improvements, it was clear there were still plenty of hurdles to overcome. Though they had triumphed at Saint-Lô and fought successfully across northern France, the soldiers of Company D were still relatively untested. Some were skittish. There was still a tendency to overreact to every foreign sound and duck at every bang. They were prone to making mistakes and being jumpy, firing off the first shot knowing the great advantage the German gunners had. In one unfortunate incident, an infantryman crawled underneath one of the tanks to escape a shelling. One of the tankers took him for an infiltrating German and threw a grenade under the tank, and it killed the poor boy. Crews were worried about not getting a chance to defend themselves, like the bow gunner who kept firing his 30mm machine gun, shells bouncing all over the road at nothing, because he was worried "something might be out there."

Problems still arose inside the tanks. Gears malfunctioned, springs leaked oil, radios died. Sometimes a round would get stuck in the floor lockers, clogging the escape hatch when they needed to bail. Sometimes hatches jammed. In some cases, crewmen were known to push others aside and try to bail out first. They had to get faster and better at getting everyone out.

And there were the inevitable accidents: the tanker who stepped on a mine while going to relieve himself in a field; one who caught fire when he fell asleep with a lit cigarette that fell onto his chest.

With Captain McDowell drifting in and out of the picture more and more, Elmer took matters into his own hands. Tankers' lives and

BAPTISM

the mission depended on rising above their fears and learning lessons fast. They needed to have faith, Elmer thought, to have trust in one another and operate not as separate individuals but as one united team. Believing their toughest days were ahead, Elmer prayed for God to watch over every tanker in every tank.

"Lord, help us through every day of this. Guide us and help me make the right decisions."

Then he turned to Myers and said, "We have a lot of work to do."

EIGHTEEN

NORTH PLANT

Jews are a race that must be totally exterminated.
—Hans Frank, governor-general in Nazi-occupied Poland, 1944

THREE MILES FROM the *Judenlager*, the column of Blechhammer's four thousand Jews arrived at "the worksite." Before them loomed a gargantuan industrial complex that stretched as far as the eye could see. Adjacent to the Adolf Hitler Canal lay a cold, bleak, sprawling expanse of backbreaking slave labor toiling in a colossus of human misery. This was the epicenter of the Auschwitz Nazi slave-labor system.

Inside the perimeter of the complex lay a jungle of steel and concrete spread out over nearly three miles in a space more than twice the size of New York City's Central Park. Eddie, Mike, and Siegfried looked out at the sooty factory of chimneys and smokestacks that rose to the sky, belching out noxious black smoke, and at coke ovens and gas plants ablaze, filling the air with a pungent sulfuric odor. Cogs of machinery in motion, boilers, distillers, compressors, and injectors hissed and clanged, steam-puffing furnaces blazed, and coal-pulverizing

NORTH PLANT

units roared as prisoners slaved away, tens of thousands of workers wielding pickaxes and shovels, pulling carts, moving iron pipes and steel beams. This was forced labor on an industrial scale.

The Upper Silesia Oberschlesische Hydrierwerke synthetic oil factory, also known as Blechhammer North, was one of the largest industrial complexes in the Nazi slave-labor system: an oil refinery turning bituminous coal into high-octane synthetic oil and jet fuel—a production plant absolutely critical to powering Hitler's vast war machine.

Nearby the North plant, also part of the Auschwitz system, was Blechhammer South. Together the two industrial sites would churn out an enormous amount of synthetic liquid fuel estimated at around 200,000 tons a year.

The plants were so critical to the German war effort that their locations had been carefully chosen by the Nazis in part because they were out of range of Allied bombers.

Run partly by some of Germany's most renowned civilian firms, the two sites were manned by some sixty thousand forced workers, including Blechhammer's Jewish slave laborers, and also French, Belgian, Soviet, and some two thousand British POWs housed at nearby Stalag VIIIB.

Jews were singled out as the lowest caste in the prison hierarchy, forbidden even to make eye contact with other laborers. They were the only group overseen by the Death's Head SS, the only group to wear the distinctive blue-and-white-striped uniforms, and the only group to be systematically starved, ruthlessly beaten, and killed without provocation. Other workers witnessed daily the SS depravity directed against the Jewish inmates, but there was nothing they could do about it.

The massive Blechhammer group was called to attention. Those with special skills like engineers or welders were pulled out of formation;

the greater majority of "unskilled labor," those without expertise of use to the Nazis, including Eddie, Mike, and Siegfried, were set to hard manual labor.

"*Arbeitskommandos formieren!*" ("Form up work details!"), Klipp shouted. Counted out in groups of one hundred to two hundred, the prisoners were marched to assigned work sites.

Eddie and Mike stuck together, the two young teens constantly jockeying to be picked for the same *Arbeitskommando*. Siegfried was frequently detailed to another crew. Blechhammer's two hundred guards circulated with machine guns and killer dogs, prodding or beating prisoners with rubber truncheons as they labored, calling them "pigs" and "shit," and berating them with comments like "Dirty Jew, work faster."

Eddie and Mike were loading a truck with rock the first time they encountered Tom Mix, the guard the prisoners had named for the Hollywood cowboy movie star who headlined in Wild West blockbusters like *The Rider of Death Valley* and *Flaming Guns*, movies well-loved in both America and in Europe. Like Tom Mix the actor, Tom Mix the SS guard wore double holstered pistols. Unlike the American actor, who wore chaps and cowboy boots, however, Nazi Tom Mix wore gray jodhpurs and shiny black jackboots and, instead of riding a horse, he rode around the North plant on a bicycle, swinging his whip in circles like a lasso before cracking it on unsuspecting prisoners.

His reputation preceded him as the most sadistic of all the guards, his torment so random and unpredictable, it kept inmates in a perpetual state of terror. He was known to kill prisoners for pure sport. He wasn't the highest-ranking guard—in fact, he was only a corporal—but he was the incarnation of pure evil, a man who seemed to enjoy being feared by everyone. Prior to the war he may have been inconsequential, but now he wielded life-and-death authority over thousands in a job that gave him license to kill at whim.

Tom Mix had an ophidian quality, a searing stare, and a volcanic temper. A lean physique in an immaculate uniform, he was in his mid-thirties, and had a short-cropped Hitler-style brush-over and an angular, high-cheekboned, "cold, mean face."

As he approached Mike and Eddie's detail, prisoners tried to tip each other off with a prison code of nervous throat clearings, careful whispers, and darting glances. The mere sight of Tom Mix threw everyone into a panic. He got off his bike and moved between the prisoners, arbitrarily whipping his way from one to the next with a vacuous expression.

He stopped, stood off to the side, smoking a cigarette, and watched the prisoners work for a while. Then suddenly, striking like a viper, he whipped out both his revolvers and fired. One of the bullets hit a prisoner in the head and the man fell over dead. Pleased with himself, he casually re-holstered his guns.

After that day, Eddie, Mike, and Siegfried understood what the others had told them—that Tom Mix was a sociopath and a monster, and to stay off his radar.

Unlike Nazi Tom Mix, the real Tom Mix was a good guy. Wildly popular in Europe, even Hitler loved his movies, though they were officially banned by the Nazis. Despite the ban, Hitler once personally telephoned Mix in Hollywood to invite him to Berlin.

"Tell him," Tom Mix told Hitler's interpreter, "I'll tour Germany again to see my fans, but only over Hitler's dead body!"

Every move brought risk, and Eddie, Siegfried, and Mike knew that the sooner they mastered prison conditions, the better their chances were for survival. They constantly sized up every situation, studying guards' habits, reading their body language, anticipating their moves, and learning prison yard tricks, like positioning oneself in the middle of a marching column because the guys on the outside copped the most abuse.

Surviving a selection was paramount. The goal was to look more fit than the man standing next to them, and so they lived from one selection to the next.

Marching every day to and from the worksite, the Blechhammer four thousand regularly passed other work crews. Each time another group came through, the SS forced the Jewish column into the ditch to clear the way for others higher up in the hierarchy to move through, clubbing a Jew if he so much as looked in the direction of passing workers or, even worse, made eye contact. Eddie and Mike were secretly elated each time the Allied POWs came through, the French occasionally mumbling under their breaths, calling the SS *"Boches!"* and *"Imbéciles!"* ("Krauts!" and "Idiots!"). The British POWs of Stalag VIIIB were Eddie and Mike's favorites. They always had a cheerful way about them and sometimes even sang as they marched. Apparently completely unafraid of any retribution at all, they would emphatically shout words of encouragement to the Jewish prisoners as they passed: "That's right, boys, carry on, war's almost over," and then rip into the SS, shouting, "Shame!" and "Bastards!"

At the North plant, the work was arduous, the harassment relentless. If an SS guard caught a Jewish inmate moving slowly or stumbling, he could be shot dead on sight. If one didn't walk properly in formation, he was clubbed. If he stopped to rest for a minute, he was beaten. To speak to another prisoner while on work detail was suicide.

Starvation set in. Supper was nothing more than a lukewarm bowl of water, which occasionally had a potato peel or a sliver of cabbage floating in it but, more often than not, contained only liquid, which is why the inmates called it "water soup." The Nazi "kitchen goons" regularly taunted the inmates and mocked their skimpy rations.

Inmates became crazed for food. In the evening soup line, some tried to position themselves to stand in the spot where they might get the vegetable pottage at the bottom of the cauldron, which led to desperate struggles, resulting in savage beatings, even shootings, by the goons. One three-square-inch piece of bread in the morning and a bowl of water soup at night was not enough to sustain hard labor. Like everyone, Eddie and Mike lost weight. Mike's doughy belly was gone, Eddie's solid frame slipped to thinness, and their pants began to hang looser around their waists.

At night in the musty barracks, men and boys leaned on one another, lamented, slept, and died. Before lights-out, they talked about their families and their lives before the camps. Some dared to think about a future or life on the outside. Most talked simply about wanting to live or, in Mike's case, about food.

In the stillest hours of the night, one could find a man up and davening, reciting Hebrew prayers or bargaining with God, promising to be faithful if he was spared, or softly asking, "God, why have you forsaken me?"

In the cramped triple bunks, lice burrowed into new hair growth on their heads and bodies, and the inmates picked them off and pinched them in half. Week after week, sleeping huddled together in the same sweat-sogged uniforms they went to work in, with a shower and a shave only once a month, inmates sometimes went to sleep pressed into the body next to him, only to wake up to find the wide-eyed stare of his dead bunkmate.

Siegfried knew he could not always protect the boys, so he taught them as best he could, empowering them with skills they needed in order to make it through and imparting to them nuggets of wisdom, like the one from the old Yiddish proverb "Don't be scared when you have no other choice."

As a veteran of frontline combat, he had survived plenty of life-threatening situations, which had sharpened his ability to sense danger and adapt to survival—nothing compared to this, of course, but he knew that the human mind and body could sustain much more than most people believed. Where once in Łazy there had been complaints from the boys, there was little of that now. They were learning to cope, it seemed, and that was good.

Siegfried taught the boys to take care of themselves. They had to keep their feet healthy; without their feet in good condition, they would be selected out immediately. They had to keep them dry and avoid blisters—but if they got blisters, they were not to break them, so they could build calluses. Once a prisoner got diarrhea in this camp, it was the beginning of the end, so he told them to eat burnt wood and ashes wherever they found them.

Siegfried saw that the boys' once-rosy faces had lost their color and youthful fleshiness, their uniforms hanging off their bodies, so he reassured them they could live with hunger. Chewing on a piece of wood could kill the gnawing emptiness; thinking of their mothers' cooking when they ate water soup could transport them, at least for the moment, to the smells and comforts of home. The boys listened intently, and they believed him. They just couldn't become a *Muselmann*, he warned, a prisoner who was so severely emaciated and exhausted that he had lost his will to live.

Siegfried tended to their mental well-being, protecting them against becoming dehumanized. *Don't dwell on your circumstances. When you walk through this storm, hold your head up*, he urged them. *One day this will all blow over.*

NORTH PLANT

"Auf Regen folgt Sonnenschein." *After the rain, comes sunshine. Never lose hope. Never give up,* he said again and again. *If you fall down, get back up. No matter what: Get . . . back . . . up.*

Siegfried could see that the boys were better together. *When it becomes too much,* he would say, *look to each other and you'll be fine.* He told them to protect one another, to share food if one went without. If they stayed close, they would never feel hopeless. *Yes*—they nodded. They understood.

What the boys didn't understand at the time was that Siegfried was teaching them not just how to save their lives but how to save their souls. Siegfried was Eddie's role model and became Mike's, too. Eddie was just grateful his father was with him on this journey. His presence alone sustained him.

Some inmates found ways to survive through illicit "dealings." Though any underground activity, like smuggling something into camp or trading with a foreign worker, meant risking execution, opportunities existed. For most, death was too high of a price to pay, but for others it was worth the risk. One inmate traded his piece of bread for a tiny silver spoon another inmate had hidden upon his arrival. In the welding shop, he melted down the spoon and made two rings. Then he found a middleman to "sell" the rings to British POWs at Stalag VIIIB, who arranged a trade for two bags of coffee from their Red Cross packages. The inmate took the coffee to a corrupt SS man, who gave him two loaves of bread in exchange for the coffee.

Demerer, the *Judenältester*, proved remarkably adept at prison contraband dealings, which he continued to leverage to save prisoners' lives, but everyone understood the stakes. It was a gamble. If you played in that business, you dealt with the consequences if you were caught. Siegfried warned the boys not to go anywhere near those shady activities.

In time, it became clear that the Nazis operated in twisted illusions.

Arbeit macht frei, like everything else at Blechhammer, was a Nazi lie. Work did not make you free. What the SS called "education" was the term for beatings; long, torturous hours of calisthenics to cull out the weak were called "sport." A kitchen implied there was warm food cooking, but Blechhammer's "kitchen" served nothing more than sawdust bread and water soup. The bathhouse was a putrid latrine. There was an infirmary, but there was no medical aid or curative care. On the contrary, it was a death ward with a crematorium, where the living went in and disappeared forever. The SS physician was not there to help the prisoners but to aid and abet in the Final Solution. By now everyone understood that when you were sick, you didn't report sick, because that would be the end of you.

Tom Mix was omnipresent. He would disappear and then reappear suddenly, lurking and observing. On the *Appellplatz*, he walked between rows of inmates, his eyes searching for his next victim. Just when an inmate thought he had passed him by, he would turn on his heels and box the man's ears or punch him in the ribs. He beat prisoners for not understanding orders in German or because he didn't like their faces, because they didn't look him in the eye or because they *did* look him in the eye when he didn't want them to. He thought up imaginary infractions on the spot so that he could land a blow. For some unexplained reason, he hated the Viennese accent, and every time he saw a certain inmate from Vienna, he would tell him to say something, then punch him in the face. He beat them because he thought they were judging him, because they flinched when he hit them, because he accused them of something and they had the audacity to try to defend themselves. To Tom Mix, the Jew who defended himself was doubly guilty. He saw it as an act of resistance to his authority, and any attempt at self-defense became nothing more than induced suicide.

Escape was a fantasy. The few who had attempted it never got far. They were hunted down, brought back, and executed alongside relatives and friends they had made in the camp. Even if a prisoner somehow made it out, he would be easily recognizable in blue and white stripes with a shaved head and a number tattoo on his arm in the sparsely populated surrounding area. Exposed to the elements, trying to find food and safe harbor would be near impossible. These inmates were watchmakers, bankers, and shoemakers, not survivalists who could hide out in the woods for months on end in the middle of the Polish wilderness. Even if sympathetic Poles would harbor them, it was only a matter of time before they would be found.

And yet, despite the impossibility, Eddie dreamed constantly of escape.

NINETEEN

"KOM GOED THUIS"

July 7, 1944, a warm summer Friday, was like any other day at the North plant, the complex's network of factories and the oil refinery blasting at peak capacity. Eddie, Mike, and Siegfried were toiling away when suddenly they heard a strange distant humming that grew louder and louder. All over the complex, SS guards and inmates, civilian and foreign workers, British, French, and Soviet POWs, stopped what they were doing and looked up to see a swarm of planes headed toward the North plant refinery.

Many couldn't believe their eyes. Closing in, a massive formation of nearly five hundred American bombers, mostly B-24 Liberators, and around three hundred fighters approached the North and South plants. Once overhead, in a simultaneous attack, they opened their bomb bay doors and dropped their loads, which rained down on the two industrial factories and a third complex nearby.

One after another, explosions hit the North plant, smashing buildings and blowing up highly flammable fuel depots, gas storage tanks, and oil production processing units. Molten metal flew wildly in all directions as everyone scrambled for cover. The Nazis raced for the safety of concrete bunkers, which were off-limits to the prisoners,

"KOM GOED THUIS"

who were left to fend for themselves out in the open. They took cover anywhere they could, pressing up against buildings, flattening themselves on the ground, curling up into balls with their hands over their heads, trying to avoid the violent barrage that convulsed the ground. When the attack was finally over, smoke rose from the carnage, buildings were ablaze, shards of metal littered the compound, and wire hung down in twisted junk on the ground. Thousands of bombs had cratered the earth and some one hundred Jewish prisoners were dead.

An eerie quiet followed with just a crackling of fires as Eddie, Mike, Siegfried, and thousands of dazed prisoners got up and wandered around the plant in awe of what had just happened. In a complete surprise to the Germans, American war planners had prioritized the destruction of Blechhammer as their number one target in Europe to be knocked out of action. That task fell to the Fifteenth U.S. Air Force. If they disabled the Blechhammer oil refinery, Germany's war machine would be severely crippled.

The SS was stunned. Blechhammer was thought to be beyond the Allied bombers' reach. Even the closest American air force units based out of Foggia or Venosa in southern Italy, it was believed, could not reach them. The Nazis' calculations had been correct; it was technically out of range, but pilots had pushed the boundaries to the absolute maximum to reach the North and South plants to deliver this blow.

The mission had been a perilous, touch-and-go journey that had tested the limits of the B-24 aircraft and crews. Loaded down with eight or more five-hundred- and thousand-pound bombs each, they had flown 650 miles for four hours straight, traveling mostly over dangerous Nazi-held territory, to reach their remote target before turning around to make the return journey to the safety of their home base.

Despite the trauma of the bombing and the loss of their fellow prisoners, the inmates were delirious with joy to see the vast damage the raids had caused and were especially ecstatic to know that help was on the way. Back in the barracks, there was palpable excitement. Out of earshot of the Nazis, the bombing was the talk of the evening.

Tom Mix became unhinged following the successful American raid and took out his vengeance on the inmates. He was doubly infuriated to see how much the bombing raised the prisoners' spirits. At the plant, he rode through work crews, whipping furiously and stopping to pummel inmates with his fists like a street fighter in a violent rage. On the *Appellplatz*, he made the four thousand prisoners run in circles and do calisthenics as he walked around shooting his pistols into the air.

"Jump! Bounce! Leap! Up, down, jump higher!" he shouted, laughing maniacally. The torture continued all night long: "Raise your hands! Lower your bodies! Stand on your toes! Now jump like frogs! *Hüpfen, hüpfen!* Jump!" Guards with whips lashed out at the inmates, wildly amused by the ridiculousness of the bizarre scene of thousands at their mercy. Made to stand for long periods in stress positions, on their toes and bent-kneed, many prisoners could not keep their balance and toppled over. Dogs lunged, biting their legs. Those who fell and could not get back up were shot on the spot. Survivors would later recall, that was "one long night."

Over the next weeks, prisoners worked to rebuild the refinery. But then it happened again.

Exactly one month after the first attack, American B-24 bombers (escorted by P-51 fighters flown by the famed Tuskegee Airmen) hit Blechhammer a second time. Now when air-raid sirens started to wail, prisoners openly cheered as they ran for their lives. Eddie dove under a truck; Mike crawled into a metal pipe. Others fanned out, trying to find protection along the perimeter of the plant, but no place was safe. As the SS fled to their bunkers, one of them yelled to the prisoners, "Good luck, here come your friends. Let them come and kill you."

This time the Germans were prepared for the attack, activating fog machines and setting off smoke pots to obscure the locations of the most critical buildings; white smoke clouds rose to the sky, covering parts of the factory. They defended with everything they had. They launched Messerschmitt fighters to give chase and fired some four hundred heavy flak guns positioned around the perimeter of the plant, 88mm anti-aircraft rounds screaming as they went up, peppering the sky with shells that blew like hand grenades, and red-hot pieces of shrapnel and twisted metal rained down on the prisoners. Bombs tore into the ground, causing huge rippling waves of pressure, and obliterated the heart of the industrial plant: the hydrogenation chambers, injector and compressor houses, distillation chambers, pipe bridges, chimneys, baro girders, catalyst plant, and buildings in the early stages of reconstruction from the last raid. They knocked out the electric pumps and toppled the flow of the synthetic gas, causing a massive inferno when it hit the fuel storage tanks, which brought the flow of oil production to a halt.

The pilots called it Black Hammer. They came in waves like a swarm of angry hornets, the sky streaked with silver birds shining in the midday sun, American B-24 and other heavy bombers with names like *Pistol Packin' Mama*, *Yankee Lady*, and *Dakota Queen* (piloted by twenty-two-year-old George McGovern, later a senator and Democratic nominee for U.S. president in 1972). The gutsy pilots came in so low that prisoners could see the planes' markings and sometimes even pilots' faces.

Back in the barracks, the inmates hailed the Americans' accuracy. "We were in awe at the precision of the targeting," one inmate would say. "With every air raid, almost everything important was damaged or destroyed."

Despite the deadly explosions, many prisoners saw the B-24 attacks as their finest hour. Believing they were going to be killed at some point anyway, at least it showed them that the world had not forgotten them, that someone was coming to save them. One inmate would later say, "When planes were dropping bombs, there was total glee. Everyone knew they could get killed, but there was total glee."

In his memoir *Night*, Nobel Prize winner Elie Wiesel, who was a Jewish slave laborer at Blechhammer South, recalled how he and his fellow Auschwitz prisoners reacted during the raids:

"We were not afraid. And yet, if a bomb had fallen on the blocks, it alone would have claimed hundreds of victims on the spot. But we were no longer afraid of death; at any rate, not of that death. Every bomb that exploded filled us with joy and gave us new confidence in life. The raid lasted over an hour. If it could only have lasted ten times ten hours!"

Sabotage was punishable by death. Nevertheless, some risked it when they believed they could get away with it. Engineers and welders made tiny alterations that could pass perfunctory inspection but rendered parts ineffective. Others took opportunities to sever telephone wires, slice rubber treads, puncture storage tanks, or, in the workshops, damage the flannel filters separating the carbon dust from the impurities. As American air raids continued, the inmates especially took advantage of moments when the plant was being bombed, destroying insulation that would render a malfunction in the cracking tower process and smashing valuable precision equipment.

It was the purest, most satisfying form of defiance and revenge, and it gave the prisoners a profound sense of release from which they found endless humor and joy in knowing that, by fooling the Ger-

"KOM GOED THUIS"

mans or destroying something important, in some small way they were exacting revenge on the Nazis and asserting a precious rare moment of unassailable personal liberty.

Acts of subversion in labor camps became so widespread that Hitler himself finally issued a decree to halt it, and, suddenly, now even civilian German foremen were authorized to shoot Jewish inmates on the spot if they were caught in the act or simply even suspected of sabotage.

Though Siegfried had warned Eddie on many occasions against mischief, he wasn't always aware of what the boys were up to. One day during a bombing raid, Eddie and Mike unexpectedly had a chance to commit an act of sabotage, and they went for it.

As the siren sounded the approach of the American bombers, smoke pots were activated and the SS raced to take cover in their shelters, Eddie and Mike dared to jump into an unoccupied *Einmannbunker*, a small, thimble-shaped, one-man bunker with concrete walls one foot thick and strictly off-limits to the prisoners. The shelter was big enough to hold a single grown man, but the two skinny teens easily wedged themselves into one *Einmannbunker* together. From inside, they looked out through an observation slit in the concrete and gleefully watched the bombing devastation happening all around them. Within minutes, fire trucks arrived to put out raging twenty-foot-high flames at the main oil production facility. Inside their tiny shelter, carnage raining down all around them, Eddie noticed an emergency telephone that connected directly to the refinery's fire brigades. He reached over Mike, grabbed the receiver, and, in his native German, did his best impression of an SS officer's rant, barking orders into the phone:

"*Nein Nein Nein!* Divert! Divert! You *must* go to Building 5. Much bigger fire there! Go *now!*"

But Building 5, the area that housed the critical hydrogenation stalls and cooling towers, was not on fire.

"Building 5?!" came the alarmed SS voice on the other end of the line. "How big is the damage there?"

"*Wahhhnsinn!* Maaaaajor damage!" Eddie yelled. "Get over there *now*!"

Eddie and Mike observed from the slit in awe as the firemen hastily retracted their hoses, scrambled to abandon the main production facility, and raced to Building 5, as the boys watched the main depot go up in flames. It was an immensely satisfying moment of temporary triumph, leaving Eddie and Mike laughing so hard their sides hurt, and Eddie delighted that the prank, like the ones he enjoyed so much as a youngster, had paid off perfectly.

The American bombings continued throughout the summer and into the fall, and after every raid slave labor was made to rebuild what had been destroyed. Just two weeks after a bombing, thanks to grueling, around-the-clock reconstruction, oil processing units were repaired and production was back in action. But just as fast as the inmates could build the refinery back up, the Americans reappeared and knocked it back down again.

The air raids continued to buoy the inmates' spirits, which pushed Tom Mix to the breaking point. He became manic and might even have taken out his vengeance on some Americans. During one raid, two crewmen who parachuted to the ground were, unfortunately, greeted by Tom Mix. He was seen viciously beating them, then leading them away. No one really knew for sure what happened to them after that, but all suspected the worst.

Though they did all they could to avoid his wrath, it was only a matter of time before Tom Mix's blows found Eddie and Mike. Fortunately for them, their encounter was brief. The boys stood absorbing the madman's pummeling without flinching, just as Siegfried had taught them. After a few hits, Tom Mix moved on to terrorize other inmates. In the end, it wasn't nearly as bad as the day Mike got a flogging that almost killed him.

On that day, Eddie and Mike thought how nice it would be to be able to, just once, shirk barracks cleanup duty for ten minutes. So they hid in the rafters while others swept the floors, but they were soon discovered. The typical punishment for such an infraction was twenty-five lashes, but the incensed SS guard doubled it to fifty, a beating that could easily result in the death of an already frail inmate. A *kapo* was called to administer the punishment. Eddie was ordered to go first and readied himself for the blows. The flogging began but, after a few lashes, the guard stepped out for a smoke. The *kapo*, protecting Eddie, told him to scream like hell as he barely whipped him. It was a convincing performance. Eddie had been lucky but, by the time it was Mike's turn, the guard had returned and the *kapo* had to follow through with his grisly task. He delivered all fifty lashes with such force that it left Mike's buttocks raw and bleeding, and he was unable to sit for several weeks. Eddie did everything he could to nurse Mike back to health, making sure he got his bread and water soup rations. In the barracks, he turned him on his side at night, and he and Siegfried pushed off other bodies to give Mike space in the bunk. It was nearly a miracle, but, with Eddie and Siegfried's help, Mike beat the odds.

By September 1944, the tide of war had shifted. Allied troops had raced across northern France into Belgium and were knocking on Germany's door. Great Britain had successfully withstood the Nazis' "Blitz," the Allies had beaten the Germans in North Africa, Soviet forces had handed the German army a stunning defeat at the Battle of Stalingrad, and Italy had capitulated. The three Allied leaders,

Churchill, Stalin, and Roosevelt, met to agree on an endgame strategy to defeat Hitler.

In concentration camps throughout Europe, prisoners wondered how long their ordeal would last and why the German people weren't rising up to try to overthrow or even assassinate their insane leader. Then one day it happened.

A group of disgruntled senior German military officers banded together to kill Hitler, planting a briefcase bomb that exploded at a meeting attended by Hitler and his staff. The assassination attempt failed and the Führer took to the airwaves to reassure the German people that he was not hurt. "I take this opportunity, my old comrades in arms, to greet you, joyful that I have once again been spared a fate which, while it held no terror for me personally, would have had terrible consequences for the German People. I interpret this as a sign from Providence, that I must continue my work, and therefore I shall continue it."

Like Tom Mix's reaction to the bombings, Hitler's response to the attempt on his life was swift and brutal, with thousands being arrested, tortured, and executed.

After five months in Auschwitz, the boys were thin as rails. Despite Siegfried's best efforts to guide them through hunger, they were getting weaker by the day. At around that time, the SS called for volunteers for the "dud commando," to defuse bombs dropped during the raids that had not blown up, luring volunteers with an extra piece of bread. Everyone knew it was near-certain suicide. In the process of digging out and disarming a bomb, it often exploded, sometimes killing the entire team. The average lifespan of a defuser was a matter of weeks. Most did not live to tell their story. Even Demerer warned prisoners that a small bit of bread was not worth the risk.

"KOM GOED THUIS"

Nevertheless, when the SS called for volunteers, the promise of an extra ration was just too great for Eddie and Mike, and they stepped forward. It is likely that Siegfried was unaware the boys had volunteered, as he surely would not have approved.

The job required teams to slowly dig out around the massive cylindrical explosive that was lodged in the ground. With their bare hands, prisoners carefully clawed away the dirt that surrounded the gargantuan shell. Then one inmate was ordered to straddle it. He cautiously wrapped his entire body around the bomb's girth, his legs giving him leverage to hit the spanner mounted on the bore head with a hammer, leaving intact the trigger mechanism with the yellow "USA" lettering. Occasionally a shell would be marked with messages scrawled by GIs: "A present for the Nazis," "Special delivery for Adolf," "To Hitler from Joe," and other, sometimes more profane tidings.

Any false move could set off a charge. The tension was enormous. If a bomb detonated, the explosion could be heard for miles. When it was over, Eddie and Mike got their extra piece of bread, which motivated them to do more defusing. Ironically, the boys grew even closer doing something they knew could kill them.

On his sixteenth birthday, Eddie was stomping grapes in picturesque Ortaffa. Two years later, sometime around his eighteenth birthday, he was shot in the head at Auschwitz.

That day, Eddie had been assigned to a hundred-man work detail on the *Judenlager* compound; Mike and Siegfried were in other work groups. The overseeing SS guard seemed excessively agitated, taunting the workers with insults:

"You're working too slow, you filthy Jews! There's a war going on. Speed it up!"

THE BOYS IN THE LIGHT

Without warning, the Nazi guard opened fire. Other guards joined in, in a mass shooting, the clatter of machine guns canvassing back and forth, mowing down dozens of prisoners where they stood. Eddie fell. Lying among the carnage, he struggled to remain conscious and to make sense of what was happening when an order was called out to load the dead and wounded onto a cart that would take them to the crematorium. Somehow Eddie collected his wits, got to his feet, and tried to blend in with those now loading bodies. The guard noticed his blood-soaked uniform and the wound on the back of his head bleeding profusely as he continued to help load the other victims. The SS man watched for a while, finally calling out to Eddie to stop, then told him to turn around and run. Expecting the guard to shoot him in the back and finish the job as some Nazis often did, Eddie turned to run, but instead of firing his weapon, the guard let Eddie make his way to the barracks.

Siegfried arrived in a panic. Eddie was losing a lot of blood. With no medical supplies or even clean water, he was left to the mercy of what the men in the barracks could do to help pull him through. A doctor, a fellow inmate, arrived and set to work. Someone produced a rag, another pulled threads from a uniform, and, with no anesthesia and no sterile supplies, the doctor did his best to patch up Eddie's head, closing the wound with a contraband sewing needle. With no way to cauterize the gash, he worked against the clock to battle deadly infection, hoping to stabilize Eddie before lights-out, over and over again putting his mouth to the wound, sucking in and spitting out the suppurating discharge. While the bullet had not lodged in his head, it had carved out a chunk of Eddie's scalp.

In the end, the doctor miraculously managed to sew the wound together and slow the bleeding. That night, it was touch and go. Siegfried and Mike watched over Eddie through fever and bouts of intense pain. A quick recovery was impossible, but the next day Eddie would have to stand on the *Appellplatz* without anyone holding him up and face a selection with a bandage on his head, a telltale sign to the SS that an inmate was unfit to work.

The next morning, the three left the barracks to face the *Appellplatz*. Eddie was weak but he could stand, and he walked on his own to the daily lineup, taking his place among the prisoners. A guard walking the ranks stopped in front of Eddie and scanned him from head to toe. Siegfried and Mike, eyes straight ahead, listened and waited, devastated at what they feared was the inevitable. With everything he had, Eddie pulled himself up as tall as he could, chest thrust out, shoulders back, hoping he would not pass out.

The guard asked him about his injury, but before he had finished his question, Eddie barked with conviction, "*S'gut! Ich kann arbeiten!*" ("I'm fine. I'm ready to work!") Apparently satisfied, the guard moved on.

By mid-September 1944, autumn winds were blowing through the camp. On September 27, Deputy Commandant Kurt Klipp called for the inmates to assemble on the *Appellplatz* for a "special event."

It was Yom Kippur, the holiest day of the year in Judaism, when Jews atone for wrongs committed in the past year. All of Blechhammer's two hundred SS guards showed up on the *Appellplatz* armed with machine guns, something that had never happened before. Gallows had been set up on a stage to accommodate three prisoners.

Eddie, Mike, Siegfried, and the thousands of inmates stood at attention, looking on as the doomed Jews, a sixteen-year-old Dutch boy, a *kapo*, and a Belgian boy, were paraded out and ordered to face the mass of prisoners. Days earlier, after a bombing at the North plant, Tom Mix had seen the Dutch boy pick up a three-inch wire he found on the ground amid bombing debris. The boy had used the wire to tie up his pants. Tom Mix accused the teen of bringing the wire into the camp as part of a plan to make explosives. It was an absurd accusation. The *kapo* had tried to intervene on the boy's behalf, explaining it away as a harmless act, that the lad was simply losing weight and needed to keep his pants up, so Tom Mix fingered the *kapo* as an accomplice. The boy's Belgian friend was guilty for having witnessed the Dutch boy picking up the wire and not alerting a guard. This was a clear act of sabotage, Tom Mix proclaimed, and all three were in on it.

Commandant Brossmann appeared and, through the loudspeaker, someone yelled, *"Augen g'radeaus!"* ("Eyes front!") That was followed by an announcement that anyone looking away would be shot. Kurt Klipp and others milled about to ensure all were focused on the gallows, and the "special event" was underway.

One by one, the three condemned prisoners were ordered to climb the scaffold, each stepping up onto a stool. Their hands and feet were bound. Tom Mix placed the nooses around the prisoners' necks. Then, with an air of stentorian authority, an SS man heel-clicked to attention and read the verdict. It was theater of the absurd. The whole thing a twisted illusion made to appear like a lawful proceeding, he delivered his proclamation with officious elocution:

"By order of the Reichsführer and Reichs Chancellor Heinrich Himmler, these three men are condemned to death for committing an act of sabotage for attempting to smuggle explosive material into the camp. On the basis of their crimes which constitute sabotage . . . they are condemned to the punishment of death by hanging."

At Brossmann's command, one by one, Tom Mix kicked the stools out from under the victims' feet. The *kapo* and the Belgian died quickly, but the Dutch boy flailed. His noose having been improperly positioned, he jerked wildly in a horrible fight with death. Then his rope broke, and he fell to the platform. An audible gasp rose from the crowd. More than one prisoner thought, *God has spoken. The accused is innocent and should live.*

"KOM GOED THUIS"

Eddie, Mike, and Siegfried watched as Demerer rushed forward and pushed his way in, pleading with the SS to halt the procedure. Since the SS were supposedly citing legal grounds for the execution, Demerer appealed, trying to sound lawyerlike, arguing that there was a law that stated that a hanging should be swift and complete the first time and that automatic amnesty should be rendered should the rope fail. He pleaded desperately for a pardon for the boy, but Brossmann cut him off, shouting, "Jews have no rights," and promptly ordered, "Hang him again!"

A wave of anguished murmurs rippled through the crowd, and the SS men, perhaps fearing revolt, gripped their machine guns, closed ranks, and fired shots into the air.

Brossmann ordered another rope. In the time it took for another rope to be brought and slipped around the boy's neck, Demerer continued to plead. Once again the teen was hoisted onto the stool, the second noose placed around his neck. But then he did something no one expected. He called out to his fellow inmates, almost in a whisper.

"Comrades," he said, softly at first, barely audibly. Everything stopped. There was total silence as prisoners were struck by the young man's audacity to speak, and they strained to hear his words. He lifted his head and, his voice growing stronger, offered a gentle Dutch farewell: *"Kom goed thuis,"* he said simply. "Come home well." The entire camp was riveted to the scene of the boy who, facing death, had dared utter a most tender human message in his last moments of a heinous end, encouraging his comrades to make it through their ordeal and get home safely.

"Halt's Maul!" ("Shut up!") Tom Mix shouted.

With his last ounce of strength and with nothing left to lose, the boy spoke again. This time, his voice stronger and more determined, he called out, "Friends, do not lose courage!"

Prisoners became overwhelmed; some began to weep. Eddie and

Mike were astounded to see the remarkable bravery of a boy their own age. Some guards and even the commandant stood stunned and seemed not to know how, at that moment, to handle the situation. One SS man turned his head away from the gallows and faced the crowd as if he were monitoring the prisoners. Eddie could see he had tears in his eyes.

"Shut up!" Tom Mix screamed again, and kicked the stool.

The corpses hung for three days, dangling back and forth so the prisoners could see them as they marched out to work in the morning and when they returned to camp in the evening. The hanging was intended to demoralize and to intimidate, to remind the inmates who was master and who was slave. But the real lesson that day was the Dutch boy's courage. His quiet defiance in his last moments greatly inspired the prisoners, who would remember the scene for the rest of their lives.

Others would follow.

At the next hangings, all five of the condemned called out in their last breaths:

"Keep your heads up!"

"Do not despair!"

"This cannot last forever!"

"Be courageous!"

"Do not forget us!"

It had now been more than ten years since Hitler had come to power. Millions had been murdered. Eddie, Mike, and Siegfried had been locked away in Nazi prisons for over four years. Many who once believed in miracles no longer did. Many were angry at God. Some stopped believing. Others continued, praying only for rescue.

Despite their ordeal, Eddie and Mike had cheated death so far, at the worksite, at the camp, through bombings, defusings, beatings, and a shooting. Living every day in the reality that life was fleeting, they had evaded close calls, had not contracted diseases, were starving, but were otherwise fit. Siegfried was grateful the boys were holding up.

One morning, as the column of Jewish prisoners was marching to the North plant, once again the SS forced their prisoners off the road and into the muddy ditch to allow the British POWs to pass. As usual, the Brits were in fine spirits, singing and whistling as they went along and, as usual, changed their tune when they spotted the tormented souls, belting out contempt for the Nazis, shouting, "Shame!" "Swine!" "*Bahstads!*"

The Jews looked downward and away, when suddenly Eddie felt something hit his chest. It was a little square of chocolate that one of the Brits had received in a Red Cross care package and had thrown over. In a world devoid of humanity, Eddie's spirit soared when he was struck by this one tiny act of kindness.

TWENTY

THANKSGIVING

They had been through blasts, shattered limbs, watched their buddies die together. That is how they spent their early twenties. They were a witness to each other's coming of age, and a witness to each other's manhood.

—Private Stuart Thayer, loader, D Company

BY EARLY AUTUMN 1944, the Allies were in complete control of France, and the Red Army was approaching the outskirts of Warsaw. Germany had lost almost 2 million men in battle; another 2 million were missing or had been taken prisoner. With every available German male now in uniform, more and more, forced labor was required to churn out war machinery for Hitler. All the while, the 3rd Armored Division surged on.

Having made their way across France and Belgium, D Company was now called upon to help spearhead the assault at the Siegfried Line, the entry point to Germany. The mammoth "Dragon's Teeth" obstacle stretched four hundred miles across from the Netherlands in the north to the Swiss border in the south. Made up of two thick

THANKSGIVING

rows of four-foot-tall, jagged, pyramid-shaped concrete "teeth" reinforced with barbed wire and mines, it looked like the jowls of a giant monster. With an enormous amount of enemy firepower directed at it, it was a barrier the Germans called impenetrable, erected to thwart any Allied attack into Germany, but also designed to lure them into killing zones.

By the time D Company neared the German border, Elmer, Myers, Vance, Fred, and the crews had developed their playbook of being quicker, bolder, and more adept at outmaneuvering more powerful enemy tanks by attacking them on their sides. While they perfected that tactic, they also perfected bailing out through their escape hatches or up through the turrets, a panic situation every time because the Germans had a practice of machine-gunning crews as they evacuated the tank. By now most tankers had been forced to bail multiple times.

Despite their improving battlefield acumen, fear never left them.

"Fear was like an oversized coat that dragged on the ground," one of Myers's crewmen said. "You wore it every day yet had to do your work despite its drag. You hoped it wouldn't get in the way. You couldn't take it off."

Some had never prayed in their lives but found religion inside the tank. Others said Hail Marys and crossed themselves for the first time since they were kids in church. In Myers's tank, even non-Catholics were crossing themselves. One tanker was so stressed by combat that his body shook uncontrollably. His buddies cruelly named him Shaky. Months later, when he became a seasoned tank commander, they still called him Shaky, and he still answered to it.

Even the bravest lost his nerve. The first sergeant would sometimes take a despondent tanker to go see Pepsi in the mess tent and Pepsi would cook up whatever he had on hand, fried eggs with toast or leftovers from the night before. If it was cold out, Pepsi would heat up some milk. Sometimes the soldier would sit in silence; other times he'd want to talk it out. Occasionally Pepsi would send word back to the first sergeant that the soldier probably needed to be seen by a doctor, who could prescribe something more than warm milk to settle the tanker's nerves, but more often than not, after just a short time, the crewman would finish his meal, say thanks to Pepsi and the mess crew, and hurry back to the front.

Crews learned to live with the Shermans' shortcomings. They praised their tanks for their protection but, in the next minute, cursed them for their lack of protection. They loved their tanks, hated them, prayed for them, sweet-talked them to get them to perform the way they were supposed to, and then, just as quickly, cursed them when they jammed, pleased when they worked until they didn't. Riding on rural roads and dipping in and out of ditches and cratered trails in their steel cocoons, thirty tons shifting back and forth, tossing them up and down inside, they rolled on, riding a fine line between fear and hope.

Although the unit's skills were improving by the day, crews couldn't dismiss the fact that their commander was becoming a liability: erratic and unpredictable, satisfied one minute and angry the next, then indifferent, almost vacant, when it seemed he should have something to say. Some of the more seasoned sergeants started to distrust him. One day, he was going to shoot four or five German prisoners and only backed off when a platoon sergeant yelled at the captain to "stand down." Whether it was true or not, the GI rumor mill had it that McDowell had a drinking problem.

One afternoon, Captain McDowell showed up after attending a briefing at battalion. He laid out his orders for the next day's mission, giving detailed instructions, but the platoon leaders and sergeants saw that his plan was dangerously flawed. It betrayed his lack of

THANKSGIVING

knowledge about even the most basic armor tactics. After McDowell issued his disjointed instructions, realizing their commander's hapless plan would likely get troops killed, the sergeants' eyes shifted to Elmer, looking for his reaction.

"Got it, sir," he said. McDowell seemed satisfied, climbed back into his jeep, and sped off.

"Okay, guys," Elmer said, "this is what I think the captain just told us," and then went on to present a clear-eyed, tactically sound plan to accomplish the mission, which had the sergeants breathing a sigh of relief and feeling grateful they had a real leader.

More and more, Elmer took charge. Part of the company commander's job was to learn what was around each bend before committing his tanks to battle. But with McDowell absent, it was not unusual to see Elmer dismount from his tank and walk up with a resolute gait to see what lay over the next ridge, unaffected by small-arms fire buzzing around him.

Elmer was turning out to be a natural-born leader who had good instincts and a no-nonsense way and was steady as a rock. He exuded competence and spoke sparingly but with conviction: "Got a challenge up ahead," or "Let's get on it. Eyes open."

He constantly came up with innovative ways to attack problems that left others scratching their heads. As Company D moved toward the Dragon's Teeth, they found themselves in a tiny hamlet with one sliver of a main road running through it. But there was a problem. A huge bomb blast had cratered the entire road, leaving an eight-foot-deep hole that made passage impossible. The convoy ground to a halt, leaving the crews wondering how they were going to move forward and deciding they would have to go back about a mile to take another road. Elmer came up on foot and looked into the cavern. Within seconds, he was up on the back deck of Myers's tank. Myers gave him the radio mike and Elmer ordered everyone to shift over to the left side of the road to let a bulldozer through. The crews watched, wondering how he would handle this, what he had in mind.

He sent a couple of infantrymen to clear out a building that stood close to the road near the crater. Then he guided the dozer driver to use his blade to knock down the front facade of the building at just the right angle. The building's bricks tumbled right into the cavity, the rubble filling the hole in the road and allowing the tanks to drive over it. It was a simple fix no one had thought of until Elmer did it.

Elmer never stopped working. He was constantly poring over maps, studying the terrain, looking over spot reports.

He stayed up nights with the enlisted leaders, brainstorming over attack plans for the next day's fight. With a twig, he drew tactics in the dirt, the sergeants puffing away on their cigarettes and chiming in, gaming out their ideas with their lieutenant. He was quick to mine the brainpower and instincts of those around him, seeking out what others with more experience had to say and taking in their opinions to come up with the best plan. As one tanker said, "He listened, then he led."

Unlike some officers with higher education, Elmer possessed something you couldn't learn in college: a combination of a farmer's horse sense, prairie toughness, humility, and a firm belief that the group was always more important than the individual. Elmer had no ego. He didn't crave the spotlight, wasn't motivated by accolades or promotions. He was impervious to rank. From the colonel to the cook, everyone mattered just the same. He thought a soldier's character and skills were far more important than the grade on their sleeve; Captain McDowell had proved that for him. Despite his casual manner, crews grew to deeply respect Elmer, whom they now referred to as "the Lieutenant," and they stood a little taller when they spoke with him. In a break from military protocol, Elmer called all the

THANKSGIVING

sergeants by their first names or nicknames: "Laddie . . . Shaky . . . Haag." In reply, they called him "sir."

Like a football coach with truculent confidence, Elmer reassured his crews to believe in themselves and to trust in their collective strength. His confidence was intoxicating and set the tone for the rest of the war. As they fought their way into Germany, the NCOs knew that their best chances were with the Minnesota farm boy at the helm.

General Rose earned a reputation for being a fearless leader who spent time out in front, close to the enemy. At over six feet tall, it was hard to miss the general as he walked among the troops. He could often be seen in his jeep with only his aide and his driver by his side, darting around the front lines, reconnoitering the way ahead, and directing the battle.

Myers had the same DNA. He frequently volunteered his platoon to scout out the situation ahead of the company, most of the time his own tank taking the lead. His fearlessness and keen instincts had already saved the unit from destruction more than once.

Lieutenant Myers had an uncanny knack for detecting danger, often sensing incoming rounds before anyone else did. In one instance, all was quiet, Fred looking through his periscope, when it simply dropped into his lap. Everyone in the tank looked at each other after the odd mishap and Fred shrugged. Suddenly, Myers yelled, "Incoming!" Sure enough, rounds descended. Another time, they got the all clear to stand down after a battle. Just when they thought the danger had passed, hatches opened and tankers began climbing out of their turrets. Despite no indication of another imminent attack, Myers yelled on the radio, "No! Get back in!" seconds before a volley of rounds rained down on the company.

Elmer and Myers continued to work hand in glove, forging what they knew would be a lifelong friendship. Myers respected Elmer for his lack of ego and his steady leadership. Elmer looked up to Myers for his smarts, his fearlessness, and his unfiltered counsel.

Elmer often turned to his little pocket Bible or recited verses to himself from memory. At some point, Myers began praying with him, together reading from Elmer's combat catechism that provided words of inspiration, passages that offered "a fountain of strength."

Through long days and nights inside Myers's tank, Redhead Fred and Baby Face Vance grew close over shared interests in sports, music, and books, though it was the cerebral Vance who had actually read the novels, and so he detailed the plots of books to Fred, who had only seen the movies. Fred's easy smile through everything rounded out everyone's edges. He had a way of chuckling almost as if to himself, then looking around, hoping others would be just as amused as he was, like when they got the call to move back into battle: "We better git to it, the war ain't gonna fight itself."

Vance remained in Fred's shadow. Inside the tank, he was conversational, but outside he was invisible in the company of others, an awkward kid who was easy to miss in a group, preferring to stay in the background, observing others in quiet reflection. Yet he still drew good-natured ribbing from other tankers for his taciturn manner and his boyish face. In truth, Vance was simply a thinker, introspective and sensitive, perhaps deeper than some. It affected him greatly when a soldier was wounded or killed in action.

"What're we doing all this for?" he would ask Fred.

"We just gotta do what we gotta do, kid. Take care of each other an' keep movin' forward. Do our best and get home in one piece."

At the Dragon's Teeth, a powerful American offense supported by infantry, tanks, and artillery assaulted the heavily fortified obstacles as the Germans pushed back with all they had. As the 3rd Armored Division busted through a wall of enemy machine-gun nests, engi-

THANKSGIVING

neers darted forward, attached explosives, and detonated the multi-rowed concrete incisors, blasting a gaping hole in the jaws of the monster, opening the first gateway into Germany, and giving passage for Allied units to stream through. And into the dark heart of Nazi Germany they moved.

Victory at the Dragon's Teeth earned D Company a short reprieve, so they set up a temporary camp in Stolberg, just inside the German border.

Elmer and Myers were promoted to first lieutenant, Fred and Pepsi became Tec-5s. Baby Face Vance turned nineteen and became Private First Class Vance.

Tankers came and went. Fresh-faced replacements took the place of those killed or wounded. Somehow the character of D Company remained the same despite the revolving door of new faces and personalities. Elmer greeted each replacement personally, shaking their hands and assuring them they would fit right in. In most units, the new guy was treated as an outsider. In D Company, however, often to the surprise of the newbie, Elmer and the sergeants quickly pulled them into the fraternal fabric that was building in the unit in what by now Elmer was calling "a family."

Though Captain McDowell was still officially in command, by October the senior sergeants and tankers had thrown in their lot behind Elmer, who had become the guiding force of D Company, working in close tandem with Myers, the bold leader at the front with a nose for danger.

After nearly ninety straight days in combat, in Stolberg, Pepsi and the mess crew took center stage, where they whipped up a hot meal for the deserving hungry hordes. As the troops made their way through the chow line, Pepsi greeted them with sharp wit and backslaps. Newer troops had to get used to Pepsi's outsize personality and brand of humor. When he told a joke, he often laughed so hard, he could barely get out the punch line, then laughed harder than anyone else when he was finally able to deliver it.

"So I got on the bus," he said, sidling up to a newbie downing his chow, "and the driver said, 'Blacks to the back of the bus,' and I said, 'I'm not Black, I'm Italian,' and he said, 'In that case, get off the bus!'"

He asked the company clerk for every soldier's birth date, then on that day he greeted him with birthday wishes and a second helping of anything he wanted, sometimes even a little cake made out of anything the kitchen happened to have: a piled-up plate of mashed potatoes, a stack of fresh biscuits, a C-rat can of pork and beans with a little wiener that looked like a candle.

Despite his upbeat nature, Pepsi also had a salty side and occasionally his short fuse landed him in hot water. At one point he was demoted for talking back to Captain McDowell, but his rank was reinstated by the first sergeant two days later.

Just three months in, Company D had come to accept the reality that crews never had control over their destiny. Knowing they could be gone the next day, they valued every smile, joke, prayer, shared cigarette, and cup of coffee. Any day could be their or their buddy's last, and all too often it was. Every day was a lottery in which they hoped their number didn't come up. Their safe place was the trust they had in one another. Confined inside their tanks, the crews got to know each other intimately, talked about their families, their girlfriends, women they had bedded or pretended to have. They talked about their dreams and their fears. They talked about not wanting to die heroes, but just wanted to do their duty and go home to their loved ones. Young men who were once total strangers became closer than brothers.

By October, the crews were doing their best not just for themselves but because they didn't want to let their brothers down, and they

THANKSGIVING

didn't want others to suffer because of something they had done or hadn't done. Said one crewman, "These men had prayed and cursed and cried their way through combat, hating it but feeling a compulsion to stay the course for the sake of each other."

Despite Elmer's leadership, there was still the inevitable misbehaving typical in any army unit, like the tankers who attempted to take unauthorized R&R trips into local villages in search of female companionship. There was occasional looting. One crew ransacked a house, plundering preserved meats and fruits—"I'm not leaving these goddam Krauts anything"—or the tankers who drank too much whenever they could. Alcohol was prized loot. One lucky tanker found a full barrel and loaded up the five-gallon cans on both sides of the tank with red wine instead of water.

Then there was Private Bizjack, who spent time in the stockade for refusing to give up a donkey he found in a field. He gave it a cracker and it followed him back to camp, and he wouldn't stop feeding it from his C-rats. Eventually they brought in Pepsi to talk to him. "Biz, you gotta let the donkey go, okay? . . . because we're fightin' a wah."

At Stolberg, they set up outdoor showers, drew clean coveralls, gave each other shaves and haircuts, and played cards using cigarettes and candy from care packages sent from home as currency; "What's a Clark bar worth to ya?"

Elmer never drew his officer's alcohol rations, but Lieutenant Myers became a company favorite for drawing his every time, then passing them off to the enlisted crews. Fred was happy to partake. Never having tried alcohol before, Vance abstained, though he envied those who could drink, imagining the power of booze could take the edge off, perhaps allowing a tanker to forget for a fleeting moment where he was and what had been done to his comrades.

Nothing cured their ills faster than mail from home. Their greatest joy was hearing their names shouted out at mail call, especially if they were called more than once.

Elmer got a flood of letters from his beautiful Harriet, who must have written every few days about this or that, about church activities or her wives' support group and about the developments of her pregnancy. He wrote back about his pride in his unit, penning, "We have a lot of faith in our company. Men of faith in the Lord and family and country. It's important to be part of a good group, in a spirit of cooperation and believing in each other."

In one letter, Harriet wrote of her fears after Elmer had sent her a card embossed with the Spearhead Division logo: "I do hope your being in a 'Spearhead' unit does not mean you are on the frontlines," to which he replied: "Darling, don't let the 'Spearhead' part bother you," then quickly changed the subject: "I have to go, love. I have letters to censor," a reference to having to blacken out parts of the crews' outgoing letters so that no operational information could accidentally fall into enemy hands. "In my heart there is love for you darling," he closed, "that mere words could not begin to describe. With all my love, Elmer."

Myers wrote to his parents in York. Pepsi missed Pa in Waltham and wondered how he was getting along at the diner. Pa wrote back, "I'm proud of you, my boy, and what you are doing over there." Fred received sweet letters from his wife, Bobbie, in Chattanooga, and wondered if his three-year-old son, Fred Jr., would remember him when he returned home.

Back in the mess area, Pepsi's pal George, a kitchen half-track driver, showed Pepsi a black-and-white picture of his sister, telling him she had the bluest eyes. One look and Pepsi fell in love.

A few days later, he asked George if he could hold on to the picture for a while.

THANKSGIVING

"Ya know that pictah of ya sistah? Would it be okay if I carried it with me?"

George agreed and gave it to him. It would be that black-and-white photograph of "Blue Eyes" that Pepsi would carry in his breast pocket, close to his heart, for the rest of the war.

When battalion called "church," a battlefield worship service, Elmer and Myers went, and the rest of the company followed. Typically, Company D showed up en masse with the largest contingent, more than all the other companies in the battalion combined. That fact would become one of Elmer's proudest accomplishments during the war.

At Thanksgiving, battalion orders came down for cooks to serve troops a proper holiday meal. Fresh turkeys, vegetables, and basic trimmings were provided, but that wasn't good enough for Pepsi, who wanted to take it up a notch. He wanted the D Company crews to have the best Thanksgiving feast of any unit in the division. Determined to pull off the impossible, he became single-mindedly fixated on the challenge.

He fanned out his crews to scour for ingredients from local farmers and housewives and to haggle, swap, and barter with other company cooks for two pounds of this for four packages of that. They came back with dozens of eggs, milk, butter, and cabbage. Others returned with bread or potatoes, which they spent hours peeling, cooking, and mashing, then whipping by hand. They basted the turkeys and stretched the gravy with water and milk. Whatever local fruit they could find was added to canned fruit to help fill out what Pepsi would call "cranberry sauce." On Thanksgiving Day, the kitchen crew presented their feast to the eagerly awaiting boys of D Company. It was a beautiful sight, Pepsi thought, that would have made Pa proud.

Captain McDowell asked Elmer to lead the men in prayer: "Lord, we give thanks. Let us never forget those we have lost in battle, and give us the strength to see this war through to the end in your good graces. Amen."

But their respite couldn't last forever.

In December 1944, the front lines unexpectedly erupted when the Germans launched a massive surprise attack in Belgium that caught the Allies off guard. The idea of having finally reached Germany, then having to backtrack, was a terrible psychological blow to the crews and no pep talk from Elmer could assuage their disappointment. Dreams of an easy enemy defeat by Christmas were dashed. With only hours' notice, D Company and the rest of the 3rd Armored Division made a hurried trek back to Belgium and into the thick Ardennes Forest.

TWENTY-ONE

SIEGFRIED'S PROPHECY

Hope for miracles but don't rely on one.

—Yiddish proverb

THE BEGINNING OF winter brought gray skies and Blechhammer's prisoners saw their first snow. As a chill set in, their canvas uniforms, now thinned and frayed, no longer provided any protection against the cold. B-24 Liberators kept coming, each bomb blast further chipping away at the refineries' fuel production and reminding the prisoners the Allies were on their way. But with inmates dying from exhaustion and starvation or from the Nazis' psychopathic sadism and random and systematic executions, Eddie, Mike, and Siegfried hoped help wouldn't come too late.

Prisoners who still held faith prayed constantly, waiting for a miracle. Why had God not answered their calls? Did he not see what was happening? Was he simply looking away from it all? *Sh'ma Yisrael, God, take me out of here.* While some wondered where God was, others felt he was coming in the form of American B-24 bombers. Siegfried, the German war veteran who had fought against the Russians, British, and Americans in World War I, prayed the forces that were once his enemies would now save Europe's Jews.

The boys grew thinner and thinner, and the fight to stay alive grew more arduous. At this point Eddie and Mike were hitching up their pants by rolling up the waistbands to tighten them just enough so they did not fall down.

The welts on Mike's back healed, as did Eddie's head wound, though he now had a three-inch gouge carved out of the back of his head.

Siegfried continued to buoy the boys as best he could.

"They're coming," he would say one day. "Stick together, take care of each other and you will make it." The next day, he would reassure them again. "Have no doubt you will make it." His words were uttered with such conviction, it was as if he knew something.

At around that same time, Siegfried began making Eddie memorize the names of the twenty-six members of the immediate Willner family: "Josef Willner, Margot Willner, Jakob, Elise, Isidor Willner..." Eddie did as he was told, going over the list again and again in his mind at the worksite and in the barracks at night, reciting them until he fell asleep.

Over time, it became obvious that Siegfried's health was deteriorating. At fifty years old, he had reached the Nazis' upper age limit for Jewish slave laborers. He was looking tired and worn and had edema in his leg, which was swollen from malnutrition. One day, after returning from the worksite, Eddie arrived at the barracks to find Siegfried missing. Someone told him his father had been sent to the infirmary. Frantic, Eddie went to find him and saw Siegfried standing behind the barbed-wire fence that cordoned off the infirmary from the main prison population.

Siegfried stood at the fence, waiting for Eddie to arrive.

Terrified, Eddie called out to his father. Siegfried had a placid look on his face, likely meant to keep Eddie calm, and said simply, "They're sending me for a rest."

Eddie was devastated. In the back of his mind, he had known this day might come, but he still wasn't prepared for it. He lunged forward, extending his arms, trying to reach out to touch his father, but the guard ordered him away from the fence.

The next day, Siegfried was gone. In an ultimate betrayal, this honorable man and proud German, good family man and good neighbor, a war hero who had fought on the front lines for the Fatherland, earning one of the country's highest combat decorations for valor and service to Germany, was murdered at the hands of his own countrymen.

In the days following Siegfried's death, Eddie realized that his father had made him memorize the family names so that he could find their relatives if he survived. Siegfried had made the importance of this clear.

The loss of Siegfried left Eddie with an immense loneliness. Against the forces of evil, Eddie's father had anchored him. Siegfried had rooted the boys in the faith that they could, and would, carry on. Siegfried hadn't been able to shield the boys from the madness, but he had protected and guided them as best he could. But now Eddie's anchor was gone. He and Mike would have to go it alone.

Eddie's loss loomed like a heavy cloud. In his darkest moments, reaching for some kind of strength, he turned to a Goethe poem that he was made to memorize in his German school.

Against every power
Defiantly tower
Never once bending
Brazenly standing

Resolute strength
Will call the arms
of the gods to you

To combat despair, he retreated to the golden days of his youth, to the sweetness of his childhood.

Flashbacks came to him in a rich cache of memories—in the blue skies and green grasses of his childhood on Weiherstrasse, a carefree boyhood playing soccer with his friends in the park; making Opa Josef laugh, digging in his pockets to offer his grandson a sweet; a welcome from the baker who gave him free cookies; his mother playing sonatas on the piano; his father wearing his Iron Cross lapel pin and everyone on the street tipping their hats to him.

More than anything, Eddie wanted to go back home, to lie in his bed under his downy blue feather *Bettdecke*, to see his mother's smile, to feel her stroke his cheek again, her silvery touch and the dulcet tones of her voice reassuring him that everything was going to be all right. He imagined escaping and running back home to find Fritz, the neighbor, asking him to hide him somewhere, anywhere, in the attic, in the back room, under the floorboards, and he was sure Fritz would do it.

But now his former friends were German soldiers. Opa Josef had disappeared, his parents were gone, and there was simply no escaping to Fritz.

With Siegfried no longer by his side, and nothing left in the world but each other, Eddie and Mike made a pact, pledging to one another that, no matter what may come, they would look after each other to the very end. Eddie began to think of nothing else but escape with Mike, doubling down on his intent to make a break for freedom the first chance they got.

SIEGFRIED'S PROPHECY

Like a prayer, Eddie recited the names of his twenty-six relatives in his head over and over again, repeating the sequence in a constant refrain. Unbeknownst to Eddie, however, every one of those twenty-six relatives had already been murdered.

Eddie was now the only one of his entire family left alive.

PART III

TWENTY-TWO

CHRISTMAS EVE

We'll fight our way out.

—The boys of Company D

As American bombers continued to pummel Blechhammer, D Company made a hasty sixty-mile retreat back to Belgium, into the Ardennes Forest, to fight the Battle of the Bulge, Hitler's all-or-nothing gambit to drive the Allies back to the sea.

Due to relentless Allied pounding of the Nazis' synthetic fuel plants, the German military machine literally began running out of fuel on the battlefield. Given their desperate situation, Hitler launched the Ardennes Offensive aimed in part at capturing Allied fuel supplies at Antwerp.

Freezing temperatures, deep snow, and a frozen misty ground fog met the company upon their return to Belgium. These harsh weather conditions handed the Germans a huge advantage, as they grounded Allied airplanes.

In the Ardennes, the generals looked up from their maps and saw chaos everywhere. They didn't even know where the front lines were.

The 3rd Armored Division had learned to fight as one, but once they entered the Ardennes, it all fell apart. The German attack blindsided the Allies, throwing the Americans into a disorienting tailspin, splintering several divisions into small groups that were left isolated, confused, and fending for themselves. Enemy tanks would appear without warning out of the mist only a hundred yards away, forcing split-second reactions and hasty retreats.

By December 22, D Company was fighting for its very survival. Germans boasted of their successes as they rammed through feeble U.S. defenses: "You cannot imagine," a German officer wrote to his wife, "what glorious hours we are experiencing now. The snow must turn red with American blood."

Somewhere in all the chaos, near Lamormenil, D Company found itself completely cut off from U.S. lines, out of communication with headquarters, and surrounded by the enemy. They had become detached from Pepsi and their supply and service units. They had no food and were running out of fuel and ammunition. They had wounded in need of aid, were freezing, and hadn't slept in days. D Company was trapped and in danger of being overrun.

It was a dire situation. Just days earlier, only twenty miles away, near a small village called Malmedy, a Waffen-SS unit tore up the Vienna Convention rules of war by ordering eighty-four American POWs to stand in an open field with their arms raised, then machine-gunned them down in cold blood. News of that atrocity had spread through U.S. troops like wildfire.

Things were getting grimmer by the hour. The company was taking sporadic fire from nearly all directions. For a bunch of Americans barely older than boys, many believed the end was near. No one knew what to do, especially Captain McDowell, who was seized with uncertainty. To try to confuse the enemy, he ordered a haphazard diver-

CHRISTMAS EVE

sionary attack that failed miserably and only helped the Germans to pinpoint their location, which left the sergeants shaking their heads. "It surely was obvious to the Germans," one crewman lamented, "that we had either lost our minds or were trying to attract their attention."

Feeling the unit was doomed, McDowell went out to his tank and returned with a bottle under each arm: scotch and crème de menthe.

"It's a helluva mixture," he said. "I was saving it for New Year's Eve. But it looks as though we might not be around come New Year's." He and a few others shared it, becoming "pleasantly numb."

With the captain off and drinking, Elmer had seen enough.

He gathered the platoon leaders and sergeants and said, "We're floatin' out here alone."

Elmer knew what he wanted to do but didn't want to hold the fate of the entire company entirely in his hands.

"We're completely surrounded," he said. "What do you guys want to do?"

Standing in the freezing cold, he searched their faces.

"The way I see it," he continued, "we got two options. We can stay here and let the Germans move on us, or we can fight our way out."

He looked around.

"We're takin' a vote."

The answer was unanimous: "We'll fight our way out."

They stayed up all night planning it. Elmer had constantly studied maps and unit spot reports before they were trapped, trying to keep up with the confusing battlefield picture, but with the Germans set to overrun them at any moment, and with all connections to the outside world cut off, he rolled out the map again and worked it out as best he could with the company leaders.

At around midnight, Elmer, Myers, and a few others set out on foot to probe through the forest of tall fir trees, searching for any trace of the enemy and looking for the best path out. They fanned out in all directions, walking, listening, and looking for any sign of German activity. Aside from the crunching of their footsteps on the crusty snow, they found only silence. Elmer, Myers, and the sergeants looked over the map one final time, discussed their options, and decided on an escape route. Elmer ordered all working tanks to be lined up in a tight single file, one behind the other.

That night, Elmer made a personal plea to God.

"Lord, I'm gonna need more than just a little bit of help on this one. You gotta watch over me, watch over my men. . . ." He thought about his beautiful Harriet and his unborn child. Other men thought about their families and sweethearts. Elmer read, "By thy great mercy defend us from all perils and dangers of this night."

After a nearly sleepless night, in the frigid, predawn hours, Elmer gathered the crews and told them, simply, to "Stay tight. Have faith."

With Elmer in the lead tank, Myers had taken up the trail position to ensure everyone would make it out safely. In the darkness, crews waited, shivering in the cold.

"'Fear thou not; for I am with thee. . . . I will help thee.' Isaiah 41:10," Elmer read, and tucked the catechism back into his pocket.

Then Elmer got on the radio and, after syncing with Myers, said, "Turn 'em over. Follow me."

In the frozen blackness with headlights off and little moonlight to guide them, Elmer's driver struggled to make out the trail. Packed tightly together, each Sherman following closely on the heels of the tank in front, they moved out quickly, picking up the pace as they went. Soon the thundering convoy was racing through the shadows down the narrow logging trail at near top speed. Within minutes, the wood line opened up and they busted out into a clearing, where they were spotted by the enemy. The Germans realized that the Americans

CHRISTMAS EVE

were making a break for it and opened fire, but it was too late. The tanks had made it far enough to evade the German guns. Company D had somehow found a small, unguarded seam between enemy units and had snuck out. Elmer's prayers had been answered.

The boys of Company D would never forget Elmer's coolheaded leadership that day, which saved them from being killed or captured, and from that day onward the once reluctant twenty-three-year-old lieutenant, who never wanted to be in the spotlight in the first place, became their North Star.

In what was one of the biggest intelligence failures in the history of the U.S. Army, right under their noses the Nazis were somehow able to secretly amass some thirty divisions, almost half a million men, and pierce the American lines at a weak point in the Ardennes Forest. With U.S. generals caught completely off guard, it had been left to small-unit leaders like Elmer and the heroics of individual soldiers to save the day. In the first week of the battle alone, tens of thousands of American GIs had been captured or lay dead or wounded in the snow. The main thrust of Hitler's plan relied on the surprise of two Panzer armies searing through Allied defenses to reach Antwerp. Hitler pinned his hopes on bad weather that would ground Allied aircraft and on a stealthy and swift attack led by two of his most prized and experienced SS Panzer divisions.

Two days before Christmas, exhausted but happy to be alive, D Company rejoined friendly forces. Having lost crews and tanks along the way, Elmer, Myers, Fred, Vance, and the rest of the unit rolled into the tiny Belgian village of Freyneux. They were down to just ten tanks, with only three or four crew members per tank. They were told to defend a critical road juncture near the crossroads at Manhay. A large convoy of a hundred or more enemy tanks and vehicles had been sighted heading their way. General Rose warned the impending battle would be "the hottest spot on the western front."

In Freyneux, a little hamlet of 42 homes and 130 villagers, D Company tankers made good use of the rolling terrain to set up positions to help defend against the enemy attack expected the next day. Short of crewmen, Fred was temporarily moved to another tank. Myers positioned his tank on the grounds of the St. Isidore Church. The little chapel that, in ordinary times, would be the center of cheerful holiday celebrations, bells ringing and candles alight, now lay eerily abandoned as fat snowflakes fell silently around it.

Buttoned up and trying to stay warm inside their unheated tanks, the dirty, tired, and cold boys of Company D settled in for a night of waiting. In freezing conditions, all they did was think of home.

Back home, families went to church to pray for their loved ones "over there." Harriet, now eight months pregnant, spent Christmas with her family. Myers's parents gathered around the holiday dinner table, their thoughts never very far away from their only son, who was their pride and joy. Pa kept the diner open, listening constantly to the radio to try to keep up with the latest news from overseas. In his tank, Fred watched the snowfall through his periscope, softly singing to himself, "I'm dreamin' of a white Christmas," and thought of his wife Bobbie's holiday cinnamon-sugar cookies as he picked through his dry ten-in-one rations.

The St. Isidore Church was a tiny one-room brownstone structure with a small, well-kept cemetery in the yard. Along with a screen of trees, a stone wall gave Myers's tank good concealment but for its turret and gun, which cleared the top of the wall by a few inches. His head up and out of the hatch, Vance admired the tranquility of the scene and the beauty of the church's simple stained glass window before he sat back down, curled up, and settled in for the night, as a few soldiers were

CHRISTMAS EVE

posted to sentry duty. Myers walked out a few hundred yards to ensure the tank had the best fields of fire, and all went quiet.

The next day, Christmas Eve morning, cast a haze over the undulating fields of Freyneux. Before dawn, Elmer, Myers, and the other platoon leaders were called to a final officers' briefing before the impending German attack, which was expected to take place sometime later that day. Myers left Vance in command.

Vance moved to Myers's seat, feeling the weight of his temporary role as the man in charge. He stood back up and looked into the darkness of the fields that lay before him.

Suddenly, in the first hint of daylight, an infantry soldier excitedly ran up and jumped onto the turret, alerting Vance through gasping breaths that four enemy tanks were making their way up the hill and would be in his sights within seconds. Vance yelled to his driver to start the engine and, with an AP round already in the breech, he rotated the Sherman's gun to face the oncoming Germans.

Out of the semidarkness, the quiet was broken by the roar of powerful engines as a platoon of four giant Panzers from Hitler's notorious 2nd SS "Das Reich" Panzer Division (infamous for their war crimes, including the executions of over 640 innocent civilians at Oradour-sur-Glane just months earlier) heaved up over the hidden bluff and were momentarily silhouetted into Vance's view.

Vance couldn't believe his eyes. Passing in front of him at less than five hundred yards, the four Panzers, unaware that Vance had spotted them, crawled up and crested with their vulnerable sides exposed.

It was an unbelievable, make-or-break moment, and in that split second no one but Vance could do anything about it. Unless the Panzers were stopped, they could easily overrun the company, have a clear path onward to Manhay, and, ultimately, have a chance of reaching Hitler's objective at Antwerp.

THE BOYS IN THE LIGHT

Vance, of course, had no way of knowing that the four enemy tanks were led by young tank ace SS Untersturmführer (Lieutenant) Fritz Langanke, who had been awarded the Knight's Cross, Germany's highest combat award, for his daring and successes on the battlefield. The young German prodigy, as it would turn out, was helping to spearhead Hitler's main attack that day. Hitler was getting minute-by-minute spot reports. With his other prized SS Panzer division all but destroyed and now in retreat, Hitler's high-stakes gamble rested on the success of this attack, led by these four tanks.

Vance dropped from the commander's hatch into the gunner's seat. Without the advantage of Lieutenant Myers calculating the distance and calling down firing instructions, Vance was on his own. He zeroed in on the first Panzer and fired.

It was a bull's-eye. The round smashed into the Panzer's side, instantly setting the tank ablaze. Vance stared in astonishment as he watched the crew bail out. He screamed for a reload, picked out the next Panzer, made a quick adjustment, and fired again. It was another direct hit. Then Vance trained on Langanke's Panzer, whose heavy gun was slowly hand-cranking its way to face and fire on Vance's tank, and he fired again. Now aided by other D Company Shermans joining in the fight after hearing the uproar, Langanke's tank was struck and forced into retreat.

The attack now stalled, the platoon following Langanke's was caught out in the open, which made them an easy target.

Alerted by the sounds of gunfire, Elmer and Myers abandoned their officers' meeting and dashed back to join the company. To get a better look at what was happening down in the valley, Elmer scaled the church steeple. From atop the belfry, he yelled instructions down to Myers, who called in artillery, and soon even U.S. fighter bombers were swooping in to join in the attack. It all worked well until the Germans realized there was a man in the steeple directing fire and

CHRISTMAS EVE

blasted it. Elmer crashed to the ground, barely making it out alive, and darted back to his tank.

When it was over, burning Panzers littered the battlefield. The American Christmas Eve victory had been decisive.

Elmer, Myers, and the rest of the crews were in awe of Vance. Thanks to his cool head, quick action, and superior marksmanship, the mild-mannered nineteen-year-old cotton farmer's son from Chickasaw, Mississippi, had miraculously saved the day, outdueled one of Germany's most experienced Panzer aces, and played a key role in almost single-handedly blunting a major German attack, which would ultimately help turn the tide of the Battle of the Bulge. His heroics would be the subject of books and articles by military historians for years to come.

Having finally met his match, Lieutenant Langanke would later remember the Christmas Eve engagement with Vance as the defining moment of his wartime career.

Vance's pivotal role in history that day would become a main topic of conversation in Company D for their rest of their lives and would earn Baby Face Vance the honor "best gunner in the company."

TWENTY-THREE

BUTCH

Now I understand why my brother died—to make this evil stop.
—Sister of Michael Papadopulos, tail gunner on B-24 *Butch*

BY CHRISTMAS, IN Germany there were no men around except for Nazi officials; fathers and sons had gone off to war and the only ones who remained behind were very old, very young, or wounded. Boys as young as fifteen were being called up to serve as German losses mounted.

In some ardent Nazi homes, Christmas trees were topped not with a five-pointed star, because that was a symbol of communism, and certainly not a six-pointed Jewish Star of David, but with a shiny glass swastika or an ornament that bore Hitler's likeness. After more than ten years of Nazism, there were now attempts by the regime to even bring Christmas in line with Nazi ideology.

For example, "Stille Nacht" ("Silent Night"), a traditional favorite Christmas carol sung all over the world, was changed by dropping mention of Christ, a Jew, and replacing it with a new stanza aimed to inspire devotion not to Jesus but to Hitler. "Silent night, holy night,

Auguste and Siegfried Willner, 1924. *Courtesy of the Willner Family*

The house on Weiherstrasse, Mönchengladbach (MG), 1922. *Stadtarchiv Mönchengladbach*

Eddie in his German public school (first row standing, sixth from right in lederhosen). Soon he would be expelled, and his friends would join the Hitler Youth, MG, 1934. *Courtesy of the Willner Family*

Opa Josef (third from left, standing) in the *Altersheim* Jewish senior home. Residents pose for a photograph before being deported to concentration camps, Rheydt, July 1942. *Stadtarchiv Mönchengladbach*

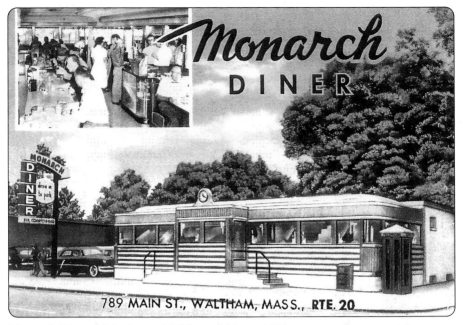

Monarch Diner, Main Street, Waltham, MA, ca. 1935. *Courtesy of Louis DeCola*

Elmer called his new girlfriend, Harriet, "a fancy thing from the city," 1942. *Courtesy of the Hovland Family*

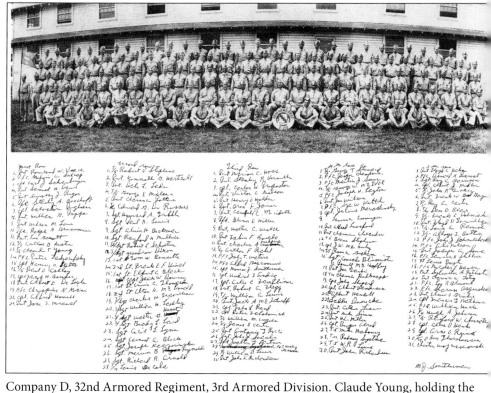

Company D, 32nd Armored Regiment, 3rd Armored Division. Claude Young, holding the unit crest at center, was the first crewman to be killed in action. *Courtesy of Fred Headrick*

Tankers of Company D, 1944. *Courtesy of Fred Headrick*

Tankers of Company D, 1944. *Courtesy of Fred Headrick*

Crews attached logs to the sides of their tanks to try to protect their vulnerable Shermans. *Courtesy of Fred Headrick*

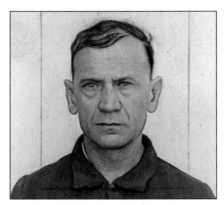

SS Hauptsturmführer Otto Brossmann (7th SS *Totenkopf Wach*, Death's Head Battalion), former high school principal and Auschwitz-Blechhammer camp commandant, 1945. *Instytut Pamięci Narodowej Poland*

SS Untersturmführer Kurt Klipp, deputy commandant and overseer of the death march, ca. 1944. *Yad Vashem*

Mother and children walk to the gas chamber. *Yad Vashem / ABMAP*

Prisoners stand at attention on the *Appellplatz,* roll call square, Buchenwald, 1941. *United States Holocaust Memorial Museum*

Blechhammer North oil refinery, Auschwitz III, October 1944. *Bundesarchiv*

British POWs at Stalag VIIIB, Lamsdorf, Silesia, near Blechhammer, 1944. *Courtesy of Peter Hayes*

Under their junior officer leadership, Company D lieutenants Charles Myers (left) and Elmer Hovland (right) turned things around, reduced fear, and motivated their crews. *Courtesy of the Hovland Family (Elmer Hovland) and the Lettieri Family (Charles Myers)*

Private "Pepsi" DeCola, the cook, 1944. *Courtesy of Louis DeCola*

Tec-5 "Redhead Fred" Headrick sits on Company D's Pershing tank, 1945. *Courtesy of Fred Headrick*

Private James "Baby Face" Vance, ca. 1943. *Courtesy of Fred Headrick*

Armorers prepare to load a thousand-pound bomb on a B-24. *National Archives and Records Administration (NARA)*

B-24 Liberators (15th U.S. Air Force) bomb Blechhammer oil refinery, August 27, 1944. *NARA*

The crew of *Butch*, including twenty-year-old pilot Lieutenant Arthur Lindell (first from left, standing). *485th Bomb Group Association*

Project Malachit tunnels (Buchenwald subcamp Langenstein) in the Harz Zwieberge Mountains. Life expectancy was six weeks. *Reinhard Arndt / Gedenkstätte Langenstein-Zwieberge*

The long march lasted thirteen days in the bone-chilling freeze of an exceptionally cold winter; a 180-mile odyssey in which the SS killed many. Painting by survivor Nikolai Kuzniecow, 1947. *Muzeum Stutthof*

SS Obersturmführer Wilhelm Lübeck, tunnels site manager, said, "If you kill a thousand, it doesn't matter because you can get a thousand to replace them." *Bundesarchiv*

Eddie and Mike atop a Company D Sherman tank. Elmer sent this photograph to Harriet. On the back he wrote: "Two little Jewish boys we picked up," 1945. *Courtesy of the Hovland Family*

Eddie (right), with a Colt .45, stayed glued to the lieutenant, 1945. *Courtesy of the Willner Family*

Eddie Willner (left), U.S. Army liaison officer to the French military (Paris). Head scar received in Auschwitz-Blechhammer SS killing spree, ca. 1953. *Courtesy of the Willner Family*

Liberation of Langenstein concentration camp. A U.S. Army medic speaks with survivors, April 11, 1945. *Associated Press photo / Henry L. Griffin*

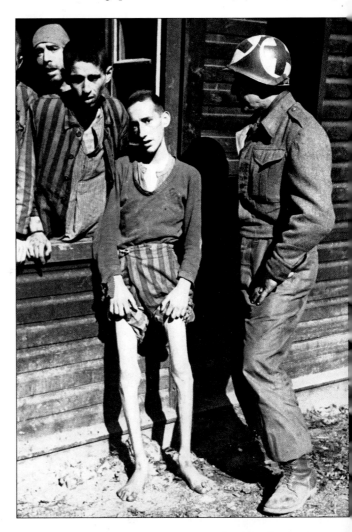

Pepsi married Blue Eyes. George was his best man, 1947. *Courtesy of Louis DeCola*

Lieutenant Myers's parents kept this photo up on their mantel for the rest of their lives, ca. 1943. *Courtesy of the Keeley Family*

Lieutenant Eddie Willner, U.S. Army, 1953.
Courtesy of the Willner Family

Airman Mike Swaab, U.S. Air Force, 1954.
Courtesy of the Swaab Family

There was nothing that could separate Mike (left) and Eddie (right), 1979.
Courtesy of the Willner Family

Eddie (left) age seventy-six with Pepsi (right) age eighty-three. They last saw each other nearly sixty years earlier in 1945 when Pepsi brought the two boy survivors back from the brink of death, September 2002. *Courtesy of the Willner Family*

Elmer (left) and Eddie (right) at Arlington National Cemetery paying respects to World War II soldiers, 2005.
Courtesy of the Willner Family

"Both boys had lost their entire families in the concentration camps, and with no one else left in the world to claim them, Company D did," September 16, 2002. Fred (left) with *Spearhead* book, Pepsi, Vance, Eddie (center), and Elmer (in striped shirt). *The Washington Post*

The boys of Company D at an annual reunion. Pepsi is seated center with the unit placard. Elmer (in white shirt) is seated next to Pepsi, 1972. *Courtesy of Fred Headrick*

Elmer (left), Eddie, and Pepsi celebrate Eddie's son, Al Willner's promotion to full colonel. World War II monument, Washington, DC, 2004. *Courtesy of the Willner Family*

The author's son, Michael, named for his grandfather Eddie's "brother" in the camps, takes a selfie with Uncle Pepsi and Celia (Blue Eyes), 2016. *Courtesy of the Willner Family*

all is calm, all is bright" was now followed by the lyrics "Only the Chancellor stays on guard, Germany's future to watch and to ward, guiding our nation aright." An attempt was also made to replace the coming of Christ the Savior with the coming of "the Savior Führer." In Nazi Germany, Hitler had eclipsed even Jesus. Now *he* had become the Almighty.

At holiday glitterati parties that year, Hitler was the man of the hour. In great marble halls, while Goebbels, Hitler's propaganda chief, smiled and doled out gifts to little blond children, Nazis drank champagne and ate lavish meals on fine bone china as if everything was right on course and Germany was headed for victory.

Back in Mönchengladbach, no one played Santa for Fritz's children on Christmas, there was little meat on offer in Fritz's butcher store, and almost every family had known the loss of a German soldier: their son, father, uncle, or nephew.

By now, it had been five years since Fritz had last seen his best friend, Siegfried, or anyone in the Willner family. All had been hauled away when the streets were purged of Jews. Fritz wondered if he would ever see any of them again or if anyone was ever coming back to get their belongings, which he still kept in the trunk that was hidden in the attic.

By late December, a total of sixteen U.S. air raids had wreaked havoc on Blechhammer.

On Christmas morning at Venosa Airfield in southern Italy, twenty-year-old American B-24 pilot First Lieutenant Arthur Lindell from Russell, Pennsylvania, woke up, washed, shaved, and went to Christmas service.

That evening, in the mess hall, Lindell sat alongside his fellow pilots and crews eating a holiday meal. They chattered about missing their families back home but were grateful for the close friendships they had made in the squadron in the middle of war. Later they stood in a circle around a decorated Christmas tree outside the chapel singing "Silent Night" with its traditional lyrics and other Christmas carols.

The next morning, Art Lindell and other B-24 pilots and crewmen attended a targeting briefing. Their mission that day: the final bombing raid to knock the Blechhammer refinery out of action once and for all. With the Germans determined to defend the refinery to the bitter end, crews were aware that they would be risking their lives on every mission. The military chaplain ended the briefing with a blessing and wished the crews "Godspeed and a safe return."

Outside, crisp, newly fallen snow had powdered the runway. Crews played in the snow, built a snowman, then, at the call, suited up in their leather and heavy sheepskin bomber jackets and climbed into the cockpits and gun turrets of their planes.

Lindell and his copilot made their preflight checks and started up the B-24 that Lindell had named *Butch* as crews settled in: navigators, bombardiers, engineers, waist gunners, and nose, top, ball, and tail gunners.

Lindell flashed a thumbs-up, which was returned by a crisp salute from the ground crew chief, and at 8:00 a.m. sharp a mammoth armada of just over five hundred American B-24 and B-17 bombers taxied down the runway and, one by one, took off into the open skies. Like the other bombers, *Butch* was grossly overloaded. One of the heaviest planes in the world now lumbered aloft carrying thirty-five tons: a crew of nine with ten five-hundred-pound bombs instead of the usual eight, in addition to .50-caliber machine-gun shells, oxygen tanks, and a maximum load of high-octane fuel. Engines turned over, *Butch* groaned and shook violently to get off the ground, and the crew inside prayed for a smooth takeoff and a successful mission ahead.

Once airborne, clouds of exhaust trailing in their wake, the massive procession of American warplanes flew above the clouds in icebox conditions at fifty degrees below zero, crews' oxygen masks freezing to their faces.

At 11:00 a.m., the Americans crossed over the Danube. Just past the Sudeten Mountains, they turned eastward to approach their target. As Christmas music played down below on radios in homes all over Nazi-occupied Europe, *Butch* and his accompanying aircraft entered Polish airspace. After traveling 650 miles for over four hours, the bombers neared their target.

Sirens sounding, once again Blechhammer's prisoners and guards looked up to see the B-24s flying in a tight formation. Smoke pots popped and anti-aircraft guns fired, sending shells whistling up and exploding, streams of burning metal and glistening tinfoil strips that looked like Christmas tree tinsel falling through the air.

At "bombs away," crews dropped their loads. *Butch*'s doors opened and released the first bomb rack, but one minute later enemy flak landed a direct hit on *Butch*. The plane exploded into a fireball, broke in half, and hurtled violently to earth.

Butch's tail spiraled downward and hit a nearby farmhouse. The front half of the plane became a missile that slammed into the electricity power station at the South plant, and Blechhammer went dark.

That day, the American aircrews delivered a fatal blow to Blechhammer, destroying the electricity grid and much of the refinery, and fuel production ground to a final halt.

December 26, 1944: Mission accomplished.

Sadly, none of the brave young crew of *Butch* survived.

After six months and seventeen air-raid missions, dropping more than 33,000 bombs on the Silesian targets, and the loss of 137 U.S. airmen, the Fifteenth Air Force's campaign to destroy Blechhammer was completed. American aircrews had turned the factories to rubble. In the end, the plants had produced only a fraction of their intended goal before being destroyed. Overall, Allied bombers had cut Germany's fuel production from synthetic plants by 97 percent. Albert Speer, the German minister for armaments and war production, called the situation "catastrophic."

German field marshal Gerd von Rundstedt sent a report to Hitler warning him of the seriousness of the situation. With Blechhammer and other oil refineries put out of action, the Reich was desperate and running out of gas. After the success of Allied bombing missions, Hitler began the process of driving Germany's war production underground.

TWENTY-FOUR

THE LONG MARCH

IN EARLY JANUARY 1945, the Soviets were rapidly approaching Auschwitz. The North and South plants in ruins, Himmler ordered all Auschwitz and surrounding camps in the path of the advancing Russians to be evacuated and the prisoners marched westward toward Germany. In a mass exodus of tens of thousands of prisoners and laborers (including British POWs) from twenty-nine camps, Eddie, Mike, and the nearly four thousand Jews of Blechhammer were set on a long march from Poland to Germany in what would become one of the largest, most arduous forced marches of the war during one of the coldest winters Poland had ever seen.

For his outstanding performance as deputy, Kurt Klipp was promoted and Brossmann was transferred out. In his first official role as commandant, Obersturmführer Klipp was given the task of driving the forlorn prisoners westward and out of the reach of the approaching Red Army.

On the *Appellplatz*, Eddie, now eighteen years old, and Mike, seventeen, formed up next to each other. In the bone-chilling freeze, on

THE BOYS IN THE LIGHT

January 21, 1945, Kurt Klipp, Tom Mix, the goons, and the rest of Blechhammer's two hundred guards, all of whom were warmly cloaked in heavy woolen coats and thick boots, prepared to march their legions of shivering prisoners, clad only in threadbare prison uniforms, some with blankets around their shoulders, out of the camp. Eddie believed that he and Mike would finally get their chance to escape while in transit, and he fully intended that they would make a run for it.

On the *Appellplatz*, each prisoner received a loaf of bread. The heavily armed SS and their killer dogs took up their positions, and the migration began.

The sounds of Soviet artillery fire in the distance raised the prisoners' spirits. Excited at the prospect of liberation, a few made a run for it back in the direction of the Russians and were shot dead. This dashed Eddie's hopes of any chance to make an easy break. It was painful to know that freedom was so close yet still completely out of reach, especially since the SS made it clear they would shoot if they sensed a prisoner was even thinking about running.

On back roads and through small towns, facing biting winds, the Blechhammer slave laborers were marched at a brisk pace, guards whipping those who moved too slowly.

A few days into the march, they passed through the German town of Oppeln. Villagers came out to see the tormented Jewish prisoners trudge past in the snow. Some looked on with hate in their faces. Eddie and Mike were spit on and cursed by villagers, who called them "*dreckliche Juden*" ("dirty Jews") and "*ekliches Ungeziefer*" ("disgusting vermin"). An old man tried to hit prisoners with his cane. Hitler Youth and schoolchildren threw stones. But several old women held handkerchiefs over their mouths; one woman was crying. Almost

THE LONG MARCH

inaudibly, her voice countered the scathing taunts. "Don't despair," she assured. "It won't last much longer." The guards shoved her away.

Occasionally a peasant tried to toss the prisoners bread or feed them. One farmer laid out a pail of hot cooked potatoes, but the guards wouldn't allow it, kicking over buckets of water, milk, anything anyone brought forward. So prisoners ate snow.

Tom Mix had no pity for those who could not walk on their own and forbade any prisoner from assisting another. Out of villagers' eyesight, he simply shot those who could not keep up. It didn't matter to Tom Mix why they moved slower, whether succumbing to frostbite or exhaustion or because snow had clumped unevenly on the bottoms of their wooden clogs, causing them to stumble. Regardless of the reason, he and other guards watched for those who faltered and promptly shot them dead, which left the trail marred for miles by bodies and red splotches in the crystalline white snow.

Freezing nights, with temperatures dropping into the teens, gave way to each new morning. Those who had not frozen to death formed up and marched on. With thousands of German soldiers and refugees fleeing the Russians, clogging the roads with carts full of their possessions, the Jewish prisoners of Blechhammer were driven off-road and into the bleak, unforgiving countryside.

In the face of a glacial wind, they slogged onward, moving through knee-deep snowdrifts. Flurries became a blinding snowstorm. Whipping winds and narcotic cold searing their skin like razors, they mechanically forced one foot in front of the other. For many, nature's fury became too much to withstand, especially when they looked up at the endless expanse of snow that lay before them. Others resigned themselves to pressing on. Some, unable to keep up due to the snow now packing like rocks on the soles of their fraying clogs and not wanting to risk being shot, simply discarded them and walked in bare feet.

Mike and Eddie lost all sense of time. They looked at one another occasionally to check in, no longer considering escape in the vastness of the endless snowy landscape. On the verge of complete exhaustion and close to succumbing, Eddie turned to Mike and said, "Brother, we're going to make it." Mike looked back at Eddie with sunken eyes and blue lips and nodded.

Suddenly, the plodding trek was interrupted by a thunderous explosion from one side of the field. That blast was soon followed by a deluge of screaming artillery shells from the opposite end of the horizon, which ignited a volley of counter-barrages. A German blast triggering a Russian salvo followed by another German round of fire, all of it lobbing back and forth over the prisoners' heads as they continued to move straight through the field.

Six days after the march began, Soviet forces liberated Auschwitz, including Blechhammer.

As the march neared Breslau, with his Thousand-Year Reich crumbling around him, a delusional Hitler was on the radio again, declaring that "tremendous feats" had been achieved. He praised the German people for their devotion, charging them to "strengthen the heart" more than ever before and to "steel" themselves "until final victory crowns our efforts."

After thirteen days and 180 miles, their arctic nightmare ended when what was left of the Blechhammer column finally arrived at Gross-Rosen. On their way into the camp, they passed an SS casino. Inside, guards escaped the icy temperatures and daily drudgery of concentration camp duty to sit in the warm arcade and play roulette or relax in the lounge and enjoy a meal, listen to music, have a cognac and a cigar. A couple of buildings away, freezing inmates were feeding bodies into the crematorium.

Gross-Rosen absorbed tens of thousands of prisoners arriv-

THE LONG MARCH

ing from all over Poland. Mike and Eddie stood on the *Appellplatz* as Commandant Kurt Klipp of the now-defunct Auschwitz-Blechhammer camp reported in to the Gross-Rosen commandant and turned over what was left of his frozen prisoners. Out of around four thousand marchers who began the trek, some eight hundred had perished along the way.

In a cruel twist of fate, after surviving the long march, a selection weeded out hundreds whose feet had rotted from frostbite; the rest were made to stand on the overcrowded *Appellplatz* for three days straight, where a torrential shower pummeled them, turning the lot into a floor of slush and mud. Some sank into the bogs and suffocated to death.

The survivors were loaded onto a cargo train and sent farther west into Germany, relieved to have survived the grueling death march and the dire reception at Gross-Rosen and thankful that was the last they would see of Kurt Klipp, the goons, and Tom Mix.

Little did they know the worst was yet to come.

In a surprising turn of events, upon arrival at the Buchenwald concentration camp, Eddie and Mike found themselves standing on the *Appellplatz* among bigger inmates with different patches on their uniforms from the Jewish star patches the two boys wore. These were the "Reds," red-patched political "leftists," Hitler's so-called "enemy of the people"; the "Greens," hardened professional criminals; and the "Blacks," so-called asocials and non-Nazi conformists, and other men from twenty-three countries: Russian and Ukrainian POWs, Poles, Yugoslavs, Czechs, French and Belgian resistance fighters, and Italian partisans.

At the *Selektion*, Eddie snapped to attention, lifting his skinny chest, trying to look strong, but next to these more robust-looking inmates the odds were not in his favor. The guard looked Eddie over and hesitated. With little muscle left, Eddie stared straight ahead, an intensely determined expression on his face, and shouted out, as he had done before: "I'm ready to work!"

The SS man lingered, then, apparently satisfied, flicked his finger to the right and logged into his book "A-5662." Eddie had made it. But now he was worried about Mike, who looked utterly anorexic. Mike stood exaggeratedly inflated, his bony chest puffed up almost to his chin. Eddie waited on edge. The SS man looked Mike over.

"I'm also ready to work!" Mike yelled out.

The guard turned to his book and wrote down: "A-5636." To the right.

The "unfit left" were led away to their deaths, the "fit right" put on a train to go to work on Hitler's supersecret project taking place underground, deep inside the Harz Mountains.

TWENTY-FIVE

THE TALISMAN

The love these men have for him is a rare thing. They would have followed that man anywhere.
—Private Stuart Thayer, loader, D Company

I would gladly have stayed with D Company until I died.
—Private Stuart Thayer

IN JANUARY, THE whole of Belgium was frozen solid like a block of ice. Despite being clothed in heavy coveralls and thick layers, the brumal freeze gripped tankers as D Company shifted to the offense. Having withstood the German attack at the Ardennes, the Allies regained the upper hand as they fought their way back toward Germany.

Occasionally, an infantryman would appear, asking the tankers, "We're cold as hell. Can we get in there?" which, once inside, was quickly followed by "Dang, it's colder in here than it is outside!" as he climbed back out and returned to his foxhole. "They prolly thought we had a stove in here, an' that it was all toasty," Fred snickered.

Elmer, who had spent his first twenty winters on the cold Minnesota plains, didn't seem bothered by the cold. He demanded troops take care of themselves, especially their feet. In some cases, severe frostbite in other units had led to amputations.

Myers heaped praise on Vance after his performance at Freyneux, which Fred hailed as "sending an entire Nazi armored task force into retreat." Vance was promoted to corporal and every tank commander fought to get him for their gunner, but Myers wouldn't give him up. And so Vance remained in Myers's tank and now, anytime Myers left the tank, he put Vance in charge.

Company D was preparing for an all-out attack on Mont le Ban when an officer somehow found Elmer in the field, told him, "Congratulations," and handed him a telegram. Harriet had given birth to a boy.

It's impossible to know what was going through Elmer's mind after hearing he had become a father, but at Brisy he led with an incredible intensity until his tank was hit. Ignoring the barrage of machine-gun fire that met tankers as they bailed, Elmer helped pull a wounded crewman out of the tank, then hoisted up and fireman-carried the bleeding man through the woods for nearly a mile, telling him all the while, "Hang on, we're gonna make it." Thanks to Elmer, the tanker survived.

Pepsi and the food service crews were trailing the company, when suddenly the mess trucks were hit by enemy artillery. One strike wiped out half the kitchen crew. All were shocked to realize that no one was safe, not even the cooks, who were supposed to be out of range of enemy fire. Shattered at the loss of his men, Pepsi placed his hand on his breast pocket, attributing his own survival to the lucky charm he carried, his talisman—the picture of Blue Eyes.

THE TALISMAN

. . .

At some point, McDowell rejoined the unit briefly, only to be wounded in Brisy and evacuated.

Word came down that battalion was dispatching a new company commander.

As battalion expedited another captain to replace McDowell, unbeknownst to Elmer, the D Company sergeants banded together and marched up to headquarters. Fresh off of the battlefield, unshaven and grimy yet clear-eyed, with a single purpose in mind and led by senior NCO Master Sergeant Haag, who had been with the company since day one, they confronted the battalion commander.

They demanded Lieutenant Hovland be officially named D Company commander. That idea was summarily rejected, the battalion commander saying Hovland was too young, too junior, and too unproven to take command of a frontline "Spearhead" company in the middle of combat.

"R'spectfully disagree, sir," Sergeant Haag, the gruff, leather-faced first sergeant pushed back in his Texas cowboy drawl.

"There's no discussion," the colonel barked back. "That job calls for a captain."

"Ain't gonna happen, sir," Laddie Devecka counterpunched. An intimidating, broad-shouldered, six-foot-two heavyweight boxer of a man, a strapping coal miner from Pennsylvania, the crews had named him Hardrock. He looked the colonel squarely in the eye and said, "Colonel, we're only followin' Hovland."

"You're out of line," the colonel cut him off.

It was a scene that started looking to the colonel like a mutiny.

"Fer krissakes, he's only a high school grad. I can't give a command to a ninety-day wonder who only has a couple of months of combat under his belt," he railed, referring to officer candidate training that turned buck privates with no army experience into lieutenants in only three months. He fired back again, "He's a *junior* lieutenant with no goddam experience! We got a West Pointer comin' your way."

"Truth is, sir," said Haag, "he's already been leadin' us for months."

Looking into their eyes and seeing the depth of the respect these no-nonsense, hardened combat veterans had for Elmer and seeing that they were not backing down, the colonel conceded.

"All right," he relented. "Let's see what your boy can do."

Sobered by the enormous official responsibility for combat decision-making and the lives and welfare of around a hundred men that now rested on his young shoulders, Elmer implored the Lord to guide him.

With his characteristic humility, the lieutenant addressed his men for the first time officially as their leader, men who had looked up to him since Normandy. Tankers, cooks, and maintenance crews drew in close to hear what their new commander had to say. Using few words, his delivery was, as usual, understated, but clear.

"We're all here to do a job," he said simply. "So let's stick together and get it done." That's all they needed to hear.

Myers, proud of his friend and feeling relieved knowing the company was now squarely in good hands, beamed. "Yes, sir."

Morale in the company soared. Years after the war, one D Company soldier would say about Elmer, "The love these men have for him is a rare thing. They would have followed that man anywhere."

Long before he was made company commander, Elmer had two driving concerns: to get the job done and to bring as many men home safely as he could.

Just a few weeks after he was appointed CO, a colonel from an infantry unit ordered him to take his tanks down a road to flush out the Germans. Believing it to be a suicide mission, Elmer refused. The colonel chewed him out.

"Lieutenant, I am *ordering* you to..." But but when he saw Elmer's hand move to rest on his Colt .45, he backed off. Years later, crews who witnessed the incident would say that Elmer's insubordination in that moment could have gotten him immediately relieved of command and even brought up on charges, but his audacious actions likely saved lives that day. As it turned out, the road was, in fact, found to be mined, with an ambush lying in wait.

By the end of the Bulge, there was no glory, only exhaustion. A pyrrhic victory, thought Vance, at too great a cost. Having just lost his new friend Tom Church in the next tank over, Vance sank into melancholy, questioning if it was all worth it. What was the point of war, of losing your buddies, of killing another human being? What were they really fighting for?

The Battle of the Bulge was Hitler's last-ditch gamble to keep his head above water—and he had lost. In truth, both sides had lost a great deal. During the brutal monthlong battle, the largest fought by Americans in World War II, the U.S. suffered some 75,000 casualties; the Germans lost perhaps as many as 100,000. By the end of January, American units had retaken all the ground they had lost and pushed on to reenter Germany. For his leadership and heroism in the Battle of the Bulge, Elmer would be awarded the Silver Star.

Despite their losses, the miserable winter, and the savagery of unending combat fought in chaos and confusion, for the crews of D Company who had survived it, by the end of the Bulge, they were tribal, devoted to each other and to Elmer.

Much to Vance's great disappointment, one day Fred was

transferred to H Company, but just five days later, without any kind of permission, having decided on his own that he had spent enough time helping out the other unit, Fred simply walked back and rejoined D Company. The first sergeant shook his head as Fred walked past and said, "I'm back." Years later Fred would say, "I was hell-bent on getting back into Myers's tank and back with my crew." Others told of feeling empty when they were transferred or wounded and evacuated and felt whole only after returning back to their brothers in D. In the hospital, one injured loader was told they were shipping him home, but he said that if D Company was still fighting, he was resigned to do it with them, so he went back.

Wrecked from combat, they needed a pick-me-up, so before they left Belgium, en route back to Germany, Elmer pulled Pepsi aside and told him to make the boys a good hot breakfast the next morning.

Frustrated he hadn't been able to feed the boys a hot meal through much of the Bulge, Pepsi threw up his arms in exasperation.

"With *what*?" he said, raising his voice. "We're outta *everything*! We can't pull off somethin' like that for tomorrow mornin'." Highly agitated, he explained that they hadn't been resupplied in weeks and had only a small stock of C-rats left, then sarcastically snapped, "Whattya want me to do? . . . You know what? How 'bout this. . . . I'll just run down to the cornah stoah, pick up everything we need to feed a hundred hungry men. I'm telling ya," he shouted, "I got *nothin'* left!"

Elmer put a gentle hand on Pepsi's shoulder, looked him in the eye, and said, "Pepsi, make the boys happy."

Pepsi returned to the kitchen and huddled with his crew.

"Where are we gonna get this stuff *this* time? How the hell are we gonna pull this one off, fellas?"

THE TALISMAN

* * *

With the sun setting, Pepsi sent his team out knocking on farm doors and mostly being turned away. With virtually nothing left to barter, they traded cigarettes, gum, and candy from their personal stashes for whatever the locals could provide. They came back with a paltry find: some coarse farm flour and only a few dozen eggs. One private returned with a live goat. The mess crew was reduced to picking through C-rats and opening up tiny packets of sugar. Finally, with barely enough ingredients to eke out some weak batter for enough pancakes to feed all the tankers, Pepsi's plan came to a halt when he realized there was no lard, no shortening, or butter to be found anywhere with which to grease the cooking pans. What to do? Pepsi thought long and hard.

It had been the habit of Company D's kitchen crew to pick up discarded weapons they found lying around the battlefield as they came through and toss them into a trailer—mostly M1 rifles but also German rifles and burp guns.

Suddenly, Pepsi had an idea.

Out of view of the mess crew, he opened up the trailer and went from one rifle to the next, undoing the butt plate and siphoning the tiny vial of oil in the stock used to keep the weapon lubricated. After draining the weapons, he returned to the mess crew with a small jar of gun oil.

At around four o'clock the next morning, they fired up the stoves. The kitchen crew mixed the flour, combined the last of the canned milk with goat's milk, added powdered eggs to their supply of real eggs, and made the pancakes, which they cooked in gun oil.

Pepsi burned the sugar to brown it, then boiled it, hoping it would at least look a little like maple syrup. Then, feeling apprehensive, he sat back and watched as the men sat down to their breakfast.

THE BOYS IN THE LIGHT

The soldiers devoured the pancakes. They congratulated the cooks, slapped Pepsi on the back, and asked for more, which further terrified him. Pepsi kept the secret to himself, worrying that everyone was going to get sick and land in sick bay and he was going to land in the stockade, or worse yet, kill somebody.

Days later, he was finally relieved that no one complained about getting sick. Fred even told him, "Best hotcakes I ever ate."

TWENTY-SIX

THE TUNNELS

When you talk of something that is unbelievably more horrible than hell could ever be, then you have to say: It was a [Langenstein] Zwieberge.

—Bernard Klieger, Langenstein survivor

I doubt that in another month I would have been alive.

—Eddie Willner

DEEP IN THE Harz Mountains, swathed in a topography of dense forest, the blue, mist-covered mountains held a secret.

As factories aboveground were being obliterated to rubble by Allied bombers, Hitler ordered tunnels to be carved into the mountains so the Germans could continue building weapons of war below the earth's surface.

Hidden away in central Germany's Harz Zwieberge Mountains near the village of Halberstadt, well camouflaged from above by a vast canopy of pines, Hitler's underground plan was in full swing. Beneath the forest floor, throngs of slave laborers at the Langenstein concentration camp were blasting out a huge complex of subterranean tunnels.

Project Malachit was Hitler's top secret program to build an extensive network of tunnels to house underground factories to make parts for a new kind of airplane engine that used jet technology to power Germany's new fleet of Messerschmitts that, at top speed, could fly a hundred miles per hour faster than any conventional Allied fighter. Rumor had it that inmates working in the shafts and galleys would also produce parts for Hitler's secret V-2 *Vergeltungswaffe* ("wonder weapon") being built in an underground factory by slave labor at nearby Dora-Mittelbau concentration camp. The V-2 was a long-range guided ballistic missile capable of flying four times faster than the speed of sound; it had a one-ton warhead and a range of two hundred miles. Combined with the Messerschmitt jet fighter, these weapons represented the Nazis' last hope in a war they were badly losing.

Eddie and Mike arrived to join a colony of some five thousand tunnel laborers.

Carving out a rocky mountain was an ambitious and dangerous operation that relied on disposable slave labor driven to work at a frenetic pace by a Nazi guard force who had complete disregard for suffering and massive loss of life in pursuing Hitler's psychotic, last-ditch illusion of victory.

Due to the clandestine nature of the project, word of the existence of Project Malachit could not get out to the world. To protect Hitler's secret, the SS had implemented a "kill all" rule, *Vernichtung durch Arbeit* ("extermination through labor"), with the objective of getting maximum productivity out of an inmate until he "expired." Inmates would be worked to death. There would be no further transfers. This was the end of the road. Life expectancy was six weeks.

A steady stream of replacement prisoners from Buchenwald was brought in to take the place of the dead as camp functionary SS Obersturmführer Lübeck matter-of-factly remarked: *"Schlagt sie nur, und wenn ihr tausend von denen totschlagt, das tut nichts, ihr kriegt tausend andere"* ("If you kill a thousand, it doesn't matter because you can get a thousand to replace them").

In an apocalyptic scene, a constant conveyor belt of human beings brought new prisoners in, and a daily body run took the dead out. So routine had it become that a local farmer quietly puffing on a clay pipe and driving a horse-drawn cart casually came into the camp every day, waited while bodies were loaded onto his flatbed dray, then drove his wagon to the crematorium in the nearby town of Quedlinburg.

The size of around eight football fields, the Langenstein camp was surrounded by the typical electrified fence and watchtowers and had a hidden machine-gun nest just outside the camp entrance. Some five hundred Death's Head SS guards oversaw five thousand inmates who were crammed into a camp built to house just two thousand.

By the time Mike and Eddie arrived, the vast majority of Europe's Jews had already been murdered, and so Jews were by far the minority at Langenstein. The two teens filtered in with the latest fresh crop of prisoners, men from twenty-three different countries. Groups formed naturally along common ethnic lines, culture, or language: the Eastern Europeans (Russians and their brother Slavs, Ukrainians, Poles); the Western Europeans (French, Belgians, Dutch, Italians); with criminals and others blending in with any group that would have them.

Eddie, Mike, and the other Jews were separated out from the rest, their nationalities of no interest to the SS; Jews were simply Jews, stateless and inconsequential, and targeted with typical extreme hate by the SS. They were housed separately in *Blok* 4, the only barracks with no bunks, so they slept crowded together on the cold, barren floor.

Oberscharführer Paul Tscheu (pronounced *Choi*) ran the camp. A short, squat bulldog of a man with a helmet of black hair, he stood on the *Appellplatz* and ordered a selection. The unfit were removed, and guards marched the remaining prisoners into the tunnels.

Filing in through the "railway" entrance, they descended into the belly of the beast.

Inside the giant caverns, thousands of emaciated prisoners toiled around the clock in back-to-back twelve-hour shifts seven days a week at a blistering pace, working toward a brutally ambitious objective. In just eleven months, prisoners had already carved out an eight-mile-long web of interlocking galleys and catacombs thirty feet high and thirty feet wide. And now, with the Allies attacking into Germany, Hitler forced Project Malachit into overdrive.

Deep inside the tunnels, fluorescent tubes and metal filament lamps cast yellow artificial light on dank shafts that smelled of sulfur. The constant echo of explosions, the gearwheels of heavy machinery, jackhammering, and heavy pneumatic drills boring at full throttle made for discordant clanging in a sea of backbreaking slave labor in a continuous cycle of blasting, drilling, and hammering. With no protective gear and poor ventilation, the prisoners choked on the fine dust that coated their bodies and turned their faces black, seeped into their unprotected eyes, and parched their lungs. Moving concrete bricks and iron and wooden beams, wielding sledgehammers and pickaxes, inmates labored to position steel rib girders and precast slabs in place to buttress the tunnel walls. Roof collapses due to the friable sandstone were a common occurrence, and it was not unusual to see men injured or killed when a weak prisoner dropped his end of a steel beam, or to hear a scream from an inmate high on a ladder

THE TUNNELS

installing electric lights who had been electrocuted. By January, the first electricity, air ducts, and panels with advanced industrial control systems were being installed in the workshops.

Eddie and Mike were assigned to the blasting crews. Dynamiting the inside of a mountain with no safety precautions killed prisoners almost by the hour. While the SS stood at a safe distance, the force of explosions sent rock flying in all directions, striking prisoners who were not allowed to evacuate the area. At full bore, progress saw blasting teams carving out an average of five feet every eight hours. And so the two boys went on, dynamiting and drilling their way from one day to the next, holding out a kind of useless gray hope that the tunnels would not devour them.

If Blechhammer was dystopian, Langenstein was a living hell. Prisoners were delirious from hunger. Siegfried had cautioned the boys not to become *Muselmänner*, but here at Langenstein everyone but the newcomers were withered to languid skeletons. Men became automatons, comatose with thousand-mile stares, walking ghosts no longer tethered to reality. Some couldn't even swallow their bread anymore. Even the big Russians withered.

By now, Eddie and Mike were alarmingly thin. On the *Appellplatz*, they stood alongside men who sometimes just dropped dead. Men who had made it this far who, through it all, had never given up their will to survive finally did so at Langenstein, where, at the absolute end of their endurance, they had not one ounce of fight left.

Now, every day on the *Appellplatz*, when an SS guard called, "Is anyone sick?" inmates stepped forward, knowing they were going to die, looking toward the end of their suffering with relief. Where once they prayed to stay alive, now they prayed to die in the night.

Others committed suicide, hanging themselves from the rafters in the barracks.

THE BOYS IN THE LIGHT

For Eddie and Mike, too, it became an intense struggle to make it to each new day. Unlike *Muselmänner*, however, they refused to make peace with death and were consumed instead with finding a way to live. They knew they needed to somehow summon superhuman strength to get through this nightmare.

When the crematorium in Quedlinburg broke down due to overuse, the farmer with the clay pipe, who so matter-of-factly drove his cart heaped with the dead, stopped coming and mass graves were dug on the grounds of the camp to bury the dead. Eddie was detailed to digging mass graves, where some prisoners were now forced to throw in *Muselmänner*, even if they were still alive.

After eight weeks in Langenstein, Eddie and Mike had already beaten the odds. Skin stretched over bones, they knew they were living on borrowed time. Every morning, they woke up and looked over to see if the other was still breathing. They were relieved to know that they were still alive, and still alive together, and realized that, after all they had been through, one would be lost without the other. Teetering on the brink of death, the two boys were now in the greatest fight of their lives.

TWENTY-SEVEN

THE PRAYER

Through the long arc of war, the tankers of D Company became battle-hardened, dog weary–wasted, and bonded for life. Nine months in, they existed in a perpetual state of near burnout in their smelly field jackets, greasy, unshaven war-creased faces, sleep deprived, and depleted. Their nerves were shot. Their young faces looked like shoe leather.

Where once they lived in shock and fear, wide-eyed innocents, by now they had developed a sixth sense about things: they could tell the type of round by its whistle, whether it had been fired by friend or foe, and now the whizz of an enemy projectile hardly even fazed them unless it hit close by. Vance and the crew would continue their card game as if nothing had happened, until they heard Elmer on the radio: "Dick to all dick stations, prepare to move out," to which Fred would mutter, "Here we go again."

By this stage, the veteran unit had developed a signature company swag: helmets cocked at rakish angles, cigarettes dangling from their mouths. Fred started wearing his olive-drab scarf tucked crosswise in the front of his filthy jacket, which gave him the aplomb of a gentleman wearing an ascot. One tanker wore a knit cap and traditional German boiled-wool house slippers he had found in a bombed-out house. Another tank was brightened by a cheery flowered comforter, making the inside of its hull look more like a schoolgirls' sleepover than the inside of an armored vehicle. Private Stubbins wore a top hat he had taken from a landowner's estate. Rocco had looted porcelain teacups and comically poured water from his canteen into a tiny demitasse and drank from it, pinkie extended.

By now, the insides of their tanks were decorated with smiling photos of wives and girlfriends, bawdy photos of pinup girls, and a few trophies here and there: an SS helmet, a dagger, a Nazi flag. To ward off the cold, Fred had "borrowed" a blowtorch for a while to warm up Myers's tank, only returning it when the maintenance sergeant put out a plea that he didn't know who had it but that he needed it back.

Hitler's speeches became increasingly frenetic and detached from reality. In a radio address, he issued a warning to his soldiers not to surrender. If they laid down their arms, they would be considered traitors and their relatives would suffer the consequences. He called on all Germans to unite, take up arms, and fight to the death:

"I expect every German to do his duty to the last and that he be willing to take upon himself every sacrifice he will be asked to make; I expect every able-bodied German to fight with complete disregard for his personal safety; I expect the sick and the weak or those otherwise unavailable for military duty to work with their last strength." There would be no surrender. Growing even more delusional and reckless, Hitler seemed determined to take Germany down with him.

Having reentered Germany, General Rose was given the mission to command the attack on the "fortress city" of Cologne. It would be the first major assault on a large German city, and D Company was picked to help lead the charge.

Recognized for their winning record in the Bulge, D Company was one of the few units to receive a new super tank: the M26 Pershing. At almost fifty tons, the Pershing was a titanic beast compared to the Sherman, had thick armor, and was equipped with a powerful 90mm high-velocity gun. "The first time they fired it," said one crewman, "it blew Lieutenant Myers's steel helmet right off his head and the goddam shell went right through a German tank destroyer and knocked out another one behind it." Now, suddenly, ten months into the war, the Spearhead Division finally had a tank in their hands that could stand up to German Panzers. "If we'd had fifteen of them nineties," said the crewman, "the war'd been over two months quicker."

As the Germans lost tanks, they turned more and more to using the Panzerfaust, a three-foot-long tube with a bell-shaped projectile about the size of a football. Launched by a single soldier tucking the tube under his arm and fired from close range at just twenty yards away, it was deadly, and the handheld missile left American crews terrified. "It was almost suicidal to advance without infantry protection," said one D Company tanker.

Allied bombing turned Cologne into a city of rubble, making it a perfect hiding place for small bands of Germans to hide and ambush. Fighting from street to street in the shell-pocked city, a German leaned out of a second-story window and fired a Panzerfaust. Like a ton of dynamite, it obliterated the Sherman, turning the inside of the tank to molten metal and terrorizing all who witnessed it. Inching forward, tankers became hypervigilant to any sign of the lethal weapon. What was worse, rumor had it that enemy troops were now delivering Panzerfausts into the hands of the Volkssturm, or the People's Storm, a home-guard militia made up of old men and boys Hitler had called to take up arms and defend their villages to the death.

As the company approached Cologne's famed Cathedral Square, Elmer felt a tug, sensing that something wasn't right, and thought, *Lord, give me a sign about danger coming our way.*

Positioned in the third tank, from where he could best control the company, Elmer ordered everyone to button up, and he alone stood with his head and torso out of the turret, using binoculars to survey the buildings ahead. Suddenly his gut told him to drop back down into his tank. As he started to go down, a sniper's bullet pierced his helmet, snapping his neck back. The shot went through his helmet, sheared his tanker's cap, missed his head by a whisker, and went clean out the other side, leaving a little feather of sharp steel curling up from the crown of his helmet.

Laddie Devecka saw the whole thing. The entire company was shaken by Elmer's close call. Myers chastised his friend for not being more careful.

For the rest of his life, Elmer would believe that it was God's providence that had told him to get down at that moment.

"If I didn't listen to that voice, that sniper would have gotten me right in the chest."

Later, the battalion commander came by, saw the helmet, and said, "Hovland, you all right?" With his characteristic dry wit, Elmer said, "Colonel, I'm a damn Norwegian. It takes more than that to scare me." Despite his joking, the nagging feeling did not dissipate, and Elmer warned his tankers to "Stay sharp out there."

Elmer sent a photo of Cologne to Harriet. He wrote about the

THE PRAYER

"magnificent cathedral" but failed to tell her he'd been shot through the helmet in front of it. Following the incident, it occurred to him, as it surely did to many others who had children, that he might not make it home to raise his boy, so he wrote even more earnest letters to Harriet and also to his newborn son. In the letters, he spoke of how faith had seen them through every battle. "We have done our best here and with God's grace, we will win this war and come home." He wrote of how proud he was of his unit: "men of courage... who have built a brotherhood."

German troops fought for every inch of Cologne, but when the American flag went up, the city that had once been one of the great jewels of Germany lay in ruins. Rising from the rubble, the grand cathedral with its soaring twin spires was heavily damaged but, miraculously, was still standing. Germany's first major city had fallen. After building temporary bridges across the Rhine, the Americans plowed deeper into Germany.

It was a morning shrouded in fog when D Company made their way toward Altenkirchen, south of Paderborn, ever alert to pockets of resistance and locals with Panzerfausts.

Just as he so often did, Myers scouted forward to get a sense of things, to test the waters before Elmer committed the company to the unknown that lay up ahead. In a scene that had played out so many times before, standing chest-high out of his tank, his throat microphone at his neck, as the tank dipped and lurched, Myers bobbed and weaved, sliding like a boxer up and down and from side to side, Fred looking through the periscope, Vance's gun at the ready. Arturo Casillas, a nineteen-year-old replacement who had been in the company for less than two months, had joined Myers's tank as the new loader. Casillas had already slammed a round into the chamber as the driver edged the tank forward, then moved it down a hill where Myers told him to go.

Suddenly, from the wood line, spears of flame shot out, accompanied by the simultaneous blast of an 88mm gun. The high-velocity round rocketed through the air and careened straight into the left side of Myers's tank and exploded.

The hatch popped open and Fred jumped out, Hamilton the driver right behind him. A German machine gunner now fired off a hail of bullets, and Fred was hit with shrapnel as the two rolled into a ditch and looked back as they fell, expecting to see the others bail out behind them, but the others, Lieutenant Myers, Vance, and Casillas, did not follow.

Suddenly, a bloodied Vance appeared, standing up out of the hatch, but he did not get out. Instead, he looked off into the distance, guessed the range, sat down again, put his eye to the gunsight, and fired a round, knocking out a tank destroyer.

Fred could not believe what he was seeing. The tank now totally in flames, Vance finally emerged again, climbed up and spilled out, fell off the tank, then crawled away as fast as he could. Seconds later, the enemy launched another 88, which slammed into Myers's tank, and the Sherman erupted into a ball of flames.

Lieutenant Myers and Arturo Casillas were dead inside, entombed in a pyre of flames, the turret glowing from the intense heat. Fred, Vance, and Hamilton watched from the ditch, black smoke rising from the burning wreckage as the ammo cooked off.

It was a devastating blow for the entire company. After months of taking point on the front line, the fearless Gettysburg College scholar and star athlete—who, by all accounts, was on a path to do something great with his life—and Casillas, the nineteen-year-old newbie with a young wife and new baby, were lost to the flames.

THE PRAYER

· · ·

Elmer was heartbroken.

Three weeks earlier, Myers had been relieved when Elmer had survived his helmet piercing, but Elmer's nagging feeling after that incident had not relented, and now he understood why.

A few days later, Elmer inventoried Myers's belongings, packed them up, and sent them to his family with a personal letter of grief expressing his deep admiration for his best friend, his attributes as a great combat leader, and as a Christian. In Myers's possessions were numerous personal letters from his parents, a photo of a pretty young girl, and a book titled *Our Two Democracies at Work* about America and Britain's successful peace and wartime partnership. A letter from the chaplain also accompanied his things home; it read "Charles was an excellent soldier. His courage and devotion to duty gained him the respect and admiration of those who served with him," adding, "Charles died while fighting for the people and the country he loved. We have lost one of our finest."

On the field, Myers's tank stood in place like a ghastly reminder to the fallen crew who remained inside and, ultimately, as a monument to the tragic toll of human beings in war.

The only thing the recovery crew found was Casillas's silver ID bracelet.

Three days after Lieutenant Myers was killed in action leading from the front, General Rose, whom Myers had so admired, was killed just up the road at Paderborn, likewise leading from the front. Rose, the highest-ranking American of Jewish heritage in World War II, who hailed from a family of Polish rabbis, was killed leading the fight against Hitler.

Myers's crew was disbanded. Vance and Fred were patched up and returned to duty, where they were assigned to separate tanks. Reeling from the loss, the normally jovial Fred, who had been a rock throughout the war to those around him, sank into depression. He could not seem to get over the loss of Myers and kept vigil for his dead platoon leader inside his tank, refusing to come out for days. With Fred in a dismal state and not eating, Vance brought food to him and tried to see him through his despair.

TWENTY-EIGHT

BREAKOUT

This is the end; I sense it clearly.
—H. G. Adler, Langenstein survivor, realizing his imminent demise at Langenstein

RUMORS THAT THE Allies were closing in sent shock waves through the Langenstein concentration camp. In fact, the Americans were only thirty miles away and would soon discover the nearby Dora V-2 production tunnels at Nordhausen. Just days earlier, Dora inmates had been evacuated but, heeding Himmler's orders that "no prisoners shall be allowed to fall into the hands of the enemy alive," and with American forces getting closer by the minute, the SS, aided by the home guard Volkssturm militia and Hitler Youth, trapped over a thousand in a barn in the town of Gardelegen and set it on fire, burning the prisoners alive.

With the Americans now headed north and coming around the mountain, Oberscharführer Tscheu called for the camp to be evacuated early the next morning, which alerted the Langenstein prisoners that they might be massacred before the Americans could reach them.

That evening, in *Blok* 4, Eddie and Mike overheard four prisoners making plans to escape and they wanted in on it. Having not dared any earlier attempt to try to make a dash to freedom, they realized it was now or never. In whispers in the near darkness, the team brought the boys in, swore them to secrecy, and hammered out a plan.

They would try to make their break at nightfall, the leader said. Darkness would make it harder for guards to see and fire on six fleeing prisoners. Taking off near a river or a stream was ideal, one man offered. The dogs were trained to attack on land but not to follow a man into the water. Escape during a moment of distraction could also be a good time to launch. Any single one of these factors, they agreed, might up their chances.

The plan was set. They would maintain close contact throughout the march without calling attention to themselves, sending messages through movements of their eyes and glances imperceptible to the guards. At "Go," they would scatter in different directions, which would make it hard for the SS to zero in on every escapee. Perhaps some would not make it, but others might. It was a long shot at best, but it was their only chance. That night, they got little sleep.

The next morning, three thousand of Langenstein's surviving prisoners dragged themselves one last time to the *Appellplatz*. Around a thousand others who were too frail decided not to answer the call to form up and stayed behind, ready to accept whatever fate awaited them in the barracks.

Fear rippled through the ranks when more guards than they had ever seen all at once showed up heavily armed with machine guns. Minds raced, prisoners suddenly alarmed they would be executed right where they stood. The escape team was a hairsbreadth from bolting right then, when Tscheu ordered the column to attention to march them out of the camp. Any momentary relief they may have had being spared on the *Appellplatz*, however, instantly evaporated

BREAKOUT

as some now feared the rumor to be true: that the guards were marching them into the tunnels, which would then be sealed and dynamited, killing them all or burying them alive.

Divided into groups of five hundred so the guards could better control them, the escape team positioned themselves near one another, Eddie next to Mike. At the shout of "First column, march!" the SS moved their blighted prisoners out of the camp for the last time.

Under heavy guard, the escape team on edge and constantly trading looks, the column moved down the path toward the tunnels. Suddenly, they were ordered to a halt. There appeared to be confusion among the guards. Perhaps fearing the Americans might reach them before they could make it to the tunnels or for whatever other reason, the SS abruptly changed plans and ordered the column onto a dirt road leading away from the tunnels. Breathing a collective sigh of relief, the prisoners turned onto a path they had never taken before. The column moved out of the pine forest and into the wide-open German countryside.

Over the next few hours, the skeletal prisoners plodded onward through the rolling landscape, many slowing or falling down to meet their end, shot for being too exhausted to continue. At some point, one inmate stumbled ahead. Apparently feeling he had nothing left to lose or perhaps too far gone to know the difference, arms extended up to the heavens, he strangely held out a precious tiny piece of bread like he was a priest leading a funeral procession, muttering, "I carry the Hosts of the Eucharistic with me." It was something he could easily have been shot for, but the guards ignored it in their push to move the column forward.

As they marched in silence, Eddie and Mike waited for the signal from their leader, but it did not come.

. . .

At the entrance to the next village, the SS ordered the inhabitants into their basements, warning, "Criminals coming through!" Pastor Hager of the local church remembered, "What we saw were ashen emaciated figures . . . a column of prisoners in blue-white garb and wooden clogs, accompanied by guards and dogs." Others heard the approaching thousands. "Before you could see the battered creatures in their striped suits," said one villager, "you could hear the shuffling of their wooden clogs from afar." The inmates, he observed, were pleading for water. "It was clear that the prisoners were in their last stages of life."

In Halberstadt, one little boy was rushed into the cellar by his grandparents and looked up through the coal window to see a long line of ghostlike forms, just their bottom half, striped pant legs and clogs shuffling past, a scene that would haunt the boy for the rest of his life.

The column labored onward, the escape team surveying the rolling countryside, trading glances from time to time, looking for any small window of opportunity, watching to see if there was a lapse in the guards' vigilance, if they dropped back or became distracted, but they did not.

At the end of that first day, the SS herded the prisoners into an abandoned and overgrown soccer stadium for the night. Looking for relief from their hunger, they ate weeds, fir buds, pine cones, whatever they could find on the grassy stadium floor.

"At this point," one prisoner would later recall, "we were so hungry we would literally sacrifice our life if we knew we could eat a potato."

In what many believed were their last moments, it was here in the soccer stadium that some made peace with death, wanting to pass on to the next life in some kind of brotherly prison solidarity. Feeling the breeze on their faces just one more time, looking out over the masses who had been his fellow prisoners and friends, one of those prisoners described a surreal, "heavenly" scene the next morning as he lay among "hundreds of intertwined bodies." Another prisoner believed his life to be ending, until someone handed him a handful of dandelion leaves. That was the moment he decided to try to live a little longer.

The second day, those who could get back up again marched all day under an overcast sky.

At one point, a woman appeared on the path with her children and set down two buckets of water for the prisoners. The SS man told her, "Scram, before I shoot you. *Das sind alles Schweine und die müssen verrecken.*" ("These inmates are all pigs and they must die.") She fled with her children but left her buckets behind.

Later that day a group of prisoners did make a break for it—a successful escape, until members of the local Volkssturm militia and Hitler Youth, actively on the lookout for escaped prisoners, found them and, making a game of it, drove them like hares into an open field and shot them as if they were on a hunt.

On the third day, the clouds broke to a clear blue sky. After trudging all day and preparing to be halted for the night, at sunset they approached the village of Welbsleben. Up ahead they could make out what looked to be a small bridge. As they drew closer, they could see a river running beneath it. The escape team shifted glances at one another to get a pulse on what others were thinking and put each other on notice. The barracks conversation raced through Eddie's head: *Nightfall . . . a river . . .* , and then, *a distraction!*

In the last light of day, they heard a distant humming and looked up to see a lone British fighter approaching overhead. The guards quickly ordered the prisoners off the road so they could not be seen from the air.

As they began stepping off to one side of the road or the other, the escape team locked glances and blinked. Hearts hammered a frantic beat.

Suddenly the leader yelled, "Go!" and the six inmates took off, scattering in different directions. Chaos erupted. The SS fired, bullets flying wildly in all directions, and the dogs were released. Through a hail of bullets, the six prisoners ran for their lives.

One of the inmates was shot in the stomach and fell to the ground. When Eddie turned to him, he groaned, "I'm done. *Go!*" Then a bullet pierced Eddie's arm, but he kept running. His heart beating like a jackhammer, he chased Mike down to the river.

Hot on their trail, a German shepherd sprinted to catch them. At the river's edge, it caught Mike and clamped its powerful jaws on to his leg. Viciously snarling and gripping tightly, it twisted its head wildly as it dragged Mike back onto the bank. Eddie grabbed the canine by the throat and together, using what little strength their ruined bodies could muster, the two boys strangled the dog until it stopped breathing and finally released its grip.

Amid shouts and shooting and complete confusion, Eddie and Mike flung themselves into the river. Running and stumbling over rocks, they pulled and pushed each other along in a mad race for their lives. Breaking free of their shackles, they exploded forward, propelled by a primal urge to get to freedom.

Struggling in waist-deep water, the two skinny boys fought to keep upright in the churning swells, which spilled and spiraled, and pushed them farther downstream.

The river, swollen by the Harz Mountains' winter snowmelt, pulled them into deeper, swiftly moving waters. Caught up in the rushing torrent, thrashing and clawing wildly, they were swept along in the turbulent flow and fought to keep their footing, falling under, then coming up, gasping for air, then righting themselves and forging ahead, every stroke drawing them onward and away, and over to the other side.

Once they sensed they were out of the guards' crosshairs, and when their frail bodies could no longer fight the force of nature, they gave in to the roiling waters and let the current take them, until they drifted, the river Eine carrying them along, farther and farther downstream and around a bend, where the sounds of chaos finally gave way to the peace of more gentle waters and an eerie tranquility. Suddenly they were alone. The shouting and shooting and barking behind them, the quiet embraced them in a sea of calm, and the night swathed them in the safety of its shadows.

At the river's edge, they collapsed onto the muddy bank. Their first triumphant moments of freedom were a free fall of delirious rapture. Lost in a spiral of awe and breathtaking joy, they fell into each other. It was a dream beyond belief. They had done it. They had accomplished the impossible.

Ringing from unimaginable relief, they looked at one another. They had never seen each other's face like that.

TWENTY-NINE

ANGELS

They looked at the Yanks with that special gaze reserved for deities.
—Spearhead in the West

We are told the American soldier does not know what he is fighting for. Now, at least, we know what he is fighting against.
—General Dwight D. Eisenhower

IN THE DARKNESS of that moonless night, the boys stood on the bank, exhausted but exhilarated. Riding high on adrenaline, they were, for the moment, able to almost ignore their injuries. But their ordeal was far from over. Now they had to resist succumbing to their wounds, exposure to the elements, and being discovered by the home guard Volkssturm militias, who had shown no mercy to escaping prisoners.

After nearly five years in captivity, they had beaten unimaginable odds. Resolved not to let anyone jeopardize their treasured newfound freedom, they made a pact: should anyone threaten them in any way or try to take them into custody, they would kill him.

Drenched and cold, they wrung out their clothes as best they could, then took off into the night. Moving through farm fields and backyards, Mike pushing through the pain as he limped along, they made their way from shadow to shadow, resting only long enough until they could dart off for the next safe place. With little light to guide them, they felt more than saw their way through the darkness and eventually came upon a barn.

Inside they found a dish of milk left out for a cat, which they shared, slurping it up in seconds. They loosely patched up Mike's dog-bite wound with a rag, and Eddie picked the bullet out of his arm with a stick, then they slipped into an underground potato cellar to hide. Once inside, they each ate a single potato, careful not to consume more than their fragile bodies could handle. They spent the rest of that night hiding, covered by potatoes should the farmer come to retrieve some or Volkssturm hunters come looking for them, and they fell into a deep sleep.

The next morning, before sunrise, they were gone. By day they hid in the woods, taking turns sleeping, one of them always on watch, and trying to guess where the front was from the distant sounds of battle. After sundown, they ran through the night, through fields and forests and streams, in the direction of where they believed the front might be, eating wild berries in the forest or anything they found edible in farmers' barns, all the while listening and looking, trying to steer clear of any sign of human activity. For five nights they ran toward the sounds of artillery fire, the exploding guns of the front line only feeding their dreams of freedom.

Then, one night, they found them. For nearly a week, the boys had remained undetected, but as they moved through the woods, suddenly they froze in their tracks when they realized they were not alone. Hearing whispers in the dark, they saw faint outlines of people in prone and dug-in positions. Eddie could make out the glint of a rifle and the faint but unmistakable bell shape of a Panzerfaust.

This was the home guard militia that Hitler had called upon to defend their villages to the death and to capture and kill escaped prisoners. Eddie and Mike had wandered right smack into the middle of a Volkssturm ambush setting a trap for the enemy.

From the darkness, a child's voice issued a military challenge: "*Halt, wer's da!*" ("Halt! Who goes there?") The challenge required a password. The moment went quiet.

Eddie's and Mike's hearts raced. Having made it so far, they were suddenly faced with the reality that their newfound freedom was in peril.

With their backs up against the wall, thinking fast, Eddie barked back in a whisper shout,

"*Halt d' Klappe, Idiot! Normale Streife!*" ("Shut up, you idiot! Regular army patrol coming through!")

The response was dead silence. The two boys sneaked past and disappeared back into the woods.

On the sixth day, in the early hours just before dawn, hiding in the woods somewhere between the villages of Bernburg and Köthen, the boys were jarred by the grinding of engines and felt the ground rumble beneath them. What started as a tremor picked up in intensity until it shook the stillness of the morning. Ideas raced through the boys' minds. What could cause such a thunderous chorus? They were likely tanks, but were they Russian, Allied, or, God forbid, German?

Staggering through dense undergrowth, the boys darted up an incline and, covered by a cluster of pine brush, inched closer, trying to get a better look. The growling of engines and clacking of tracks growing louder and louder, excitement thrummed through them like a live wire. Eyes glued, they waited and watched to see what iron beast would appear through the trees.

Now almost deafening, the roar of powerful revving engines accelerated, churning until it vibrated the earth itself. Locked onto the moment, the boys' adrenaline raced in equal parts excitement and fear.

Then, in the haze of the day's first light, an American Sherman tank burst onto the scene—a turret, a gun, a helmeted figure standing up and out of the hatch—and came thundering down the road toward them, followed close on its heels by other tanks.

Like a shot, Eddie and Mike sprang out of the wood line, planted themselves squarely in the center of the road, faced the speeding tanks head-on, and threw their hands up into the air.

Just yards away, a bow gunner peered through his periscope and shouted at the driver to stop. The driver jammed on the breaks and the tank lurched to a sudden halt. The tank commander squinted to get a closer look. Trying to process what he was seeing, he finally radioed in, "Lieutenant, you better get up here. There's something you're gonna wanna see."

In the first morning rays of light streaming through the canopy of trees, two emaciated figures in tattered blue-and-white-striped uniforms stood rooted to the road, hands raised high in the air.

The lieutenant came up the line to see what the holdup was. Other tankers dismounted and came forward but stopped in their tracks when they saw what appeared to be two teenagers withered to skeletons, with eyes like saucers and twig-like arms and legs, barely clinging to life. They were trembling terribly but, unable to contain their euphoria, had huge smiles on their parched blue faces, and in that moment, Elmer and the boys of D Company found themselves standing face-to-face with Eddie and Mike.

It was a disturbing discovery. Fred, Vance, Bernie, Sal, Fats, George, Rocco, and Mahoney formed a semicircle around the boys, unsure of what they were looking at or what to do.

"They were shaking and extremely exhilarated," Elmer would recall years later, ". . . sunken corpses . . . repulsively emaciated."

No one spoke as the soldiers looked over the boys, staring at them in a silent exchange of so many questions. What twisted depravity could possibly have caused anyone to do something like this to another human being? the crewmen wondered, as they became some of the first witnesses to the human cost of Hitler's evil.

"We stared at them and they stared at us," Fred would later say. "Man, they were hard to look at."

Vance was transfixed. "They were only a couple years younger than me."

"Those boys," said Bernie Clow, "had seen evil."

Fats Falatovich would recall, "We didn't know what they'd been through, but those huge eyes said it all."

Eddie and Mike could hardly believe it was all real as they stood staring at the Americans, gazing upon their saviors as if they were in the presence of angels.

Eddie and Mike couldn't speak any English but, still shaking, pointed to the number tattoos on their forearms to try to tell their story.

"Get Hansen up here," ordered Elmer. Sergeant Hansen, who spoke some German, came up the line.

When word went down the column that the company had encountered some escaped Jewish prisoners, Brooklyn and a couple of other tankers pushed their way to the front and inserted themselves into the circle, pointing to Eddie and Mike and asking, "*Jude? Jude? Jew?*" then tapped their chests, pointing to themselves, in a mixture of German and English, saying, "*Ich auch Jude* . . . I am also a Jew."

If the boys of D Company ever needed to know why they had just gone through the hell of almost constant combat, the treacherous slog of war, a nearly ten-month, 1,500-mile-long fight across the European continent, losing their buddies along the way, this was it, and in that moment they finally understood what they had been fighting for.

And that was the moment Eddie and Mike walked from the darkness and into the light.

THIRTY

"THEY'RE WITH US NOW"

> *They needed all the compassion that we as Americans could give them.*
>
> —Lieutenant Elmer Hovland

EDDIE WAS SPEAKING excitedly, saying something urgent.

"He says there's an ambush up ahead lying in wait for us," Sergeant Hansen translated. "Enemy dug in with Panzerfausts. These two just sneaked through their lines, say they can show us where they are."

Elmer sized up the boys and took in the moment.

"Tell 'em they're gonna lead us," Elmer ordered. "Get 'em up on the lead tank."

At that call, tankers gingerly hoisted the two fragile survivors up onto the first tank in the column.

"*Halt fast*" ("Hold tight"), Hansen called up to them, his huge hands wrapping their spindly fingers securely in place around the metal turret handrails.

High atop the first tank, the two survivors held on, loose blue-and-white-striped uniforms flapping in the wind, Eddie's bony out-

"THEY'RE WITH US NOW"

stretched arm pointing the way as he and Mike shouted out directions down to Hansen, who simultaneously shouted them to the crew, who relayed them over the radio. It was a miraculous turn of events. In the blink of an eye, Eddie and Mike had gone from the hunted to the hunters.

The company reached the outskirts of the ambush and the column halted. Elmer handed Hansen the bullhorn.

"Tell 'em they got thirty seconds to figure out whether they want to live or die or we're going to blast 'em to pieces." Hansen blared the message and, within seconds, a white flag was raised and more than a dozen gray-haired old men and young boys emerged with their hands up in surrender, taken prisoner without a shot fired.

In their first minutes of being rescued, Eddie and Mike had helped save Company D from a Panzerfaust attack.

U.S. forces were under strict orders to bypass all refugees they encountered along the way. Absolutely nothing, their commanders made clear, could be allowed to slow the momentum of the Spearhead Division's frontline advance. Refugees carried lice, typhus, and other diseases and required medical attention and food. In short, they were a burden. Orders stated refugees were to be directed to displaced persons camps, which were cropping up all over Germany, where they could be treated and cared for.

But these were no ordinary war refugees. It was clear these boys were victims of some heinous crime.

Instead of leaving them to die by the side of the road or just tossing them a box of C-rations, Elmer knew there was only one thing to do.

As old men and boys ambled past to be processed as POWs, relinquishing their weapons, an assortment of Panzerfausts, carbine rifles, and pistols, Elmer ordered Eddie and Mike be taken to the battalion aid station and "cleaned up."

"Then bring 'em back to me," Elmer said. "They're with us now."

The boys were brought back to the rear, where medics put them in a tub and tenderly washed their fragile bodies with care, bodies that had not been properly cleaned in years. Their hair was shorn and they were deloused for a final time. The battalion surgeon examined them from head to toe for diseases, gently turning over their bony arms and legs, observing their protruding ribs, diagnosing advanced malnutrition. He treated Mike's dog-bite wound, Eddie's bullet wound, their infected open sores and torn-up feet. He noted the gouge in the back of Eddie's head. Eddie weighed in at seventy-five pounds, Mike a few pounds less. Both had lost more than half their body weight. The soldiers then took the boys to a nearby farmhouse and told the woman who answered the door to clothe them. Her husband, a German soldier, was fighting at the front, and she outfitted the two boys in his shirts and pants, which draped loosely on their frames.

The boys were returned to Elmer, who called Pepsi forward from the kitchen trucks.

Pepsi was aghast at the sight of the two boys, just skin and bones, teetering on the edge of life and death.

"Put 'em to work in the kitchen," Elmer said to Pepsi.

Pepsi stared dumbfounded at the boys, then looked over at Elmer. "What exactly do you want me to have them do, sir?"

Elmer replied: "Eat."

With the two survivors in tow in the kitchen with Pepsi and the mess crew, the unit roared right back into combat, battling pockets of intense resistance, which, sadly, saw even more D Company crews killed in action. Around that time, Elmer, who viewed every life in his company as his personal responsibility, wrote a letter to Harriet, saying, "We have found two boys. They are in bad shape; I am praying they will make it."

Back in the kitchen, Pepsi understood his mission. Elmer had all but tasked him to save the boys. The survival of Eddie and Mike now rested in his hands. It was an enormous undertaking that broke his heart wide open.

"They were painful to look at," Pepsi would recall years later, about the moment he first took the boys back to the kitchen area. The mess crew was in awe: "Their chests were sunken, their ribs were showing. Their breathing was heavy, but they just kept smiling at us."

"Eddie. Mike. Come here'n sit down, boys." Pepsi patted his cot. It was clear to Pepsi that they were in a critical state, that their bodies were shutting down, and he wasn't sure where to start.

Racked with concern about doing the right thing, he worried that he had days, maybe only hours, to stabilize the boys before they could collapse, never to get up again.

"They were so fragile," he would later recall.

"I think I'm gonna staht you boys real slow. We better not feed you too much too fast, okay? Maybe staht you on these. They're no good, nobody likes 'em," he prattled on, "but it's somethin'." Though they didn't understand what he was saying, Eddie and Mike watched as he chattered away, unwrapping C-rat crackers and handing them to the boys.

They tolerated the crackers, so he made them some broth with chicken and vegetables.

They threw it back up.

Pepsi cursed himself but just chattered on.

"That's okay, boys," he reassured them. "That was my fault, that's gonna happen. You boys haven't eaten in a while; you gotta get used to food. . . . I can see that."

Over the next few days, Pepsi got the hang of it, what they could tolerate and what they couldn't. Soon, he was carefully introducing new items into their diet: eggs and canned peaches.

Like a muttering grandmother, Pepsi hobbled around the kitchen, talking incessantly as he prepared their food: "You boys are gonna be okay, I promise ya. Don't you worry 'bout a thing. You're safe now, and you're gonna be okay." He'd pat them on the back. It was the first time in years that they felt safe in the company of a kind soul who was trying to help them. Pepsi's spirited way and sparkling eyes reassured them that everything was indeed going to be okay, and they believed him.

On Elmer's orders, Pepsi kept the kitchen open around the clock for the boys.

"You boys can even wake me up in the middle of the night if you wanna eat something," he'd chirp, "or if you just wanna talk, okay?"

"I dunno what happened to you boys," he'd say, shaking his head, clanging around, looking for pans and kitchen utensils. "That shoonda happened to ya', but it's gonna be okay. We're gonna get you all fixed up, okay? . . . All fixed up like new. Don't you worry about a thing. When you getta little biggah and we get more supplies around here, I'm gonna make you somma my world-famous pancakes and fatten you right up." The boys had no idea what Pepsi was rattling on about in English, but they saw the concern and the friendly gleam in his eyes and they would remember it for the rest of their lives. One of the first phrases they would pick up in English from listening to Pepsi was "'K boys, whaddya wan' me to fix ya?"

For Eddie and Mike, it was a triumph just to go to bed every night in the company of the good men in the kitchen crew, who swaddled them in kindness and filled their bellies with something more than water soup.

"THEY'RE WITH US NOW"

Pepsi kept the boys close in those first weeks as the company drove farther into Germany. They slept next to him on cots in the mess tent along with the rest of the kitchen crew. At night, he would pat them in a fatherly way on the tops of their heads or put his arm around their shoulders, every touch a balm for their souls. Then he'd smile and say, "G'night, boys. You sleep well, now. I'll be right here next to ya."

Often, he would wake up in the night to check on them, relieved to see that they were still breathing. When they awoke from a nightmare, Pepsi comforted them and told them it was okay and to go back to sleep.

Years later he would recall, "Oh, those first days, it was touch 'n' go."

Pepsi threw everything he had into their care, trying his best to save them. Perhaps in part because he had lost his own mother at a young age, he seemed to understand the enormous upheaval the two orphans were going through.

"They didn't know us, and we didn't know them," Pepsi would later say in a newspaper interview, "but they had been terribly mistreated and that is all we needed to know."

Before long, Pepsi had put ten pounds on the boys. Their hair sprouted and their physical wounds began to heal. They imprinted on Pepsi like he was a mother duck, following him around, doing what he told them to do. They happily helped him whenever he gave them a chore: washing dishes, cleaning out the tent, sweeping out the truck, peeling potatoes and carrots. Every job, no matter how small, gave them a chance to give back in some small way for their rescue. They desperately wanted to show their worth and to prove to Elmer that he had made the right decision to take them on.

Elmer took on a paternal role. In between battles, he came back to the mess area to check on the boys. Physically, they were in rough shape, but their spirits ran high. Pepsi had lit a spark in the two boys. But they still needed extraordinary care, and if anyone could bring them back to life, Elmer thought, it was the boys of Company D.

Without any explanation to the crews, Elmer simply brought the two orphans into the D Company family, setting in motion events that would forever bond soldiers and survivors and change all of their lives.

THIRTY-ONE

BIG BROTHERS

Heavy fighting continued as they pressed their way eastward toward Kochstedt. At Wallwitzhafen, D Company faced fanatical resistance, spot reports warning of Panzerfausts: "aggressive snipers and bazookamen." German troops assaulted so violently that it forced the company into retreat. But once regrouped, they attacked with guns blazing, which saw streams of German soldiers limping out of the smoke of battle, hands raised and waving handkerchiefs.

As the company advanced, Eddie and Mike rode with Pepsi, bumping along in the kitchen truck. Immersed in English with the kitchen crew, longing to belong and being polyglots already, they picked up the language remarkably quickly, their acute sense of survival and motivation to succeed in their new environment enabling them to soak up words and phrases in record time. Pepsi would later recall, "They were like sponges."

Before long, Pepsi and the mess crew were bringing Eddie along when they needed to barter with the locals for food and supplies.

"Tell him we need ten dozen eggs."

"Bring us four bushels of potatoes tomorrow morning."

"Ask him who in this area has bread . . . butter . . . milk."

During a break in combat, the tankers went back to the chow trucks to get a hot meal. They arrived to see Pepsi, who had the two skinny survivors hustling in the kitchen, boiling water, setting up for meals, washing pots, all the while greeting the men with radiant smiles as they made their way into the mess area. To the great amusement of the crews, Eddie and Mike darted around the mess area wearing kitchen aprons as if they had been part of the team forever as Pepsi called instructions to them: "Go clean up those dirty pots, Eddie," "Gimme a hand with this, Mike," the boys answering him with the Boston accent they had picked up: "Gahtcha, Pepsi," "Yes *sah*!"

Like high school freshmen being able to hang out with the seniors, Eddie and Mike were in awe of the soldiers, who took an immediate shine to the boys, always offering a gentle word of encouragement, a pat on the back, or a handshake, especially as word spread about the depravity they had endured at the hands of the Nazis—the murder of their families, abuses, executions, starvation—which built up rage and hardened the tankers' attitude toward the enemy.

Fatigued from ten months of war, almost constantly on the edge of fear and exhaustion, losing their buddies and missing their loved ones back home, the tankers were occasionally given to bouts of melancholy. The war had taken its toll, but the young soldiers lit up when they saw the two survivors. It was magical to see the boys, who had been on death's doorstep, coming back to life. For Eddie and Mike, every day of freedom was pure joy. They reveled in soaking in the simplest things: the wonderment of a blue spring sky, feeling the sun beat down on their faces, smelling the wet earth, hearing birds twittering, and, especially, just being among the Americans.

The survivors' childlike spirit was infectious. They were a living reminder to the boys of Company D of why they had fought this war, and it became, in a sense, a sort of healing for the troops to be a party not only to Eddie and Mike's liberation but to their metamorphosis. The boys' fragile, perpetually hunted look had given way to a new confidence. Eyes etched with the ghosts of trauma now flickered with joy. They were so profoundly grateful to have been given a second chance at life.

After a time, the soldiers realized, after all they themselves had been through, the two boys were a salve for their weary souls, their presence helping them to cope with their own demons, to deal with their own war trauma. The Americans had been the rescuers, but after a while they realized there had been an unexpected reverse effect: the two concentration camp kids were helping them learn to cope with all they themselves had endured.

Eddie and Mike were captivated by the Americans and asked an endless stream of questions about where the soldiers were from and why some had foreign names—DeCola, Heinz, Haag, Devecka—and why they had different accents and mannerisms. "That's cuz I'm from Chatt'nooga, see," Fred quipped, "and Brooklyn over there . . . well, he's from another planet altogether called New York City."

Tankers produced pictures of their families, girlfriends, or fiancées. Fred showed the boys a picture of his wife and son. Pepsi pulled out his coveted picture of Blue Eyes. "That's my lucky chahm right there."

It didn't take long for Eddie and Mike to realize that America seemed to be everything Germany was not. Where Aryan purity had become the cornerstone of German society, America was a marvel of endless possibilities—filled with many cultures that had amalgamated into something wonderous, an enchanting mix of people of varied backgrounds who united to work together. The United States seemed like a magical place, and their fascination lit a flame in the two boys that would never go out. Walking out of an unimaginably dark past and facing an uncertain future, they realized that America was a place they wanted to be.

A big brother–little brother relationship took root. Crews grew protective of the boys, making every effort to bring them into their ranks, into their discussions, and into their lighthearted practical jokes and horseplay, treating them like part of the soldier brotherhood.

One day, Elmer gave Pepsi a task. A few days later, Pepsi assembled the kitchen crew and called in Eddie and Mike. With a theatrical flourish and a chuckle, he called out, "All right boys, front and *centah*!" As they snapped to attention, he handed each boy a crisp, neatly folded, size small U.S. Army field uniform. Eyes popped and a wide grin stretched across each boy's face. Overwhelmed with emotion, they teared up with pride as they donned the uniforms, which represented much more to them than just a new set of clothing. It signified that they had been accepted as part of the unit.

Pepsi beamed. "You boys look good!"

The next time the tankers came back for hot chow, they were heartened to see the boys transformed and looking like "real" American soldiers.

Somehow Elmer got the boys on the army payroll. He assigned Mike to the mess crew, where Pepsi made him his assistant in the kitchen, and he pulled Eddie up to the front line. Between battles, Elmer had Eddie accompany him as an interpreter when he needed to communicate with local government officials or to question townspeople about enemy activity that had come through their areas.

"Ask him who's in charge in this town."

"Where are the 88s and Panzerfausts located?"

"Are there regular army soldiers in this town? Where are they?"

"Where are the SS and Gestapo?"

BIG BROTHERS

"Where's the Volkssturm set up?"

Eddie stayed glued to the lieutenant, emulating Elmer's every move, his sure-footed gait, his spare but deliberate manner of speech. Eddie could see that Elmer was greatly revered by his men, and he wanted to be just like him.

Before long, Elmer made Eddie his right-hand man and from then on seldom had any interaction with locals unless he had Eddie by his side. He used Eddie's language skills to translate confiscated German documents and help the unit make sense of reports or letters POWs carried on them, screening for any valuable information that could be of interest to the division.

Then, in a move that surprised even the senior sergeants, in addition to the uniform, Elmer issued Eddie his own Colt .45-caliber pistol, which Eddie proudly wore holstered over his shoulder. It was a symbol of trust that Eddie didn't take lightly; he carried it with great care and a newfound sense of responsibility. From time to time, Elmer instructed Eddie to lean on a mayor, or question villagers for information, or even, on occasion, to interrogate a prisoner.

Eddie proved to be a natural at drawing information from the Germans. He understood what made Germans tick. He knew how to get under their skin, how to appeal to their respect for authority. He understood loyalty to Hitler and used those cultural sensitivities to his advantage. He was confident and had a toughness that got results. Each time Elmer watched Eddie in action, it brought a smile to his face.

It had been a colossal reversal of fortune. A few weeks earlier, Eddie and Mike had been standing on the *Appellplatz*, clinging desperately to life, or blasting rock in the tunnels, wondering if any given day would be their last. Now they were in American uniforms, had been embraced by the best of men, and were filled with purpose.

THIRTY-TWO

UNBREAKABLE BOND

The last days of war in the spring of 1945 were chaotic and unpredictable, with some German units fighting to the last man and others surrendering en masse, but when the Russian and U.S. armies met at the Elbe River, not far from Dessau, the war was all but over. D Company reached the Mulde River a mile away from the Elbe.

The tankers learned of the end of the war on May 8 when Corporal Blume, the company runner, announced the news:

"Hey, fellahs!" he shouted. "It just came over the wire! War's over!"

When word came that they were no longer at war, Elmer pulled the company together. The price for ridding Europe of evil had been high. Over 2,500 3rd Armored Division soldiers had been killed, more than 7,000 wounded. The division had lost 100 percent of its tanks. Company D had lost around 50 percent of its men: 34 had been killed and many more wounded. Elmer called for a moment of silence.

The tankers could not have been happier the war was over, but it was an adjustment for men who had slogged through nearly a year of combat.

"No more firing the tank. No more 88s or Panzerfausts coming for you," said one D Company tanker. "No more smelling that sour combination of hot metal, burning oil and gunpowder. No more dry-mouthed mornings when you wondered what the mists were hiding; what was in those trees up ahead."

D Company transitioned from fighters to occupiers. They moved from village to village, entering when they saw a white sheet hanging in surrender. Women and children came out of their houses to welcome the Americans, many relieved it was they who had landed in their village and not the Russians. Word was spreading that Russian soldiers had been taking revenge and raping and pillaging as they moved throughout a vanquished Germany. Historians would later estimate some 2 million German women and girls were raped by the Red Army. American troops handed out chocolate and gum. Pepsi handed out cans of peaches.

Eddie remained at Elmer's side as they rode from one village to the next, informing local mayors they were now under U.S. Army jurisdiction and handing them a new set of rules they were to follow, which Eddie had translated into German on offical 3rd Armored Division letterhead. The rules ordered them to lay down their arms and mind the curfew and called on local communities to show up with shovels and buckets to clean up streets that had turned to rubble.

Eddie helped draw up new mandates using firm, unambiguous language he knew would resonate with obstinate Germans who might not want to be told what to do by their former enemy—wording that commanded immediate compliance:

"On order of the commanding officer Lieutenant Hovland . . ."

"In order that there be no misunderstanding or excuses later on . . ."

"There will be no further discussion in this matter."

"In case of non-compliance or failure on your part, I will hold you personally accountable."

"I will not shy away from punishment."

In another directive, he added a last-minute handwritten message: "No excuses."

All were official U.S. Army orders signed by Elmer and "Eddie Willner, Company Assistant."

The end of war brought a chance for soldiers and survivors to bond in more relaxed settings. Tankers and service crews asked Eddie to teach them German phrases so they could chat up the Fräuleins, which they often mangled with hilarious results.

"How d'ya say, 'I love you?'"

"*Ich liebe dich.*'"

"'Itch leeber dish'?"

The tankers taught Eddie and Mike GI skills: how to shave using your helmet as a basin, how to salute, how to smoke a cigarette, and how to have it dangle from your mouth just so. The crews even taught the boys a little about "the birds and the bees," sharing pictures of their favorite pinup girls. It was quite the education.

The first time Eddie and Mike had gum, they munched on it, then swallowed it, leaving the soldiers chuckling and shaking their heads. One crewman took it upon himself to show them how to do it. He unwrapped a piece, put it in his mouth, and chomped on it, the boys watching the private's face intently as he gnawed, his jowls masticating for a while like a cow chewing its cud. "And then, see, you spit it out," at which point it plopped out onto the ground. The boys burst into laughter, having never before heard of something you would chew but not swallow.

Eddie and Mike absorbed it all as crews talked about their favorite sports teams and had hot, good-natured debates about the merits of the Boston Red Sox versus the Brooklyn Dodgers.

One soldier who had played semiprofessionally before the war showed Eddie and Mike how to pitch and hit a baseball, others cheering them on as they ran the bases. Another group taught the boys how to play craps and casino.

At one point, a few of the tankers dressed Eddie and Mike in their own Class B uniforms with a shirt sporting the 3rd Armored Division patch and 32nd Regiment crest, a tie, trousers, and an envelope service cap and took them into town to get an official-looking photo taken. Both amused and proud, they posed the boys and took pictures of them sitting behind the wheel of a jeep as if they were the commander's driver and pretending to fire a rifle and a pistol.

Through it all, Pepsi remained the mother hen. He continued to dote on the boys and to feed them liberally and even taught them how to cook a little. He talked endlessly about American food, describing hot dogs and root beer floats, how the tastiest food is cooked in bacon fat, how to make eggs "sunny side up, the American way."

Fred regaled the boys with his angling adventures, catching walleye and crappie, and taught them the fine art of whittling, but Vance kept his distance, watching it all from afar, perhaps still wondering what exactly the boys had been through, where their families were, and what challenges lay ahead for them.

To a man, the crew of Company D took part in helping to nurse the survivors back to health, physically and emotionally, and the two boys idolized them for it.

"They became attached to us, and we became attached to them," Pepsi would later say. "They became like our little brothers. They helped where they could, and we took care of them. Everyone loved them.

"They looked up to us and we wanted to take care of them. They needed us and, after all we'd been through, we realized we needed them, too."

In just a few months' time, D Company had completely pulled the two boys into their tribal brotherhood, forging a connection with the two survivors that would anchor them in the world, spark hope for their future, and help them to dream beyond their troubled pasts.

THIRTY-THREE

LIBERATION

Nuremberg stands firmly against the resignation of man to the inhumanity of man.
—Whitney Harris, Nuremberg prosecutor

The magnitude of the Holocaust, planned and carried out by the Nazis, must be forever seared in our collective memory.
—Stockholm Declaration signed in January 2000 by representatives of forty-six nations

MAY 8, 1945, marked the unconditional surrender of the German armed forces. Around the world, people celebrated victory in Europe and the end of a nearly six-year war that cost millions of lives and had brought untold destruction and suffering to the populations of many countries. Where once the Nazis had conquered most of the continent, Europe was now free.

As Soviet troops stormed Berlin, Hitler shot himself in his underground bunker under the ruins of the Reichstag; his new wife in a marriage just hours old died after ingesting a cyanide capsule, as did Goebbels, Hitler's propaganda minister, who once vowed, "We'll never give up power. They'll have to cart out our dead bodies." Goebbels murdered his entire family, his wife and six young children, before killing himself. One day after being arrested by the British, Himmler, the head of the SS and Hitler's architect of the Final Solution, also committed suicide by cyanide poisoning. A year and a half later, Göring, commander of the Luftwaffe and one of Hitler's closest confidants, killed himself while in Allied custody by biting down on a cyanide capsule just two hours before his scheduled execution. Many top Nazis fled the country to points unknown.

In the end, Hitler managed to achieve the exact opposite of what he had promised the German people. Instead of a triumphant return to glory by an Aryan master race in a Thousand-Year Reich, he burned his country to the ground. Berlin, which had once been the fifth largest city in the world and considered an international cultural jewel, was now obliterated and looked like an ashen moonscape. Virtually the only landmark left standing was the pockmarked Brandenburg Gate.

FDR did not live to see liberation. In fact, he died of a cerebral hemorrhage while sitting for a portrait the very day that Eddie and Mike escaped from the Langenstein death march and raced into the river to freedom. Roosevelt's vice president, Harry S. Truman, took the oath of office and became president that same day.

On May 8, 1945, he addressed the world saying:

"The western world has been freed of the evil forces which for five years and longer have imprisoned the bodies and broken the lives of millions upon millions of freeborn men. They have violated their churches, destroyed their homes, corrupted their children and murdered their loved ones. Our armies of liberation have restored free-

LIBERATION

dom to those suffering peoples, whose spirit and will the oppressor could never enslave."

Throughout Europe, the Allies entered concentrations camps to find scenes of mass carnage.

GIs flooded in with food and medical aid, setting up makeshift mobile hospitals.

In the Harz Mountains, soldiers of the American 83rd Infantry Division pushed open the gates to Langenstein, where they were met by an eerie silence.

One of the first to enter the camp was a medical team led by U.S. Army doctor Kenneth Zierler of the 8th Armored Division, who was accompanied by American war correspondent Howard K. Smith. They entered the camp to find prisoners standing on rickety legs or lying among the dead. These were inmates who had been unable to go on the march and had remained behind, taking their chance they would be executed. For some unknown reason, perhaps in their haste to abandon the camp, the SS did not kill them. Dr. Zierler would describe the scene:

"We were surrounded by human wreckage. They were beside themselves with joy to see us."

Despite their skeletal state, prisoners swarmed the American soldiers, who announced, "You are free!"

"One inmate dropped to his knees and kissed my shoes," Zierler said. "We lifted him back up."

Dr. Bernard Metrick, another U.S. Army witness to the liberation of Langenstein, said, "How they survived more than one day in this horrible torture chamber is a sign of the courage and the will to live. How they managed to live through that hell was nothing short of miraculous."

Some prisoners stared blankly back. Others put their hands

together in prayer; a few were so shocked at the arrival of the liberators, they collapsed and fell down dead.

One prisoner said, "I know I am not going to live much longer but thank God you have finally come." In fact, between twenty and twenty-five freed Langenstein prisoners a day, the trauma on their bodies irreversible, would continue to die in the weeks immediately following liberation.

A few days after liberation, a tall man with an imperious air, in knickerbockers and with a Heidelberg scar running down his cheek, strode up from the village and demanded to speak to the officer in charge. An American colonel came forward to hear the man complain about U.S. troops stealing chickens and eggs in the village and demand it cease immediately.

As he spoke, the inmates slowly drew into a circle around him. Recognizing him as a Langenstein SS guard, they stared at the man incredulously, looking him up and down and over from head to toe. Unbothered, the man continued complaining as more inmates gathered. They couldn't take their eyes off him. One survivor told the colonel that the man had been one of their SS tormentors and that he must be arrested immediately. The colonel replied that it was not within his authority at such an early point in the occupation to take anyone into custody.

As the colonel walked away, the man turned to leave but was blocked by the now two or three dozen inmates who had surrounded him. One pulled a shovel from a nearby truck, another a pickax, and, with as much strength as their frail bodies could muster, knocked him to the ground. In a macabre scene, others joined in, striking and stomping the man over and over. In the end, he did not rise again, but the inmates were too exhausted to deal a final blow. At that point, an American sergeant came over, unslung his carbine, and finished the job.

LIBERATION

. . .

The same day that Langenstein was liberated, General Eisenhower, accompanied by Generals Patton and Bradley, conducted a walk-through at another Buchenwald subcamp, Ohrdruf. Afterward, Eisenhower cabled General George Marshall in Washington, saying, "The things I saw beggar description," later adding, "I have never at any other time experienced an equal sense of shock."

He also said, "We are told the American soldier does not know what he is fighting for. Now, at least, we know what he is fighting against."

Eisenhower ordered local Germans to walk through the camps to see what they had been a party to and ordered them to assist in burying the victims.

"I visited every nook and cranny of the camp," he later wrote, "because I felt it my duty to be in a position from then on to testify at first hand about these things in case there ever grew up at home the belief or the assumption that 'the stories of Nazi brutality were just propaganda.'"

He also encouraged Marshall to immediately dispatch a congressional delegation to bear testament to the atrocities.

In the summer of 1945 and on into the fall, while Eddie and Mike remained with Company D, war crimes trials began where judges from Great Britain, the Soviet Union, the United States, and France sat in judgment of "crimes against humanity."

Where once at Nuremberg Hitler stood like Caesar beneath a hundred-foot-tall stone swastika glorifying the birth of a new Nazi nation before tens of thousands of hypnotized, torch-carrying supporters, now the Allies sought to stamp out the last vestiges of the morally reprehensible Nazi ideology, and so they organized international war tribunals in a building just two miles away, to bring the perpetrators of the atrocities to justice.

Opening the Allied case against the defendants at the Nuremberg Trials, chief American prosecutor Justice Robert H. Jackson began, "The wrongs which we seek to condemn and punish have been so calculated, so malignant and so devastating, that civilization cannot tolerate their being ignored."

Other trials were held in Germany, Poland, France, and the Soviet Union. Some SS criminals were caught, tried, and convicted. Others managed to slip away and blend right back into the civilian population, retreating to full and prosperous lives, hiding in plain sight or living openly as former SS. So many would never face accountability for their actions, having literally gotten away with mass murder.

The guilty were unapologetic about their roles in the atrocities. Many believed in Hitler to the very end, remaining proud supporters of what he, and they, had achieved. Some made statements twisting their monstrous deeds into honorable service to their Führer and to their country and maintained that there was nothing wrong with what they had done. Others excused their actions, saying it was the law at the time, they were just following orders and, therefore, they should not be held accountable.

The Auschwitz-Blechhammer guards pleaded not guilty, claiming not to have been involved. Nobody saw anything, or it was always the other guy who did it.

Typical was the trial of Blechhammer SS guard Heinrich Schaefer. Despite plenty of survivor witness testimonies that confirmed he had killed many, Schaefer denied it all; his response to nearly every question included the following string of statements:

"I cannot remember."

"I did not see anything."

"I did not kill anyone."

"I did not see anyone being killed."

LIBERATION

"I have never been a Nazi."

"I was very much against the atrocities being committed."

Commandant Otto Brossmann, who presided over many killings at Blechhammer, including the Yom Kippur hanging of the brave Dutch boy, was sentenced to death by a court in Kraków in December 1948. And yet he was subsequently acquitted and died a free man in November 1957—this despite the fact that records show that, during the war, he had received a Waffen SS medal for "splendid work in exterminating inmates."

Kurt Klipp, commandant of Blechhammer following Brossmann and leader of the death march from Blechhammer to Gross-Rosen, was also responsible for hundreds of killings and had been promoted due to his good works in Auschwitz. He was apprehended in May 1945 but, while in British custody awaiting trial, died of typhus that he had contracted when he was made to bury corpses, by order of British troops, at Bergen-Belsen concentration camp.

Tom Mix, the cowboy monster of Blechhammer, was named by many former inmates as being one of the most sadistic guards of them all. Though there is no confirmation of Tom Mix's true identity, more than a dozen survivors identified him as SS Rottenführer Hermann Leinkenjost from Bochum. Official German records show a Hermann Leinkenjost died in April 1945, listed as a "war death," in Wrocław (Breslau), Poland. In the end, Tom Mix's true identity and whereabouts were never corroborated, and questions remain about whether he actually died or simply slipped back into society.

The Blechhammer kitchen goons, Karl Francioh and Ansgar Pichen, both pleaded not guilty to their crimes but were convicted and sentenced to death for their part in torturing and killing inmates. They were hanged in December 1945.

Details are murky about what happened to the Langenstein guards at Hitler's secret Project Malachit tunnel project. No records have been found about what happened to SS Lagerführer Paul Tscheu. His whereabouts after the war remain a mystery. Wilhelm Lübeck, who said, "If you kill a thousand, it doesn't matter because you can get a thousand to replace them," was apprehended and held in confinement until 1948, when he was released and went on to work as an architect.

In the end, while some Nazi criminals were brought to justice, the large majority were never held to account, disappearing to places unknown in Germany or elsewhere in Europe or to Latin America, to Argentina, Brazil, and Chile. Some 1,600 Nazi scientists and engineers were quietly whisked off to the United States and to the Soviet Union, their war crimes ignored so that their knowledge could be exploited for their expertise in engineering, technology, chemicals, and weaponry in the new Cold War arms race. Among them was Wernher von Braun, an SS officer and head of Hitler's V-2 rocket program, which relied on concentration camp slave labor at a cost of tens of thousands of human lives.

THIRTY-FOUR

THE FINAL GOODBYE

EDDIE AND MIKE remained with D Company through the last battles of the war and into the first months of Allied occupation. Finally, after six months together, the American soldiers were going home.

In October, Company D started breaking down camp and preparing to go back to the States. They turned in their tanks, packed up their letters and photographs from home, along with their souvenir German belt buckles, pocketknives, and Nazi flags. Though happy to be returning to their families, changed forevermore, they were melancholy that their brotherhood was breaking up and especially anxious about what the future held for Eddie and Mike.

In the previous weeks, when they realized their time together was coming to a close, the young tankers had racked their brains trying to figure out ways to get their "little brothers" to the United States. The ideas were mostly bantering or harebrained GI schemes, joking they could just smuggle the boys aboard ship in their duffel bags, or that some of them, not much older than Eddie and Mike themselves, could try to adopt the two teens.

All kidding aside, everyone realized there was no viable way for the two survivors to return with them to America. With no path for the boys to emigrate, the soldiers were forced to leave them behind and felt like they were deserting what they now considered "two of their own" at the gates of an unknown future.

They dreaded the day they would have to separate from the boys and put it off to the last possible moment. In the cool temperatures of that autumn day, Elmer, Fred, Vance, Pepsi, and the rest of the company gathered to say goodbye.

Eddie and Mike stood looking at the faces of their heroes. Fate had dealt them a lucky hand in putting them in the path of these young men. They had cherished every moment with D Company. Every connection, every caring act, every new life skill, every laugh, now echoed in the coming goodbye.

They had known from the start that their time with the unit would be a fleeting gift, just a weigh station to a new beginning, but it was a chapter of their lives etched deeply on their hearts.

Thanks to Pepsi, in the half year Eddie and Mike spent with D Company, they had put on about fifty pounds. Their frames now fuller, they had regained muscle and fat and had color in their cheeks. They were stronger emotionally and that self-assured American spirit had rubbed off on them.

Their hearts were full as they stood before the boys of D Company, profoundly grateful to them and to the lieutenant, who had given them a shot at life and a family after they had lost everyone and everything.

Thanks to being on the army payroll, Eddie and Mike had enough money in their pockets to last them at least for a little while. Someone handed the boys travel orders that allowed them to make their way unhindered through U.S. military police checkpoints and skirt Allied authorities, who might try to place them in a displaced persons camp, where young Jewish survivors were being recruited to go to Palestine to help build a new Jewish state.

Elmer finally spoke.

"You've been through a lot, but you boys are gonna be all right. You'll always be a part of us. We'll never forget you," he said, and offered a solid, reassuring handshake while masking his concern about the uncertain future that awaited them.

Tankers and crews surrounded the boys to say their farewells. Fred stepped up, his face softening to a broad grin, and said gently, "F'you ever get over to Chattanooga, I'll take ya' boys fishin'."

"Ah, don't listen to him," Pepsi interjected. "Listen. You come up to see me in Bahston. I'll take you to a Red Sox game and I'll cook you up a meal you'll *nevah* fahget!" It was all meant to take the edge off of an uneasy moment as they all realized they would never see each other again.

Others filed by, patting the boys on the back and shaking their hands, some fighting back emotions.

"Eddie. Mike. See ya around."

"It's been a pleasure to know ya."

"So long, fellahs."

Finally, Pepsi, who, despite his levity, was distraught at the thought of a final goodbye, put his arms around Eddie and Mike. Choking back tears, he said simply, "You boys take care."

Then the two survivors, still wearing their army-issued GI uniforms, turned and walked away.

Later, Pepsi would recall the moment. "It was painful to separate with them. I wish we coulda taken 'em home with us."

PART IV

THIRTY-FIVE

"I WANT THOSE DAYS BACK"

We stood there once, and if we just keep the scenes alive, we can stand there again.

We sang our war songs one more time. No one else can do it for they don't know the words.

—Private Stuart Thayer

BEFORE THEY SPLIT up to go back home and go their separate ways, with Eddie and Mike now gone, the lieutenant called the troops together for a final farewell.

"It was a privilege and honor to be a member of the family of Company D," he said. "You can be proud you were in the 32nd Armored Regiment. Our record speaks for itself. When you go home to your families and your churches, hold your heads up. You did a good job.

"If any of you ever get to southern Minnesota, look me up. Stop by. I won't give you a drink, but I'll buy you a cup of coffee."

Then he shook every man's hand, climbed into his jeep, and left.

More than one soldier had a lump in his throat as they stood in silence watching Elmer's jeep disappear into the distance. There was an instant void, a sense of loss, of somehow feeling incomplete as some wondered what their lives would be like without him in it.

He had been thought by the command to be too inexperienced, too uneducated, too young, and too unpolished to lead them. Yet, they all agreed, he was the best leader they could have ever had.

Elmer, Pepsi, and the boys of Company D, with wounds both seen and unseen, returned home to ticker-tape parades and a grateful nation that honored their sacrifice. They got medals pinned to their chests, then put their uniforms aside and returned to their farms, their mills, their factories, and to the familiar surroundings of their youths to try to pick up where they had left off, to resume the simple lives that honored the values they had fought for, where hearing the national anthem and saluting the American flag had taken on an entirely new meaning.

The evil of Nazism had been defeated, but America still had work to do to address her own issues of racism. More than a million Blacks had served in uniform during the war, mostly in segregated units. Witnessing the horrors of Nazi racial ideology had exposed the hypocrisy of American discrimination. The war became the impetus for change in 1948 when President Truman announced the end of segregation in the military. It was the first step in a long and ongoing journey toward equality for Black people in America.

Those who came home lived with postwar trauma, haunted by nightmares of watching their buddies die, of those they could not save, and also of the enemy soldiers they had killed. As the scale of the horrors of the Holocaust became known to the world, the boys of D Company lived with the memories of having seen with their own eyes the cruelty man was capable of in Eddie and Mike. The tragedy of the Holocaust had become personal for them.

"I WANT THOSE DAYS BACK"

. . .

Lieutenant Elmer Hovland disembarked in New York Harbor, then hitchhiked most of the way home to his beautiful Harriet, who met him at the door holding his infant son. His father, Nels, had passed away only a few months before his son's homecoming, so Elmer became the man of the house, and he and Harriet and the baby moved in with his mother, Mary, for a time.

A few years later, Elmer and Harriet struck out on their own, got in their Studebaker, moved to Luverne, and had three more children. He put aside his Silver Star and settled into a modest life working in the Albert Lea lumberyard. He was a Fuller Brush man for a time, then became a carpenter, eventually starting his own construction company, building homes from the ground up. He became known around town for his craftsmanship and his dedication to building new communities in the spirit of his Nordic ancestors who had come to the Great Plains to build new settlements.

He became a leader in Luverne, an active member of the Blue Mound Lutheran Church, and a lay leader. He had a generous heart, visiting strangers in nursing homes, bringing meals to the elderly, and, from his modest salary, giving to charities and the needy. He remained a part of the Norwegian community, even joining the Norse Glee Club choir.

Elmer continued to be outspoken about the power of faith and taking care of one another. He frequently wrote articles that made it into the *Rock County Star Herald*, the local newspaper, about being "good citizens, good neighbors and keeping high standards," and challenged citizens to take pride in their community.

Sergeant Pepsi DeCola returned to Boston, kissed the ground, then went home to Pa in Waltham. He kissed his father on both cheeks and said, "I missed you, Pa." His father handed him an apron and Pepsi went right back into the diner business.

He also went to find his pal George's sister, Blue Eyes, and married her. George was his best man. Pepsi credited Blue Eyes for saving his life and told her so—told her that just thinking of her kept him from feeling down. He cherished her and, after that day, never left her side. Her eyes, as it turned out, were indeed the most crystal blue he had ever seen.

When Pa retired, Pepsi took over management of the Monarch Diner. He also opened two more diners in Waltham with his brothers, all of which saw enormous success.

Pepsi and Blue Eyes had two children. His greatest joy was his family and his Catholic church community. He joined the American Legion Post 156 and he and Blue Eyes joined a ballroom dance club. He spent a lot of time in his garden, where he installed a life-size statue of the Virgin Mary under a flower arbor and took meticulous care of his prized buffalo tomatoes, which he used to make authentic homemade pasta sauces the way Ma had taught him from her old-country Civitaquana recipes.

In a veteran's interview, Pepsi said, "I thank God for bringing me back to the realm of humanity." He would go on to say that, as bad as war was, it had somehow changed him for the better.

Three-time Purple Heart recipient Tech Sergeant "Redhead Fred" Headrick came back from war, took a train to Nashville, then a bus to Chattanooga, where he reunited with his wife and six-year-old son, Fred Jr., who had been just three when Fred went off to war. Fred returned to his job at the Bradley Full Fashion Hosiery Mill. A high school dropout but a man of enormous enterprise, Fred then switched careers and worked his way up in the restaurant business. He opened the Scenic Grill Restaurant, which became a well-known fixture for many years in Signal Mountain, Tennessee, and he ultimately became the wealthiest of all of them.

"I WANT THOSE DAYS BACK"

Fred never fully let go of the war and paid tribute to it every day of his life, compiling a dozen boxes of records and keepsakes and meticulously chronicling in detail virtually every aspect of the company's journey through combat, collecting assorted memorabilia, official and unofficial records, photographs that he put into scrapbooks, letters, World War II books, and newspaper articles. He became president of the local chapter of the VFW (Veterans of Foreign Wars) and helped cook dinners at the American Legion. He volunteered at the Medal of Honor Museum and was a member of the Battle of the Bulge Association, the Disabled American Veterans, and the Military Order of the Purple Heart. Fred never missed a Sunday at the Signal Crest United Methodist Church and taught Sunday school. Of his time in war, Fred said, "It made you appreciate things you have in America."

Corporal James "Baby Face" Vance was awarded two Purple Hearts, left the army, and went to college at Mississippi State University. He married and had two children. While his actions at Freyneux were hailed by every man in the company and detailed in articles and a book following the war, Vance never received any official recognition for his actions during a critical point in the Battle of the Bulge, which had helped turn the tide of the German advance, despite Fred's vehement protests: "I don't know why he wasn't given a Silver Star for that." After he got his bachelor's degree, Vance returned to active duty in 1952, became an officer, and went on to serve in Vietnam.

His proudest moment of his thirty-year career would remain knocking out those three Panzers in Freyneux. In all the years he spent in the military, that was what Vance remembered as his shining moment.

Lieutenant Charles Myers's parents in York, Pennsylvania, kept his picture up on the mantel and a gold star in the window and mourned their loss for the rest of their lives.

The Myers family had given up their only son to the war. A boy who had been raised to be the best of America, singled out by his college classmates as a future leader, he would remain twenty-four years old forever.

Lieutenant Myers was killed in action just three weeks before Company D found Eddie and Mike and only six weeks before the end of the war.

Myers's remains stayed on the land that he had helped to free. He is memorialized on the white marble Tablets of the Missing at the Henri-Chappelle American Cemetery in Hombourg, Belgium, where his name is inscribed along with about one hundred others whose remains were not recoverable.

Just two columns away, also on the Tablets of the Missing at Henri-Chappelle, is the name of Lieutenant Arthur Lindell from Russell, Pennsylvania, the twenty-year-old B-24 pilot of *Butch*, who was killed in action in the last bombing raid on Blechhammer, his remains also listed as not recoverable.

The boys of Company D reintegrated into American society and got on with their lives. For a decade or so, they let their brotherhood become a memory, but, almost to a man, they couldn't let it go. The loss of their brothers in arms still weighed on them even ten years later.

They had come home from war hoping to forget some things but, after a while, realized they missed the fraternity. More than just missing one another, they realized they needed each other. It was more than a matter of a simple desire for camaraderie. It was as if they had lost a sense of belonging and lost a sense of themselves.

The longing lingered, so Fred called for a reunion.

"I WANT THOSE DAYS BACK"

. . .

They came rolling in: Elmer, Pepsi, Fred, Vance, Sergeant Haag, Sal, Smeegie, Fats, Shaky, George the Greek, Brooklyn, Laddie Devecka. Despite the hell they had been through and the terrors they had tried to forget, they wanted to stand in their youth again, to be with the men who were a party to their coming of age, when they were "boys set down to a man's task." Men who would not have known each other but for the war were now part of each other's life stories. And so they came back together to see the scenes again, to remember their tank commander's head and shoulders rising from the turret, drivers slamming the break levers, clutching, accelerating the tank on the front line, Smeegie racing Elmer through the dust and the rain and the haze, Fred, Vance, and the crews looking on, trying to see something in his face as he went by.

From the hedgerows of Normandy to the frozen spruce forests of the Bulge, and on to victory in Germany: Fred and Vance in Myers's tank, moving past and on up to the front to scout out ahead of the column, Vance firing on Panzers in Freyneux, Pepsi's combat diner therapy sessions. Buddies who sat in their tanks together, making coffee in a little C-rat tin, sleeping curled up in a ball on the floor of the tank or hunched over on the seat, then taking hits, firing back, or bailing—and the lighter moments: the horseplay, the tomfoolery, sweet-talking the French girls.

"I want those days back," Stuart Thayer, a Company D loader, would write. "That's why I'm here."

It became an annual event. Once a year, they got in their cars and drove to the hometown of whoever was hosting: to Joe Layton's farm in Dorchester, Massachusetts; to Conrad Bleimeister's in Hooper, Illinois; to Brady Laird's in Brookhaven, Mississippi; to Nevada, Ohio, Texas, New Hampshire, Georgia; to Julius Marashinsky's on Long

Island. They stayed in motels, attended banquets, toured one another's homes, and had barbecues in their backyards. Elmer with Harriet, Pepsi and Blue Eyes, Fred and Vance with their wives.

They talked about the war and about their families and their crops—"We could use some rain. Been mighty dry"—and cars: "Been getting about twenty-two miles to the gallon." About baseball and politics, about government waste and bureaucratic carelessness and, in later years, about their angina and cataracts and bypass operations, about financial woes. "Since I retired, there ain't no money," said one.

"Mebbe you shoulda stayed in the army," said another.

"Stayed in the army, ah, Jesus, no!"

As close as they were to their wives and friends and even their own brothers, their experiences in war could not be fully understood by those who hadn't been there, and sometimes they just needed each other to make sense of it all. For some plagued by postwar nightmares, they found true solace only in each other's company.

They felt a tangible spirit at the reunions, lingering over photos of themselves and each other when they were twenty-year-old, bright-eyed, smiling kids—"boys," Thayer would write, "who remembered each other when their jaws were firm, and their bellies were hard, and they went to the moon...."

"If I ever need proof that I once rode into the mouth of Hell," said Thayer, "I can have it here. Yes, you were there, they tell me; yes, this happened, that happened. It's true, we did those things. Histories confirm the broader picture, but no one of them say I helped. It is only here in the memories of these men that my part is recognized. It is here that I was once a party to great events."

As the years went on, they gave interviews to their hometown newspapers. They steered the conversation not to the glory of their own deeds but to the glory of their brotherhood, to their good fortune to serve among "good and skilled men."

They paid tribute to Elmer's leadership and they talked about saving Eddie and Mike. Those were the stories that made their eyes light up.

Elmer took most of his interviews with a Bible in his lap.

When asked, "What kept you strong?" not surprisingly Elmer responded, "My Christian faith. I carried that catechism that they issued. I read from that every morning and every night.

"That's the reason I think I'm here today is because I put my trust in the Lord and he more than took care of me," he continued. "When you're about to face death in battle, you need something to keep you going. It made me realize there was something bigger than just me. I realized it had to be God. And I believed he was on our side."

He wrote letters to the editor of the local newspaper: "Having spent months on the front line in World War II under all kinds of enemy fire with nary a scratch, I have complete confidence that God is always in control."

And opinion pieces: "Is prayer still important today? You better believe it. On the battlefield, prayer was the first thing in the morning and the last thing at night. Was God listening? Oh, yes, all the time."

Asked about his soldiers, Elmer gave his men all the credit: "We had a lot of men, farmers, strong, a lot of faith. Men of faith in the Lord and family and country.

"As an individual, you weren't that important, until you were part of a good group. The spirit of cooperation and working together made you strong.

"They were ordinary soldiers who changed their lives from civilian to coming together as soldiers, and that speaks so highly of the American people. It was great."

When asked what kept him going, Fred said, "War was H-E-double-L. The friendships kept you going. You don't make friendships like that in regular life."

Asked about the camaraderie, Pepsi said, "They were kids and they became buddies. I fed 'em and tried to keep 'em happy, and I tried not to let 'em fall apaht."

When asked about the two survivors the company had saved in the middle of combat, Elmer said: "They needed all the compassion that we as Americans could give them, and Americans are notably compassionate.

"There were no clear manuals written on how to handle every situation. You made judgment calls. My judgment was to take care of them because it was humane."

Asked about how they felt when they first saw Eddie and Mike, Elmer became emotional, turned away, and said simply, "It was tough. . . ."

In between tapings, with cameras still rolling, Elmer would read a passage of scripture, then look off into the distance as if he might be reflecting on those wartime memories, then feeling comforted once again when he had his hand resting on his Bible.

When Pepsi was asked about caring for the survivors, he said, "They came to us hungry and beat-up. They wanted to eat. Oh, they were in rough shape. They were so happy to be alive. These kids were a step away from death, but they were so happy."

Asked in another interview why he took such good care of Eddie, he said, "He was just a human being, somebody's kid, somebody's son."

"They were just skin and bones," Fred said, "and we saved 'em. They flagged us down. We picked 'em up and moved on.

"It was our company commander's call about what to do with

them, and he said they're gonna stay." When asked what happened to those two boys, Fred said, "Well, I just wish I knew."

The reunions continued for nearly fifty years. For many of the boys of D Company, it was the most important weekend of the year. The reunions kept them going, their fidelity to one another becoming even more cemented in time. Always happy to see one another, they greeted each other joking, poking, and chiding about how they had physically changed over the years. At one reunion, Fred arrived from Chattanooga, gazed around the room, took in the balding heads and ample girths, and said, "Boys, I look at this bunch and it makes me wonder how we won the war."

They had long since put their lieutenant on a pedestal and nothing changed with time. At one reunion, in between their gin and tonics and beers, someone asked, "Anyone remember what the lieutenant got that Silver Star for?" Another answered, "I don't remember, but he should have gotten a whole chest full of 'em."

In the end, their reunions were mostly happy occasions when they recalled the things that made them laugh. Pepsi finally fessed up to using gun oil to cook them that memorable pancake breakfast after the Bulge.

"Glad we survived the war," Fred would say. "Never mind them damn Germans. You mighta killed us all, Pepsi."

At every reunion, inevitably, someone would ask, "Wonder whatever happened to those two Jewish boys we picked up."

THIRTY-SIX

THE CALL

I just want to see you guys again.
—Eddie Willner

MY FIVE SIBLINGS and I were raised with the stories told dozens of times about what these men had done for my father, Eddie, and for his best friend, Mike, after the trauma they had endured at such a young age. Though my father told us they were just "ordinary Americans," to us kids, their virtues had, over the years, reached legendary heights. Growing up, I thought they were superheroes, men ten feet tall, giants one can only read about or see on the big screen. But for their actions and sacrifices, America and her allies would not have defeated Hitler, my father would likely not have made it out alive, and I would not even be here to tell this story.

For nearly fifty years my parents looked for them, poring over the white pages of thick phone books on out-of-state family trips, rummaging through newspaper articles that listed veterans' units and names but, armed with misspellings, timeworn memories of not exact names, but just their GI monikers and war nicknames—Pepsi,

THE CALL

Fred, Baby Face Vance—and fading recollections about where they said they lived, they never found them. Nevertheless, they kept trying to piece things together, looking for a lucky break. Thanks to the advent of the internet era and my mother's determination, in the mid-1990s she turned to computer searches, scouring records of military units in World War II, cross-referencing them with those partial-name fragments, but that trail also went cold.

Would we ever find them? I wondered as a child. Would they ever know the critical role they had played in my father's life—in all of our lives? After nearly five decades of searching, we came to accept that they were lost to us forever and would just remain in my father's memory.

Despite disappointments, my mother kept searching, writing to any organization she could think of: the Veterans of the Battle of the Bulge, *Military Officer* magazine, Veterans of Foreign Wars, the *Stars and Stripes* newspaper. But she never heard anything back, or else received polite letters saying they had no record of the names she gave them. Then one day in the late 1990s, a letter arrived from the president of the 3rd Armored Division Veterans Association:

"Dear Mrs. Willner," it read. "We have a man named Lieutenant Hovland who was in Unit D Company, 32nd Armored Regiment. I do not know if this is the man you are looking for. His phone number is: xxx-xxx-xxxx."

Eddie had an immediate reaction: "That's him." It seemed my mother had found Elmer.

Almost six decades after the end of the war, Elmer, now eighty years old, having lost his beloved Harriet months earlier, was sitting alone in his favorite old easy chair, staring out the window, when the phone rang. He got up and ambled across the room to answer it.

A woman's voice spoke, said she was looking for "Lieutenant

Hovland, the commanding officer of Company D of the 32nd Armored Regiment of the 3rd Armored Division in World War II." No one had referred to him by that formal title in many years.

"Speaking. Who may I ask is calling?" Elmer replied. She identified herself as Hanna.

"I'm Eddie Willner's wife. Do you remember Eddie? He was one of the Jewish boys you saved in World War II."

The name "Eddie" took Elmer's breath away. Hanna told him that Eddie had been talking about Elmer and the boys of Company D his whole life.

"Oh my Lord," Elmer said, sitting back down.

Hardly ready for what he was about to hear, Hanna told him Eddie's story.

In 1945, after he left Company D, Eddie went first to Brussels, hoping that by some miracle his parents would show up there alive. He went to the home of the Leeks, the Jewish family who had once harbored him, who, he learned, had also suffered a tragic fate. Wandering the streets of the city, he inquired wherever he could. When word went out that a teenage survivor had returned and was looking for his parents somewhere around the city center, he was approached by a Belgian underground team of former concentration camp inmates who tried to recruit him to help "take revenge" on the Nazis. He turned them down and moved on to continue his search for his parents. With no sign of them anywhere, Eddie made his way home to Mönchengladbach. He arrived to find a vanished community, where the city had been swept clean of any trace of Jewish life. Armed only with the list of the twenty-six names his father had made him memorize, he walked the streets searching for anyone on the list, for "Josef, Margot, Jakob, Elise, Isidor Willner . . ." He longed to see just one face he recognized, to hear one familiar voice call out to him, to see Opa

THE CALL

Josef come around the bend smiling with a sweet in his pocket, to reunite with a Jewish classmate or neighbor. But now a strange German family lived in their flat on Weiherstrasse, another had taken over Opa Josef's home. Eddie would find no trace of anyone in his family, neither that day nor in the years to come. Recovered Nazi records would show that everyone in his family had perished.

Fritz, the Catholic neighbor, welcomed Eddie home with a bear hug and tears. Fritz was devastated to learn what had happened to Siegfried and Auguste. Eddie retrieved the things his parents had left secretly in Fritz's care: the silver family menorah, Siegfried's Iron Cross, Auguste's green notebook with her recipes, her favorite silver party cake tongs, a few family photos, and Opa Josef's purple velvet prayer book.

Eddie reconnected with Mike, who had gone back to Amsterdam to look for his family. As it would turn out, Mike was also left alone in the world, both boys the sole survivors of sprawling Jewish families who had lost hundreds of relatives.

Inspired by the memories of their American heroes, Eddie and Mike, still only teenagers, put in paperwork in hopes of emigrating to America. With thousands of displaced refugees in postwar Europe petitioning to get to the United States, it was a long shot, but in 1947, just two years after the end of the war, their applications were approved. Soon the two teens sailed separately to the United States, arriving in New York Harbor, where they were welcomed to her shores by the Statue of Liberty.

There, with only an eighth-grade education, nearly penniless, with no personal documentation or vocational skills, too old for an orphanage, and having picked up enough English during their time with Company D to at least pass a language test, they proudly raised their right hands and took the oath of military service to "support and defend the Constitution of the United States of America," dedicating their lives to the country that had liberated them.

They found new families in the U.S. military, Eddie in the army, Mike in the air force. Using his French and German language skills, Eddie became a military police criminal investigator and, later, an interrogator, where he worked with French police helping to break up black-market smuggling rings in France and partnered with Belgian authorities to find the remains of missing U.S. soldiers.

Eddie studied hard, got a high school equivalency diploma, and quickly rose to the rank of staff sergeant. Then, wholly inspired by Elmer, in 1952, Eddie applied for officer candidate school and was accepted, and Sergeant Willner became Lieutenant Willner, detailed as an intelligence officer. Mike rose through the ranks to become a master sergeant tech specialist.

Returning to Germany, Lieutenant Willner interrogated German POWs freed from imprisonment in the Soviet Union. Less than ten years after he immigrated to the U.S., Eddie was assigned as chief of the intelligence and analysis branch at U.S. Army headquarters in Stuttgart, and became the first American liaison officer to the newly formed *Bundesnachrichtendienst*, or BND, Germany's CIA, where he worked alongside some former SS officers, who may have felt uneasy working shoulder to shoulder with a young American officer with an Auschwitz number tattooed across his forearm.

While posted at the headquarters in Heidelberg, Eddie met Hanna, a German secretary, who had escaped from East Germany and left her family behind. (Her story is in my book *Forty Autumns*.) Both left alone in the world, they were drawn to one another and became a team. Eddie and Hanna married and went on to have six children. Mike married and had three.

They became Uncle Eddie and Uncle Mike to each other's children and remained as close as two brothers could ever be, leaning on

THE CALL

and helping one another in good times and bad, looking after each other every step of the way.

From time to time, they reflected on their days in the concentration camps, sometimes just sitting in long silences in each other's company. Eddie attributed his survival to luck, to his close friendship with Mike, and to his father's love and discipline. He also credited his unwavering will to live and his belief that human beings can withstand much more physically and mentally than they think they can.

Scarred but unbroken, Eddie and Mike found their way forward, living in the present and refusing to let their past hold them back. They became American patriots in their adopted country, wore their uniforms proudly, flew the American flag on flagpoles in the driveways of their modest suburban homes, and threw themselves into being good soldiers, good family men, and good Americans.

Eddie served in the army for over twenty years, with assignments in Japan, Korea, France, and Germany, then served for another twenty years as a civil servant. In retirement, he volunteered, helping new immigrants get settled, teaching adult literacy to inner-city elderly, and serving on the local police council. Mike served in the air force for twenty-two years and then worked in New York's JFK Airport security. Both men gave eyewitness testimony to Holocaust awareness projects, Eddie most notably at the United States Holocaust Memorial Museum and Steven Spielberg's USC Shoah Foundation project. In the mid-1980s, Eddie went back to his hometown, Mönchengladbach, and gave a presentation to the community titled "We Were Your Neighbors." Fritz had passed away, but his family came to support Eddie and sat in the front row.

Mike died of cancer in 1985. Eddie and Hanna were living in Northern Virginia with their six children and fourteen grandchildren.

After Hanna hung up, Elmer called Pepsi and Fred.

"You sittin' down?"

Pepsi would later recall, "The call gave me goosebumps." They phone tagged the others and spread the news. Over the next days, Elmer, Fred, and Pepsi couldn't sleep. They called Eddie and talked for hours. Eddie said to them, "I just want to see you guys again."

THIRTY-SEVEN

THE REUNION

NEARLY SIX DECADES after they had last seen each other, in September 2002, Eddie welcomed the surviving members of Company D to his home in Falls Church, Virginia. He would be hosting that year's reunion. The aging veterans, many of whom had stopped attending in recent years for health reasons, pulled themselves together and found a way to make the trip. For some, it would be their last. The reunion at Eddie's house was one of the most well attended in years, with many bringing their wives and children and some their grandchildren.

The Washington Post sent a reporter to cover the event and ran a front-page story, which was picked up by other major news outlets across the country, titled "Thanking 'the Boys' Who Gave Him Life."

They pulled up in their Buicks, Oldsmobiles, and Pontiacs. The boys of D Company, now old men mostly in their early eighties, arrived at Eddie's house and were greeted by a huge banner that spanned the entire front porch: "Welcome Soldiers of Company D, 32nd Armored Regiment, 3rd Armored 'Spearhead' Division."

"More than 50 years had passed without a word," wrote *The Washington Post*. "Lives were lived and lives were lost. Dashing soldiers became stooped grandfathers. Memories, like snapshots, faded away. Eddie Willner was a lost piece of Company D's history. Lost, that is, until this weekend, when the faces of a half-century ago appeared at the Willners' front door in Falls Church, and the men of Company D—the men who 57 years ago gave Eddie Willner his life back—came to his home to honor him.

"He was just 18 when they found him, half dead. After surviving five years in the camps, where both of his parents were killed, Eddie . . . and a Dutch friend Mike managed to flee their SS guards while on a death march. Both boys had lost their entire families in the concentration camps, and with no one else left in the world to claim them, Company D did."

Eddie's heart beat fast as the men came up the driveway, and he was suddenly thrust back to the war to the moment he and Mike had come out of the woods, euphoric to see the American crews dismounting from their tanks and approaching. Bent and arthritic now, they shuffled in aided by canes and supporting one another, lining up in the driveway and stepping up onto the porch.

Pepsi was first in line. His wavy black hair was now gray at the temples, but he was unmistakably the same man, still spritely as ever. Crow's-feet softened his eyes, and deep lines replaced the dimples that used to define his cheeks, but it was the same comforting face. With characteristic comic affect, he pulled Eddie into a big bear hug before Eddie could notice Pepsi's welling emotions, his Boston accent breaking the ice when he belted out, "How ah ya, buddy?"

"Thank you for saving me," Eddie choked as he embraced Pepsi.

"Well, you know, Eddie," Pepsi retorted, "it was my 'onah to help save ya, but you know, you made *me* a bettah person. You saved us, too. You taught us all a thing or two about life. You made us all bettah, buddy."

He let Eddie go, wiping away tears, and backed up to introduce Blue Eyes. "Here's my dahlin', my lucky *chahm* I told you about. 'Membah the pitchah? I went home and married her! She's been my dahlin' for fifty-foah yeahs now."

Redhead Fred, his fiery ginger hair and freckles faded, his once-lean physique filled out to an ample waistline held up by suspenders, still had that infectious ear-to-ear grin. Wearing a "Spearhead" ball cap, matching Western corded bolo tie, and leather tab suspenders, he held out his hand for a handshake. "Well, I'll be doggone. How are ya, ol' buddy? You remember me? Always did wonder what happened to ya."

Vance, only a year older than Eddie, now seventy-seven to Eddie's seventy-six, once a plump-cheeked youth, was now bald and bespectacled but in good physical form. He approached Eddie with the same contemplative expression he had always worn when he had looked at Eddie back in the day—a bit bewildered, a bit reverent, always seeming to be wondering what Eddie must have gone through.

"Eddie? Vance. It's really good to see you again," he said with a handshake and a mature, self-assured mien that Eddie barely recognized. Baby Face Vance had grown up.

Inside, Eddie's house looked like a July Fourth Independence Day celebration: red, white, and blue streamers curled through the air and bunting decorated the furniture. Bowls of pretzels and chips stood on the coffee table, finger sandwiches were set out along the buffet, and a large sheet cake with a red, yellow, and blue Spearhead battle insignia surrounded by white frosting roses was the centerpiece on the dining room table.

The old soldiers streamed into the house—Fats, George, Sal, Bernie,

Stu—leaning into one another, giving warm, weighty slaps on the back. Stiff-kneed and hard of hearing, they greeted each other, jostling and wisecracking, some wearing Spearhead shirts or jackets with 32nd Armored Regiment crest lapel pins, one in farmer's overalls, one in cowboy boots.

Someone posted the "D/32" company guidon in the corner of the room right below portraits of Eddie's parents, Siegfried and Auguste.

"How the hell are ya, buddy?"

"Hey, yer lookin' good, by God!"

"You drive down here okay?"

"How's the family?"

...and two on the couch: "You believe we're sittin' in Eddie's livin' room?" head shaking...

"Never thought I'd see this day."

They gathered around Eddie:

"Well, dang, Eddie," one tanker said, "I can't believe you made it to the United States."

"*I* can't believe you speak such good English," Fred interjected. "Lord, you speak English better'n *I* ever did," the room erupting in laughter.

Others approached Eddie, one patting him on the back, and saying with a wry smile and a wink, "I knew if we patched you up right, you'd turn out okay."

They spread out, strolling through the ground floor like they were wandering through a museum, taking in Eddie's life from personal mementos scattered around the room.

Fats looked over a photo of Eddie, his wife, and their six children. "Lordy! You've been busy!"

Vance adjusted his glasses on the end of his nose, tilted his head back to catch the bifocal lenses to look over promotion certificates and testaments to a successful military career.

THE REUNION

"Well, I'll be doggone. Look at this," Fred said, eyeing a photo of two of Eddie's kids in army uniforms. "Coupla his kids followed the old man into the service."

Suddenly, someone hollered, "Lieutenant's here." Elmer had arrived.

When he came into the house, it was as if General Eisenhower himself had entered. Those who were seated stood up; those who were already standing stood a little taller.

His blond hair now white, Elmer still had that confident gait. His square jaw had softened, but his eyes were still a bright, steely blue. He nodded all around, working his way through the room as men leaned in to shake his hand with murmurs of "Lieutenant," "Afternoon, sir."

Elmer shrugged off the attention.

He searched the room until his eyes rested on Eddie, then navigated the crowd to reach him. Offering his large, powerful workingman's hand, his eyes narrowing to that same steady gaze that Eddie instantly recognized. The room went quiet.

"Eddie," he said simply, in a moment that seemed to hang on the air forever, "I'm so proud of you."

"Who wants cake?" Pepsi chirped as he sliced pieces, carefully cutting around the unit insignia to keep it intact. As guests milled about, one of the men brought his eleven-year-old grandson over to ask Eddie about the number tattoo on his arm, his grandfather prompting, "Go ahead 'n' ask him," as Eddie's grown children moved through the room thanking the old soldiers for "saving our father."

After a while, someone called the room to order.

"As you know, it is our custom at each reunion to take a minute to think about the men we left behind. As always, we remember our brothers who have departed ... those who have passed since coming home, but especially those we lost on the battlefield.

"I'll now read the names of those who left us back in the war, men who died in France, in Belgium, in Germany ... our friends who gave the ultimate sacrifice.

"Private Claude Young, Private Sylvester Rothstein, Private Smith, PFC Arturo Casillas, Lieutenant Charles Myers ..."

Handkerchiefs move across faces as the thirty-four names were read.

A couple of the old soldiers lumbered to their feet to make speeches. One thanked Eddie and Hanna for hosting the reunion, saying, "Eddie, we're glad you found us because we been thinkin' about ya for a long time," which was followed all around by murmurs of affirmation and head nods.

Then Eddie rose. Steadied by his oldest son, Eddie raised his glass, looked around the room, and finally spoke.

"You are the best men I have ever known."

Turning to Elmer, he said, "I have no words but to thank you for what you did for me and Mike. You could have left us by the side of the road, but you didn't. You took us in and gave us back our lives. And today I have a good life as an American because of you. I know if Mike were here, he would say the same thing."

Then Elmer stood up to speak. To the boys of Company D, Elmer would forever be their twenty-three-year-old company commander on the battlefield who had led the tankers through the worst of times. To a man, everyone still called him "sir," including those who had gone on to outrank him, like Vance, who had retired four grades higher as a full colonel, and even Eddie, who had retired as a major.

Now, as Elmer began to speak, just like back in the war, they all leaned in closer to hear what their commander had to say. Elmer gathered himself and, in that sober Norwegian manner, lifted his

THE REUNION

chin slightly, looked out over the room full of his men, and said simply, "We did good together. We got the job done, we took care of each other, and we took care of those boys."

Turning to Eddie, he said, "By the grace of God, we've come together again. Eddie, we never forgot you."

The reunion of the Holocaust survivor and the soldiers who rescued him was deeply fulfilling for all. The story had finally come full circle. Eddie was at peace, having finally found his big brothers to whom he felt he owed so much, and the old soldiers were somehow made whole knowing that Eddie and Mike had made it to America and had thrived.

Following the reunion, in a newspaper interview, Elmer said to be personally thanked by Eddie brought tears to his eyes. "It really shakes me up. There are some things you can't put into words."

THIRTY-EIGHT

POSTSCRIPT

EDDIE'S ADULT CHILDREN, myself included, and grandchildren made trips back to Germany and Poland to Auschwitz-Birkenau and to subcamp Blechhammer. They stood on the train platform where Eddie last saw his mother; went into the Project Malachit tunnels at Buchenwald subcamp Langenstein; and walked along the riverbank where he and Mike made their escape. Though he returned to other internment and concentration camps where he was held prisoner, Eddie visited Langenstein only once and never returned.

In 2019, Eddie's children had brass Stolpersteine "stumbling stones" embedded in the sidewalk on Weiherstrasse, where the family once lived contently in the flat above Fritz before they were evicted and forced to flee Germany. Today, Stolpersteine brass plaques have been installed in sidewalks throughout Europe to eternalize Jewish families who met with tragedy in the Holocaust; stones begin with "Here lived . . ."

In the months after the reunion, Eddie and Elmer wrote many letters to each other.

POSTSCRIPT

"I have thanked God many times," Eddie wrote, "for your being there with your men on that day."

Elmer's letters were filled with spiritual reflection about the meaning of it all, about how he believed Providence had brought them together. His messages always ended with a blessing or a psalm about the grace of God and life's good fortune: "We have been much blessed with a wonderful family. There is nothing that can compare to family except our Christian faith."

Fred wrote to Eddie, "After everything that happened to you, that you made it to liberation and got to come to the USA, you are a hero."

Eddie wrote to Pepsi and the entire kitchen crew, "I will never forget how kind you were to me when I was hungry."

Elmer, Pepsi, and Fred spoke often with Eddie by phone in their later years and on occasion came to visit, staying overnight to attend family gatherings or to just sit with the Willner clan, which, by 2005, had grown to twenty-six members. Elmer and Pepsi even traveled in to attend Eddie's son's, my brother Albert's, promotion to U.S. Army colonel, a proud moment for all in attendance.

While Company D soldiers had taken in our father back in the war, as adults, we all but adopted a few of the aging veterans into the Willner family, in particular, Elmer and Pepsi. As we had lost all our relatives in the Holocaust, Pepsi filled a void, becoming a much-loved surrogate uncle to Eddie's children and grandchildren, filling the role so generously, sending cards and flowers and boxes of homegrown tomatoes. He even converted an entire room in his modest ranch home in Waltham into a shrine of sorts to our family, where he proudly displayed mementos of the active lives and accomplishments of the Willner children and grandchildren like we were his own, posting new photographs of every high school and college graduation, every military promotion, every wedding, every new baby. Eddie's children and grandchildren visited Pepsi and Blue Eyes often.

In the end, it would be the sacrifices, the fight, and those who lost their lives in battle that would come to make its greatest mark on Eddie and Mike, that sobering reality that a nation had given up its sons and daughters to fight to save Europe and, ultimately, the world. And they would never forget the compassion the boys of Company D had shown them after they had endured the worst of mankind, acts of kindness that restored their faith in humanity in a story of boys coming of age and finding what mattered: faith, unity, unbreakable friendship, and about the triumph of good over evil.

CODA: SUPPER WITH UNCLE PEPSI

ONE BY ONE, Elmer, Fred, Vance, and Eddie passed away, until Pepsi was the only one left.

In 2016, at ninety-seven years old, having long since sold the diner, Pepsi spent his days in his backyard cultivating his prized red buffalo tomatoes and, after nearly seventy years of marriage, still doting on Blue Eyes.

Eddie's grandson Michael, named for Eddie's "brother," Mike, a student at nearby MIT, had come by for his regular monthly visits to see his Uncle Pepsi. Though greatly slowed now, Pepsi still darted around the kitchen with the same joyful gusto he always had. Though his body was failing, his spirits were as high as ever as he navigated his kitchen, chattering away in his Boston accent, "'K, whaddya wan' me to fix ya?" and finally settling on cooking for Michael his signature Italian spaghetti and meatballs "the way Ma used to make it," perked up with garlic, basil, and, of course, tomatoes from his garden. He cooked, they talked, and they ate, Pepsi prying and advising, "Who're ya datin'? How's your ma? What are they feedin' ya in that college? Aw, you don't wanna eat that. I'll send you home with some spaghetti and *gahlic* bread."

THE BOYS IN THE LIGHT

They spent hours together laughing and joking around—somehow the story about pancakes and gun oil got funnier and funnier every time Pepsi told it.

After a few hours of lively conversation, Pepsi grew tired. Leaning forward, he labored to speak. At barely above a raspy whisper, he told Michael the story again about the old days "during the wah" when "I was a cook and I fed your gran'pa," and "Boy, was he skinny," and, shaking his head, "He didn't deserve that . . . and, well, we just had to take care of him."

Pepsi passed twenty-eight days later.

EPILOGUE

THE WAR

THE ADVENT OF the modern industrial age helped make World War II the most violent military conflict in human history. The breadth of human suffering inflicted at the hands of Germany's Nazis is almost too great to comprehend, the human destruction so vast, it is hard to fathom.

In just a few short years, the Nazis murdered an estimated 6 million Jews, wiping out the majority of Europe's prewar Jewish population. In addition to Europe's Jews, the citizens of Poland and the Soviet Union were especially brutalized. Poland lost about a fifth of its population. Tens of millions perished, mostly civilians. For the generations that immediately followed, the weight of this great suffering cast a long shadow that haunted and shaped people's attitudes about everyday life and how Western Civilization saw itself. The lessons learned about the horrors of war helped keep the world mostly at peace for the next fifty years.

For the Western Allies, the fight against Nazi Germany was truly one of good versus evil, and the resulting experience would shape the West's worldview for the next several generations. Germany's defeat would also set the stage for another dark chapter in human history, the Cold War between East and West, that would trap half of Europe behind an authoritarian Iron Curtain for the next forty-plus years.

About 16 million Americans served in uniform in World War II, roughly 11 percent of the population. Total U.S. losses topped 400,000, with almost 700,000 listed as wounded. Many more would bear the invisible scars of combat for the rest of their lives.

The UK would also lose almost 400,000 in uniform, and close to another 70,000 civilians from German "Blitz" terror bombings and, later, V-1 and V-2 rocket attacks that were launched against British cities. For their part, Canada and Australia would each lose 40,000 or more.

Germany itself paid a devastating price for following the Nazis' twisted ideology, losing some 5 million men in uniform and over 2 million more civilians, somewhere near 10 percent of Germany's entire population. After the war, the Soviets held over a million German soldiers in harsh conditions at forced labor camps, some until as late as 1956. Many German POWs held in captivity in the Soviet Union simply never returned.

The Allied invasion on D-Day remains the largest amphibious assault ever attempted in human history. Some 156,000 Allied soldiers took part in the initial attack, including 73,000 Americans, most of whom stormed ashore at the treacherous Omaha Beach. A staggering 23,000 airborne and glider forces were dropped behind enemy lines in the early hours of June 6, 1944, mostly from the American 82nd and 101st Airborne Divisions. Over 61,000 British and more than 21,000 Canadians stormed ashore on Gold and Juno Beaches. French partisans played a huge role in the success of the operation by con-

EPILOGUE

ducting sabotage operations that prevented a swift German response. Some 9,000 Allied soldiers died or were wounded on D-Day itself, including 2,500 Americans killed, most on Omaha Beach. U.S. Army Rangers suffered a casualty rate that day of about 70 percent, the highest among the Allies. But it was French civilians who paid the highest price on D-Day and in the days that followed with as many as 20,000 thought to have died, mostly as a result of Allied bombing raids.

The Battle of the Bulge was the largest and bloodiest single battle fought by the United States in World War II. Hitler's last-ditch, high-stakes gamble to hold on to his Thousand-Year Reich failed, in part due to a lack of gasoline to fuel his tanks. The United States would lose an estimated 20,000 killed, with German losses estimated at over twice that number. Hitler's surprise attack remains one of the greatest intelligence failures in U.S. military history.

At the end of the day, the U.S. Army prevailed thanks to the heroics of bands of isolated small groups of men cut off from their headquarters and led by junior officers, sergeants, and even young soldiers themselves. It was these soldiers who showed incredible bravery and knocked Hitler's carefully calculated attack timetable off schedule.

Destroying Hitler's industrial might came at a catastrophically high cost, as the number of U.S. Air Force pilots and crews lost in air action over Europe totaled a staggering 79,265 Americans. For its part, the "forgotten" Fifteenth Air Force, based in Italy (often overshadowed by the exploits of its larger counterpart, the Eighth Air Force, which flew missions from the UK), lost 21,671 personnel killed, wounded, or taken prisoner, including the loss of the Lindell crew. The Fifteenth is credited with knocking out much of the Axis's refining capability, including the two synthetic refineries at Blechhammer, ultimately bleeding the German army dry of precious gasoline and turning the tide of the war in the Allies' favor, especially during the Battle of the Bulge.

3RD ARMORED DIVISION

During its 1,460-mile drive across Europe, the 3rd Armored Division is said to have destroyed more tanks, inflicted more losses, and taken more German prisoners than any other U.S. armored division during the war. But it came at a high cost of over 2,500 fallen and over 640 Sherman tanks destroyed and another 700 knocked out, repaired, and put back into action at a loss rate of 580 percent, again higher than any other U.S. armored division. The division took over 76,000 prisoners, almost five times more than the number of men in the division itself. The 3rd Armored Division was the only U.S. division to lose its commander in combat in Europe, the first to breach the Siegfried Line and cross into Germany, and the first to capture a major German city (Cologne), and it holds the record for the longest one-day advance: a 101-mile dash into central Germany on March 29, 1945, one day before General Rose was killed.

D COMPANY, 32ND ARMORED REGIMENT

> *I know that no one outside our little group cares what we did. It was not different from what others saw in their thousands. Our day has passed; ours is an old war now. The edges of memory have gone soft; we can hear the engines only in the distance. As with most ordinary men, our deeds died before we did. And yet they were our deeds and will be so until the last of us is gone.*
>
> —Stuart Thayer, Company D loader

EPILOGUE

D Company lost thirty-four soldiers killed in action, about 24 percent of its assigned strength. Its total casualty rate was near 100 percent, with only a handful making it all the way from D-Day to the linkup with Eddie and Mike.

Some tankers, like Private Abernathy, Tec 5 Sylvester Rothstein, and Private "Big Smith," were killed after Eddie and Mike had joined the unit and just weeks before the end of the war.

THE HOLOCAUST

In 1933, there were 9 million Jews in Europe, which made up more than 60 percent of the world's Jewish population. Just twelve years later, two-thirds of them had been murdered by the Nazis. Approximately 6 million Jews perished in the Holocaust.

In addition to targeting Jews, the Nazis also killed an estimated 250,000 to 500,000 Roma/Sinti and thousands of others, including gays, Jehovah's Witnesses, the disabled, and the clergy.

According to the U.S. Holocaust Memorial Museum, between 1933 and 1945, Nazi Germany and its fascist allies established more than 44,000 concentration camps and other incarceration sites, including ghettos.

JOURNEY THROUGH THE HOLOCAUST

Eddie Willner and Mike Swaab survived incredible odds.

- Of the 638 Jews deported from Mönchengladbach, Germany, Eddie's hometown, only 27 are known to have survived the Holocaust.

- Of the 1,000 people in Transport 31 that deported Eddie, Auguste, and Siegfried from Drancy, France, to Poland, records show that only 13 survived the war.
- In total, of the 76,000 Jews and other prisoners deported in cattle cars from Drancy to the east, it is estimated that only around 2,000 survived.
- Of the 4,000 prisoners who set off on the frigid death march from Blechhammer (Auschwitz) to Gross-Rosen, around 1,320 survived.
- Life expectancy at Langenstein (Buchenwald) was six weeks. Eddie and Mike survived eight.
- Of the 3,000 who started the death march from Langenstein, only around 500 survived the march.
- More than 56,500 Dutch Jews were deported to Auschwitz, a little over 1,000 of whom survived.

THE CAMPS

Langenstein-Zwieberge

Of the more than seven thousand captives who were imprisoned in Langenstein during its existence, about two-thirds are estimated to have died due to "extermination through labor," malnutrition, exhaustion, accidents, and the death march.

After Eddie and Mike escaped, the Langenstein death march columns broke off into separate routes, the larger group ending at Wittenberg, near Dessau. Little is known about where they were headed or what finally happened to end the march in Wittenberg.

EPILOGUE

Of note: Louis Bertrand, a French resistance fighter who was an inmate at Langenstein, died in June 2013. It was his wish to have his ashes buried in the Langenstein concentration camp. "It was his way of saying," his son, Jean-Louis Bertrand said, "'I haven't forgotten the guys who died in this place, and I salute their memory.'"

For information on visiting Langenstein-Zwieberge in Halberstadt, Germany, the museum, the prison compound, and the tunnels, go to https://www.facebook.com/gdlangenstein or contact info-langenstein@stgs.sachsen-anhalt.de.

For information on visiting Blechhammer in Blachownia Śląska, Poland, the museum, and the *Judenlager* compound, go to https://www.facebook.com/blechhammer1944 or contact Ed Haduch at ehaduch@gmail.com.

For information on visiting Freyneux, Belgium, and the Manhay History Museum 44, located in Grandmenil-Manhay, go to http://www.mhm44.be/.

RESTING PLACE

Mike Swaab was buried in the Netherlands.

Elmer Hovland was buried in Luverne, Minnesota; Pepsi DeCola in Waltham, Massachusetts; Fred Headrick in Chattanooga, Tennessee; and James Vance in Canton, Georgia.

Eddie Willner was buried in Arlington National Cemetery (Section 60, Grave 15), the only grave on the ANC grounds inscribed with "Auschwitz Survivor." In essence, his gravestone stands as the one and only marker that represents not just Eddie but twenty-six members of the Willner family murdered in the Holocaust.

THE BOYS IN THE LIGHT

Eddie's headstone is featured on Arlington National Cemetery's Walk of Honor Tour, which includes notable figures in World War II. His story educates visitors about his journey through the camps and about Elmer, Pepsi, and the rest of the great American boys of Company D who saved him.

ACKNOWLEDGMENTS

This book would not have been possible without the contributions of a number of people and organizations from across the globe.

My first thanks go to my "cast of characters." It was my deep privilege to have personally known Elmer Hovland, Pepsi DeCola, and Fred Headrick, not to mention my uncle Mike Swaab and, of course, my own father, Eddie Willner: ordinary young men who came of age in a time of turmoil, who forged unbreakable bonds of brotherhood as they faced tragedy and triumph. Without their willingness to share their experiences and memories, this story would not have been possible.

Fred Headrick was a gold mine of information. I was extraordinarily lucky that Fred saved nearly everything related to Company D's time in the war. In addition to the things he personally collected, he became the unofficial repository for other D Company veterans. When they were aging and didn't know what to do with their mementos—their memoirs, photographs, letters and telegrams, scrapbooks and newspaper clippings—they gave them to Fred, and when Fred was getting on in years and he didn't know what to do with his collection, he entrusted them to my family.

ACKNOWLEDGMENTS

I am deeply indebted to Stuart Thayer, whose meaningful recollections of D Company provided background and perspective. I treasured my conversations and time with Elmer Hovland, a humble man of great character. Pepsi DeCola was a pure joy to know. He was as deep as he was loving, and his humor never failed to illuminate a room.

I am especially grateful to the families who welcomed me into their lives and supplied me with critical materials. First on that list are the Hovlands: Jon, Char, Steve, Chris, and Mark, for their generosity of spirit and unending patience in helping me to find documents, letters, and photographs and for the details of their own conversations with Elmer. To the DeCola family, simply for their years of love and embracing this project; to Lieutenant Myers's family, most notably the Lettieris and Keeleys, who supplied me with documents and photos that helped me keep the memory of their great-uncle alive; and to Fred Headrick Jr. and Barbara Headrick.

I am profoundly grateful to the concentration camp survivors who gave eyewitness testimony to Nazi crimes, whose recollections help shed light on history and added perspective to this story. While it was no doubt painful to have to relive the inhumanity they were subjected to, they did so so that Nazi Germany's crimes against mankind were recorded for all to learn from. Special thanks to the survivors of Blechhammer (Auschwitz) and Langenstein (Buchenwald) concentration camps: Arno Lustiger, Ernst Koenig, Robert Clary, John Steiner, Simon Michalowicz, Peter Strum, Karl Demerer, Marcel Dejean, Louis De Wijze, Israel Rosengarten, Edward Gastfriend, Sam Silberberg, Paul Le Goupil, Bernard Klieger, Georges Petit, Sigmund Walder, Henry S., Henry G., Paul D., Alex H., Luzer Markowicz, Alberto Berti, Georg Jänecke, Louis Bertrand, Alter Wiener, H. G. Adler, and Ivan Ivanji.

ACKNOWLEDGMENTS

My research for this book was based on interviews, archives, and a step-by-step retracing of most of the sites chronicled in this story. Whether at Pepsi's home in Waltham, Massachusetts; in the Ardennes Forest or Freyneux in Belgium; or the Blechhammer North oil refinery in Blachownia Śląska, Poland, it was important for me to follow every lead, to stand on the bridge, the train ramp, the *Appellplatz*, to wander through the forest, to go into the tunnels, to walk the battlefields, to crouch inside an *Einmannbunker*, to stand on the bank of the Eine River.

In the United States and abroad, I am indebted to those institutions whose mission it is to memorialize the Holocaust, most notably the United States Holocaust Memorial Museum (USHMM), with special thanks to Megan Lewis for her research in the National Socialist Crimes files; to Steven Spielberg's USC Shoah Foundation, which interviewed my father, and for the remarkable work they have done in capturing survivor testimonies; and to the Fortunoff Video Archive for Holocaust Testimonies at Yale University Library. Thank you to the wonderful staff at the U.S. National Archives and Records Administration (NARA), including Jacob Lusk, Michael Hancock, Robin Cookson, Ryan Bass, Corbin Apkin, and Heather Sulier. At the Library of Congress, I am particularly grateful to Megan Harris for her work with the Veterans History Project; the team at the 3rd Armored Division Association Archives at the University of Illinois, namely Dina Allen and Grace Moran; and those who assisted me at the United States Army Military History Institute, the U.S. Army Center of Military History, the U.S. Army Heritage and Education Center, and the Dwight D. Eisenhower Presidential Library.

A big shout-out to the 3rd Armored Division Veterans Association, which gave me unlimited access to their World War II files—my deep appreciation goes to Don Duckworth, Charles McFetridge, Larry

ACKNOWLEDGMENTS

Klauser, and Lou Baczewski. Thank you to my fellow authors and attendees at the World War II Conference in Gettysburg who inspired me to bring this story to life; and to Lieutenant General Thomas Griffin Jr. and Mrs. Jane Griffin. Tom, who commanded the 3rd Armored Division from 1986 to 1988, was a great supporter of this project, a contributor, a mentor, and a friend.

I must pay tribute to Sergeant Frank Wollner, who carried a portable typewriter through the war and chronicled the 3rd Armored Division's trek through combat in the book *Spearhead in the West*.

My thanks to local hometown archives: the Rock County Heritage Foundation and Rock County Historical Society, Luverne, Minnesota; Marlene Mann at Luverne Public Schools; Lori Sorenson at the *Rock County Star Herald*, Luverne; Adam Bentz and Becky Anstine at the York County History Center in York, Pennsylvania; Amy Lucadamo at Gettysburg College; Andrew Dalton at the Adams Historical Society, Gettysburg; and the York County Historical Society. To the fliers, namely Jerry Whiting of the 485th Bomb Group Association; to the Lindell family; to Ed Cornelia for his devotion to the story of Art Lindell, and to the families of the crew of *Butch*.

A number of experts patiently answered my never-ending questions. First on that list is author Steve Zaloga, leading expert in World War II armored warfare and technology. Thanks also to Stephen Harding, author and former editor of *Military History* magazine (HistoryNet), for his insights, guidance, and friendship.

This book could not have been fully researched and vetted without the tremendous efforts of Serge and Beate Klarsfeld and the Beate Klarsfeld Foundation, who spent decades piecing together evidence of atrocities, which they published in a massive volume that lists the 76,000 names and backgrounds of every passenger in every convoy that deported Jews from France, the majority of whom went directly to their deaths at Auschwitz. Likewise, Danuta Czech painstakingly

ACKNOWLEDGMENTS

assembled records from onion skin and yellowed papers, which were published in tomes of historical evidence to help survivors identify what might have happened to their loved ones. Both the Klarsfelds and Czech and organizations like JewishGen have provided findings of inestimable value to survivors and historians.

In Poland, special thanks to researcher Dr. Teresa Wontor-Cichy; Dr. Wojciech Płosa, head of archives at the Auschwitz-Birkenau State Museum in Oświęcim; and Szymon Kowalski; and to the team at the Auschwitz-Birkenau Research Center. In Łazy, I am grateful to Pani, Beate Dryja, my interpreter Marcin Bergier, and Czesław Karolczyk and the Instytut Pamięci Narodowej (Institute of National Remembrance), the Commission for the Prosecution of Crimes against the Polish Nation, and to POLIN Museum of the History of Polish Jews.

In Blechhammer, sincere thanks to two special historians who played a seminal role in my research, for their years of collaboration and valuable contributions: Edward Haduch, deputy chairman of the Blechhammer 1944 Association, and Marcin Kopytko of the Museum of the Silesian Battle for Fuel "Blechhammer-1944" in Kedzierzyn-Koźle. My thanks also to Aleksandra Kobielec and Dominik Alberski of Muzeum Gross-Rosen, and Bogusława Tartakowska and Danuta Drywa of Muzeum Stutthof.

In Germany, archivist Gerd Lamers of Stadtarchiv Mönchengladbach was instrumental to my research. Thanks also to Janine Keulertz. I must also recognize regional historian Günther Erckens, who spent many years compiling records for two massive volumes about Jewish life in MG. My appreciation also to Bernard Scherger, Armin Schuster, Irmgard and Rolf Tophoven, and Dr. Elisabeth Friese for their research on the vanished Jewish communities of Mönchengladbach, Grefrath, and Kempen.

Thanks to the Duisberg Archives, mostly notably to Dr. Sabine Eibl and Dr. Jörg Franzkowiak; and to the Arolsen Archives International

ACKNOWLEDGMENTS

Center on Nazi Persecution and International Tracing Service; the Bundesarchiv; Deutsches Historisches Museum; Landesarchiv Berlin; Landesarchiv Baden-Württemberg; Staastarchiv Ludwigsburg; the State Criminal Police Office of Baden-Württemberg; and the Stuttgart Public Prosecutor's Office on Nazi crimes, for war crimes records and tribunals.

In Langenstein, Dr. Nicolas Bertrand, Dr. Gero Fedtke, Gesine Daifi, and their dedicated team at the Langenstein-Zwieberge Memorial Museum have assisted me for years. Their commitment to preserving the concentration camp, the Project Malachit tunnels, and the stories of those who lived and died there is remarkable. Today one can still visit the grounds and the tunnels. In Welbsleben, thanks to Mayor Paul Geppert for his roundtable discussions in Holocaust awareness programs.

In Belgium, thanks to my friend Eddy Monfort, Freyneux historian and author. The Manhay History Museum, located in nearby Grandmenil and curated by the local townspeople to ensure the deeds of those young Americans are not forgotten, is one of the best World War II museums I have ever seen. Thanks also for the support of Chris Arsenault at Henri Chappelle Cemetery, and to the State Archives of Belgium.

In France, I must recognize Mémorial de la Shoah and the locals who assisted with research in Ortaffa. In the Netherlands, thanks to the NIOD Institute for War, Holocaust and Genocide Studies. In the UK, the Imperial War Museum, and Paul Johnson at the National Archives, Kew. I am grateful to Federica Tomaino for her help with Italian translations.

And in Israel, special thanks to Yad Vashem, and also to Dr. Lily Kahn, University College London, for her research and Yiddish translations, and to my friend Liz Margalit for her help and encouragement.

ACKNOWLEDGMENTS

I am grateful for my phenomenal agent, Mackenzie Brady Watson, at the Stuart Krichevsky Literary Agency, who is a relentless champion of social progress, and to my editor extraordinaire at Dutton, Cassidy Sachs, to Brent Howard, and to the whole Dutton team who embraced this story.

To those who read my early drafts and supported me through every phase of this process, my cheering team: Juliet and Neil Campbell, and Anne and Warren Grawemeyer.

I could not have written this book without the support of my family. I was fortunate that my father, Eddie, shared his past, which is not always the case with Holocaust survivors who lived with the ghosts they wanted to forget. I am indebted to my mother, Hanna, for her support and translations; to my uncle Mike, a loving soul who just wanted to live a normal life after the camps; and to Mia Van Velzen, Mike's daughter in the Netherlands, who helped navigate Dutch archives and supplied me with dozens of personal files and recollections.

My research and understanding of the context of some deeply personal events would not have been complete without the contributions of my brothers, Dr. Colonel (Ret.) Albert Willner and Michael Willner, whose own research and dedication to this story were critical to bringing it to life. I am thankful for their reviews, critiques, and support every step of the way. To my other siblings, Marcel, Maggy, and Sachi, I thank them for their insights and love.

My children and in-laws, and my nieces and nephews, have filled my life with joy and great confidence in the next generation. Thanks especially to Michael, Ryan, and Natalie Cadena, who assisted with website design and technical guidance.

A huge thanks to my partner on this journey, my husband, who helped me shape and reshape my drafts as we lived and worked around the world.

ACKNOWLEDGMENTS

And finally, to the millions of young Allied men and women who served and fought in World War II. To the tankers, the fliers, the sailors, the infantry. They answered the call so we could live in a world of peace and prosperity. We stand on their shoulders and must honor their sacrifice by protecting the democracy they so gallantly fought for.

—Nina Willner, July 2025

NOTES

CHAPTER ONE: AMERICAN INNOCENCE

5 **a million other Norwegians:** "Immigration to the United States, 1851–1900: The Norwegians," *Immigration and Relocation in U.S. History*, Library of Congress, accessed September 29, 2024, https://www.loc.gov/classroom-materials/immigration/scandinavian/the-norwegians/.
6 **as far as you could go:** Steve Hovland, interview with author, May 20, 2018.
6 **farm just outside Kenneth:** Warren Upham, *Minnesota Geographic Names: Their Origin and Historic Significance*, vol. 17 (Saint Paul: Minnesota Historical Society, 1920), 467.
6 **population 118, a tranquil town:** U.S. Census Bureau, *Minnesota, Population of Counties by Minor Civil Divisions, 1920 to 1940*, 547.
6 **the land they had left:** Washington State University Libraries, "German and Scandinavian Immigrants in the American Midwest," Gilded Age and Progressive Era, accessed September 29, 2024, http://digitalexhibits.libraries.wsu.edu/exhibits/show/2016sphist417/immigration/germans-and-scandinavians.
6 **the Hovlands stayed on:** S. Hovland, interview with author, May 20, 2018.
7 **the family's first clock:** Jon Hovland, interview with author, April 29, 2018.
7 **more important than one individual:** S. Hovland, interview with author, May 20, 2018.
8 **learned how to swim:** Chris Hovland, note to author, September 10, 2018.
8 **grounded in faith:** S. Hovland, interview with author, May 20, 2018.
9 **little-tough-guy:** Louis Sammy "Pepsi" DeCola, interview with author, June 4, 2011.
10 **cooking and eating:** L. DeCola interview.
10 **diner, as it turned out:** L. DeCola interview.
10 **Mama's sweet little tomato boy:** L. DeCola interview.
11 **Some 15 million:** Irving Bernstein, "Chapter 5: Americans in Depression and War," U.S. Department of Labor, https://www.dol.gov/general/aboutdol/history/chapter5.

NOTES

11   **Nels had scraped together:** S. Hovland, interview with author, May 20, 2018.
11   **"We're not giving up":** L. DeCola, interview with author, June 4, 2011.

CHAPTER TWO: A GERMAN JEWISH BOY

13   **named Monks Gladbach:** Günter Erckens, *Juden in Mönchengladbach*, Band 1 (Mönchengladbach: Stadtarchiv, 1988), 19–21.
13   **the city for seven generations:** Günter Erckens, *Juden in Mönchengladbach*, Band 2 (Mönchengladbach: Stadtarchiv, 1989), 484–85.
14   **clothing factories and weaving mills:** Note: Jews owned twenty-two of the city's ninety-eight clothing factories. *The Encyclopedia of Jewish Life Before and During the Holocaust*, vol. 2 (New York: NYU Press, 2001), 836–37.
14   **first appeared in MG:** Klaus-Dieter Alicke, *Aus der Geschichte der Jüdischen Gemeinden im deutschen Sprachraum*, https://www.xn--jdische-gemeinden-22b.de/index.php/home.
14   **full legal rights as citizens:** Peter Hayes, *Why?* (New York: W. W. Norton, 2017), 37.
14   **nearly 1,400 Jews:** MG population: 167,000. Alicke, *Aus der Geschichte der Judischen Gemeinden im deutschen Sprachraum*.
14   **middle-class family:** Maria Zahnen written testimony to German legal authorities, September 1957, Willner Family Archives.
14   **allegiance was, first and foremost:** Eddie Willner, conversations with author, 1977–1982.
15   **on the first floor:** Eddie Willner, conversations with author.
15   **a silver family menorah stood:** Eddie Willner, conversations with author.
15   **play Santa Claus:** Eddie Willner, interviewed by Esther Finder, Jewish Survivor, USC Shoah Foundation, June 22, 1997, Falls Church, Virginia, https://vha.usc.edu/testimony/30082?from=search&seg=7.
16   **World War I veteran:** Eddie Willner, interviewed by Esther Finder, June 22, 1997.
16   **Iron Cross for valor:** Cross of Honor for Frontline Combatants: *Siegfried Willner, Im Namen des Fuhrers (UML) und Reichskanzlers* (certificate of decoration), Willner Family Records.
16   **distinguished service fighting:** Eddie Willner, conversations with author.
16   **both the Eastern and Western:** Siegfried Willner's World War I Germany Army Service Record, Willner Family Records.
16   **representative for a silk-tie company:** Maria Zahnen written statement to West German Authorities, July 1960, Willner Family Archives.
17   **counterbalance to Siegfried's reserve:** Eddie Willner, conversations with author.
17   **Auguste adored her:** Eddie Willner, conversations with author.
17   **bone china plates:** *Wohnungseinrichtung und Inhalt der Wohnung der Eheleute Siegfried und Auguste Willner*, Stadtarchiv Duisburg, Duisburg, Germany, Willner Family Archives.
18   **his *kleinen Süßen*:** Berta Winter to Auguste, undated letter, Willner Family Archives.
18   **Opa Josef encouraged:** Eddie Willner, conversations with author.

NOTES

19 **Eddie stand at attention:** Eddie Willner, interviewed by Neal Goldenberg, Oral History Interview, March 15, 1987, Jewish Community Council of Greater Washington Oral History Collection, United States Holocaust Memorial Museum, https://collections.ushmm.org/search/catalog/irn511576.
19 **take it like a man:** Eddie Willner, conversations with author.
20 **penned a letter:** Eddie Willner, letter written to father, Siegfried Willner, Willner Family Archives.

CHAPTER THREE: PATRIOTS AND PARASITES

22 **right-wing nationalist:** Volker Ullrich, *Hitler: Ascent, 1889–1939* (New York: Vintage Books, 2016), 37–39, 42, 94–101.
23 **they had been victimized:** Ullrich, *Hitler: Ascent*, 205–8.
23 **he and he alone:** Peter Hayes, *Why?* (New York: W. W. Norton, 2017), 61.
23 **showed Jews fought:** Günter Erckens, *Juden in Mönchengladbach*, Band 1 (Mönchengladbach: Stadtarchiv, 1988), 365.
23 **of some 100,000:** Hayes, *Why?*, 53.
23 **eight male cousins:** Erckens, *Juden in Mönchengladbach*, Band I, 363–4.
23 **Jews had shirked:** Hayes, *Why?*, 53.
23 **less than 1 percent:** Hayes, *Why?*, 48–50, 55, 65–67; "German Jewish Population 1933," Holocaust Encyclopedia, United States Holocaust Memorial Museum, https://encyclopedia.ushmm.org/content/en/article/germany-jewish-population-in-1933.
23 **Help me rid the country:** Robert Clary, interviewed by Merle Goldberg, Jewish Survivor, Visual History Archive, September 12, 1994, USC Shoah Foundation, https://vha.usc.edu/testimony/95.
24 **destroy the Jews:** Ian Kershaw, *Hitler: 1889–1936: Hubris* (New York: W. W. Norton, 2000), 125–6.
24 **"removal of the Jews altogether":** "Hitler's First Writing on 'the Jewish Question,' September 16, 1919," Report of Corporal Adolf Hitler to Captain Karl Mayr, *Famous Trials, Accounts and Materials for 100 of History's Most Important Trials by Professor Douglas O. Linder*, University of Missouri–Kansas City School of Law, https://famous-trials.com/hitler/2530-hitler-s-first-writing-on-the-jewish-question-1919.
24 **"We'll beat our way":** Ullrich, *Hitler Ascent*, 113–16.
24 **Henry Ford, a virulent antisemite:** Henry Ford, *The International Jew: The World's Foremost Problem* (Dearborn, MI: Dearborn Independent, 1920), https://www.thehenryford.org/collections-and-research/digital-collections/artifact/488496/.
24 **scathing racist diatribe:** Khalid Elhassan, "These Corporations Committed the Ultimate Evil," Historycollection.com, June 7, 2021, https://historycollection.com/these-corporations-committed-the-ultimate-evil/.
24 **portrait of Ford:** Michael Dobbs, "Ford and GM Scrutinized for Alleged Nazi Collaboration," *Washington Post*, November 30, 1998, https://www.washingtonpost.com/wp-srv/national/daily/nov98/nazicars30.htm.
24 **"Ford as my inspiration":** Ullrich, *Hitler Ascent*, 176; Daniel Schulman, "America's Most Dangerous Anti-Jewish Propagandist," *Atlantic*, November 7, 2023, https://www.theatlantic.com/ideas/archive/2023/11/henry-ford-anti-semitism/675911/.

NOTES

24 **convicted of treason:** Hitler was convicted for his role in the ill-fated Munich beer hall putsch coup attempt. Ullrich, *Hitler: Ascent*, 159–64.
25 **"contaminates everything he touches":** "Extracts from *Mein Kampf* by Adolf Hitler," Yad Vashem World Holocaust Remembrance Center, https://www.yadvashem.org/docs/extracts-from-mein-kampf.html.
25 **"the personification of the devil":** "Extracts from *Mein Kampf.*"
25 **Jesus was an Aryan warrior:** Mikael Nisson, *Christianity in Hitler's Ideology, the Role of Jesus in National Socialism* (Cambridge, UK: Cambridge University Press, 2024).
25 **case for genocide:** Ullrich, *Hitler: Ascent*, 178; Kershaw, *Hitler: 1889–1936.*
25 **needed to be "exterminated":** Ullrich, *Hitler: Ascent*, 178.
25 **economic collapse and a series:** Hayes, *Why?*, 55, 70; Ullrich, *Hitler: Ascent*, 316.
25 **2.6 percent of the vote:** Ullrich, *Hitler: Ascent*, 213.
25 **largest political party:** Hayes, *Why?*, 55, 70; Ullrich, *Hitler: Ascent*, 290, 316.
25 **droves of unemployed:** Hayes, *Why?*, 55.
25 **disaffected young men:** Hayes, *Why?*, 69; Ullrich, *Hitler: Ascent*, 223, 233, 245.
25 **message of salvation:** Ullrich, *Hitler: Ascent*, 223, 233, 245.
25 **almost 3 million:** Ullrich, *Hitler: Ascent*, 431–32.
25 **process them fast enough:** Ullrich, *Hitler: Ascent*, 431–32.
25 **shouting, "*Deutschland erwache!*":** Johanna Willner, interview with author, February 2, 2022.
26 **a "witches' brew":** Hayes, *Why?*, 67.
26 **communist provocateurs and liberal:** Hayes, *Why?*, 69.
26 **atmosphere of intimidation:** Ullrich, *Hitler: Ascent*, 298.
27 **SA held book burnings:** Nazi book burnings included works by American writers like Ernest Hemingway and Helen Keller. "Book Burnings in Germany, 1933," *American Experience*, PBS, https://www.pbs.org/wgbh/americanexperience/features/goebbels-burnings/.
27 **swore an oath:** "German Military Oaths," *Holocaust Encyclopedia*, United States Holocaust Memorial Museum, https://encyclopedia.ushmm.org/content/en/article/german-military-oaths.
27 **ousted Jews from government:** Hayes, *Why?*, 73–77.
28 **Posters and pamphlets:** *Kriegsbriefe gefallener deutscher Juden, Mit Einem Geleitw von Franz Josef Strauss* (Herford, Germany: Busse Seewald Verlag, 1992).
28 **misshapen face and a large:** "Julius Streicher: Der Stürmer," *Holocaust Encyclopedia*, United States Holocaust Memorial Museum, https://encyclopedia.ushmm.org/tags/en/tag/der-sturmer.
28 **Words like "vermin" and "parasites":** G. G. Otto, *Der Jude als Weltparasit* (*The Jew as a World Parasite*) (Munich, Germany: Eher Verlag, 1943), Calvin University German Propaganda Archive, https://research.calvin.edu/german-propaganda-archive/weltparasit.htm.
28 **infect German minds:** "Julius Streicher and Der Stürmer," Michael D. Bulmash Collection, Kenyon College Digital Archive, https://digital.kenyon.edu/bulmash_streicher/.
28 **"*Die Juden sind*":** "Julius Streicher and Der Stürmer," Bulmash Collection.

NOTES

CHAPTER FOUR: RISE OF HATE

29 **returning a halfhearted salute:** Eddie Willner, interviewed by Esther Finder, Jewish Survivor, USC Shoah Foundation, Falls Church, Virginia, June 22, 1997, https://vha.usc.edu/testimony/30082?from=search&seg=7.
30 **silence for a full minute:** Albert Speer, *Inside the Third Reich* (New York: Simon & Schuster, 1997); V. Ullrich, *Hitler: Ascent*, 95–96, 297–98, 302.
30 **cult of personality:** Peter Hayes, *Why?* (New York: W. W. Norton, 2017), 69.
30 **in order for propaganda:** Ullrich, *Hitler: Ascent*, 101.
30 **claimed to be a messiah:** Thomas Weber, "Hitler Created a Fictional Persona to Recast Himself as Germany's Savior," *Smithsonian*, January 10, 2018, https://www.smithsonianmag.com/history/hitler-created-fictional-persona-to-recast-himself-as-germanys-savior-180967790/.
30 **"greatest liberator of humanity":** Hermann Rauschning, *Hitler Speaks: A Series of Political Conversations with Adolf Hitler on His Real Aims* (Whitefish, MT: Kessinger Publishing, 2010), 222.
30 **"I am convinced":** Adolf Hitler, *Mein Kampf*, 65.
30 **was a Christian movement:** Hayes, *Why?*, 69; Hitler speech, Passau, Germany, October 27, 1928, in Richard Steigmann-Gall, *The Holy Reich, Nazi Conceptions of Christianity, 1919–1945* (Cambridge, UK: University of Cambridge Press, 2003), 60–61, https://assets.cambridge.org/97805218/23715/sample/9780521823715ws.pdf.
31 **The film *Jud Süß*:** Nicholas Cull, David Culbert, and Davis Welch, *Propaganda and Mass Persuasion: A Historical Encyclopedia, 1500 to the Present* (Santa Barbara, CA: ABC-Clio, 2003), 205.
31 **granted full legal rights:** Hayes, *Why?*, 42.
31 **gone into decline:** Hayes, *Why?*, 45.
32 **boycotted Jewish businesses:** Frank Werner, *The Curse of Gurs: Way Station to Auschwitz* (Scotts Valley, CA: CreateSpace, 2012), 13–17.
32 **association with their Jewish:** Statement by Maria Zahnen, *Eidesstattliche Erklärung, Anlage zu ZK.*: 226 056, Mönchengladbach.
32 **books like *Der Giftpilz*:** "Antisemitic Children's Book Published by Julius Streicher," Michael D. Bulmash Collection, Kenyon College Digital Archive, https://digital.kenyon.edu/bulmash_streicher/.
32 ***Juden Raus!* (Jews, Get Out!):** "Juden Raus! Board Game," Wiener Holocaust Library, https://wienerholocaustlibrary.org/object/obj046/.
32 **teachers showed up:** U.S. Army Colonel (Retired) Frank Cohn, conversations with author.
32 ***Mädel* League uniforms:** Richard Evans, *The Third Reich in Power* (New York: Penguin, 2006), 264.
33 **"Our Führer loves children":** Tomi Ungerer, *Tomi: A Childhood Under the Nazis* (Boulder, CO: Roberts Rinehart, 1998), 73.
33 **New curricula immersed:** Cate Haste, *Nazi Women* (Channel 4 Books, 2001), 101.
33 **"They walk differently":** Fritz Fink, *Die Judenfrage im Unterricht (The Jewish Question in Education)* (Nuremberg: Stürmerverlag, 1937), Calvin University German Propaganda Archive, https://research.calvin.edu/german-propaganda-archive/fink.htm.

NOTES

33 **"Nordic men and lower":** Louis L. Snyder, *Encyclopedia of the Third Reich* (Cambridge, MA: De Capo Press, 1994), 79.
33 **"privilege" of honoring:** Eddie Willner, conversations with author.
34 **"wedding gift from the Führer":** Johanna Willner, interview with author, February 2, 2022.
35 **friends never came around:** Eddie Willner, conversations with author.
35 **lost his job:** M. Zahnen, official statement to West German Authorities, May 1958, Willner Family Archives; Eddie H. Willner, interviewed by Arwen Donahue and Gail Schwartz, Oral History Interview with Eddie Willner, United States Holocaust Memorial Museum, July 12, 2000, https://collections.ushmm.org/search/catalog/irn508471.
35 **kicked out of his school:** Eddie Willner, interviewed by Neal Goldenberg, Oral History Interview, March 15, 1987, Jewish Community Council of Greater Washington Oral History Collection, U.S. Holocast Memorial Museum, https://collections.ushmm.org/search/catalog/irn511576.

CHAPTER FIVE: PROMISE

38 **got only average marks:** Elmer Hovland, grade school report card, 1931, Hovland Family Records.
38 **several notorious criminals:** John Lauritsen, "Finding Minnesota: Did Bonnie and Clyde Rob a Bank in Okabena?," *CBS WCCO News*, January 31, 2024, https://www.cbsnews.com/minnesota/news/did-bonnie-and-clyde-rob-a-bank-in-okabena/.
38 **local pool hall:** S. Hovland, interview with author, May 20, 2018.
38 **loss of Ma:** Louis DeCola, *I Dedicate the Story of My Life to My Family*, unpublished manuscript, n.d.

CHAPTER SIX: KRISTALLNACHT

41 **Nazi storm troopers marched:** Peter Hayes, *Why?* (New York: W. W. Norton, 2017), 82–83.
41 **plundered and defaced:** Eddie Willner, interviewed by Ellen Epstein, Oral History Interview with Eddie Willner, May 25, 1989, United States Holocaust Memorial Museum, https://collections.ushmm.org/search/catalog/irn504739.
41 **disappeared into the bowels:** *The Encyclopedia of Jewish Life Before and During the Holocaust*, vol. 2 (New York: NYU Press, 2001) 863–67.
42 **on the Mönchengladbach synagogue:** Benjamin Rosendahl, "Moenchengladbach," *Destroyed German Synagogues and Communities*, http://germansynagogues.com/index.php/synagogues-and-communities?pid=54&sid=905:moenchengladbach.
42 **went up in flames:** Erckens, *Juden in Mönchengladbach*, Band 1, 655.
42 **local firefighter tried to douse:** Eddie Willner, interviewed by Esther Finder, Jewish Survivor, USC Shoah Foundation, Falls Church, Virginia, June 22, 1997.
42 **furniture, including a piano:** Eddie Willner, interviewed by Ellen Epstein, Oral History Interview with Eddie Willner, United States Holocaust Memorial Museum, May 25, 1989.
42 **parents were evicted:** Eddie Willner, interviewed by Neal Goldenberg, Oral History Interview, Jewish Community Council of Greater Washington, United States Holocaust Memorial Museum, March 15, 1987.

NOTES

42 **four Jewish families:** Alicke, *Aus der Geschichte der Judischen Gemeinden im deutschen Sprachraum.*

42 **Josef was removed:** Eddie Willner, interviewed by Arwen Donahue and Gail Schwartz, Oral History Interview, United States Holocaust Memorial Museum, June 12–13, 2000.

43 **fined the German Jewish community:** Göring declared Jews responsible for Kristallnacht and levied a fine of one billion reichsmarks. "Kristallnacht: Background & Overview," *Jewish Virtual Library,* https://www.jewishvirtuallibrary.org/background-and-overview-of-kristallnacht.

43 **"final reckoning with the Jews":** L. Snyder, *Encyclopedia of the Third Reich* (Cambridge, MA: De Capo Press, 1994), 201.

43 **tried to sell:** M. Zahnen, written statement to West German Authorities, May 1958.

43 **new law that required:** Michael Burleigh, *The Racial State: Germany, 1933–1945* (Cambridge, UK: Cambridge University Press, 1991), 92–96.

43 **tried desperately to find:** Eddie Willner, interviewed by Esther Finder, Jewish Survivor, USC Shoah Foundation, Falls Church, Virginia, June 22, 1997, https://vha.usc.edu/testimony/30082?from=search&seg=7.

43 **neither fund his trip:** Siegfried Willner, letter to Association of Jewish War Veterans of USA, Willner Family Archives.

44 **MS *St. Louis* sailed:** "Voyage of the S.S. *Saint Louis,*" *Holocaust Encyclopedia,* United States Holocaust Memorial Museum, https://encyclopedia.ushmm.org/content/en/article/voyage-of-the-st-louis.

44 **Gestapo continued to build:** "Akten der Geheimen Staatspolizei Siegfried Willner" (Secret State Police Files Siegfried Willner), 1938, Stadtarchiv Duisburg, Duisburg, Germany.

44 **"have a heart attack":** Eddie Willner, interviewed by Ellen Epstein, Oral History Interview with Eddie Willner, United States Holocaust Memorial Museum, May 25, 1989, https://collections.ushmm.org/search/catalog/irn504739.

44 **faith in the kindness:** Eddie Willner, interviewed by Ellen Epstein, May 25, 1989.

CHAPTER SEVEN: BLUE RIBBON AMERICA

47 **1939 World's Fair:** Keri Blakinger, "A Look Back at Some of the Coolest Attractions at the 1939 World's Fair," *New York Daily News,* April 30, 2016, https://www.nydailynews.com/2016/04/30/a-look-back-at-some-of-the-coolest-attractions-at-the-1939-worlds-fair/; "Electricity and Domestic Bliss at Expo 1939 New York," *Bureau International des Expositions,* April 6, 2017, https://www.bie-paris.org/site/en/latest/blog/entry/electricity-and-domestic-bliss-at-expo-1939-new-york; Allison Marsh, "Elektro the Moto-Man," *IEEE Spectrum,* October 5, 2018. https://ieeexplore.ieee.org/document/8482432/keywords#keywords; Betsy Golden Kellem, "The Nimatron, the World's First Video Game Made Its Debut at the Westinghouse Pavilion at the New York World's Fair in 1939," *JSTOR Daily,* March 1, 2022.

47 **"Remember, remember always":** Franklin D. Roosevelt, "Speech to the Daughters of the American Revolution," Washington, DC, April 21, 1938, American Presidency Project, UC Santa Barbara, https://www.presidency.ucsb.edu/documents/remarks-the-daughters-the-american-revolution-washington-dc.

NOTES

48 **"We are a nation":** Franklin D. Roosevelt, "Campaign Address," Brooklyn, New York, November 1, 1940, American Presidency Project, UC Santa Barbara, https://www.presidency.ucsb.edu/documents/campaign-address-brooklyn-new-york.

48 **"our strength is our unity":** Franklin D. Roosevelt, "State of the Nation Address to Congress," Washington, DC, January 6, 1942, American Presidency Project, UC Santa Barbara, https://www.presidency.ucsb.edu/documents/state-the-union-address-1.

48 *Rhapsody in Blue*: Isaac Goldberg, *George Gershwin: A Study in American Music* (New York: Ungar, 1958).

49 **"a younger generation":** Franklin D. Roosevelt, "Speech to the Daughters of the American Revolution," Washington, DC, April 21, 1938, American Presidency Project, UC Santa Barbara.

50 **German American Bund, a vocal:** Sarah Kate Kramer, "When Nazis Took Manhattan," NPR, February 20, 2019, https://www.npr.org/sections/codeswitch/2019/02/20/695941323/when-nazis-took-manhattan; Rachel Lears, *Knock Down the House* (Netflix, 2019), YouTube, https://www.youtube.com/watch?v=YCSo2hZRcXk.

50 **ten thousand Jewish children:** Ken Burns, Lynn Novick, and Sarah Botstein, dirs., *The U.S. and the Holocaust*, NPR, 2022.

51 **to keep an open mind:** Franklin D. Roosevelt, "Fire Side Chat," September 3, 1939, American Presidency Project, UC Santa Barbara, https://www.presidency.ucsb.edu/documents/fireside-chat-13.

51 **"a gift," Nels said:** Elmer Hovland, conversation with author, April 9, 2004.

51 **three-mile, one-way walk:** S. Hovland, taped interview with Elmer Hovland, 2004, Hovland Family Records, Luverne, Minnesota.

51 **high school band:** "Seniors Present Novel Drama," *Luverne Echo High School Newspaper*, May 23, 1939.

51 **newspaper lauded him:** "Our Seniors," *Luverne Echo High School Newspaper*, April 18, 1939.

52 **bought a Model T:** S. Hovland, interview with author, May 20, 2018.

52 **yearbook quote was:** Elmer Hovland's Luverne 1939 High School senior yearbook class photo caption, *Luverne High School Yearbook*, Luverne, Minnesota.

52 **"Remove all sin":** Mary's prayer book. Elmer sent passages to the *Rock County Herald*.

53 **"take care of people":** L. DeCola, interview with author, October 6, 2007.

53 **"Aw, Jeezus, Sammy":** L. DeCola interview.

54 **demands became too much:** L. DeCola interview.

54 **Elmer graduated high school:** S. Hovland, interview with author, May 20, 2018; Luverne High School 1939 Year End Report Card, Hovland Family Records.

54 **Sammy graduated one year later:** L. DeCola, unpublished manuscript, n.d.

54 **at an assembly plant:** S. Hovland, interview with author, May 20, 2018.

54 **continued to pledge:** Franklin D. Roosevelt, "Fire Side Chat," September 3, 1939, American Presidency Project, UC Santa Barbara.

NOTES

CHAPTER EIGHT: ON THE RUN

56 **Joint Distribution Committee:** Eddie Willner, conversations with author.
56 **annihilation of the Jews:** "Extract from the Speech by Adolf Hitler (Made to the Reichstag)," January 30, 1939," Yad Vashem, citing N. H. Baynes, *The Speeches of Adolf Hitler* (London, 1942), 737–41.
56 **by the name "Israel":** "Law on the Alteration of Family and Personal Names, August 1938," *Holocaust Encyclopedia*, U.S. Holocaust Memorial and Museum, https://encyclopedia.ushmm.org/content/en/timeline-event/holocaust/1933-1938/law-on-alteration-of-family-and-personal-names.
57 **on the police list:** Eddie Willner, interviewed by Ellen Epstein, Oral History Interview with Eddie Willner, United States Holocaust Memorial Museum, May 25, 1989.
57 **prepared to apprehend him:** "Akten der Geheimen Staatspolizei Siegfried Willner" (Secret State Police Files Siegfried Willner), 1938, Stadtarchiv Duisburg, Duisburg, Germany.
57 **and they took off:** Eddie Willner, conversations with author.
57 **violating strict rules:** Maria Zahnen statement, July 1960.
57 **"watch over my children":** Josef Willner family Siddur, Hebrew translation courtesy of Dr. Lily Kahn, University College, London, March 2014.
57 **"Keep these things":** Eddie Willner, conversations with author.
58 **and seized everything:** Compensation decision, State of Düsseldorf, Compensation for Victims of National Socialist Persecution, Willner Family Archives.
58 **meticulously catalogued every single:** Neighbor's Statement, May 7, 1958, Stadtarchiv Duisburg, Willner Family Archives.
58 **École Moyenne de l'État:** Eddie Willner, conversations with author.
59 **Grand Rabbi of Brussels:** Eddie Willner, interviewed by Ellen Epstein, Oral History Interview with Eddie Willner, United States Holocaust Memorial Museum, May 25, 1989.
59 **French internment camps:** Camp de Gurs, Camp de Saint-Cyprien, Camp de Rivesaltes, "Willner Family Chronology," Willner Family Archives.
60 **slip under the barbed wire:** Eddie Willner, interviewed by Esther Finder, Jewish Survivor, USC Shoah Foundation, Falls Church, Virginia, June 22, 1997.

CHAPTER NINE: TRAINING

61 **"Never before has there been":** Franklin D. Roosevelt, "Message to Congress Requesting War Declarations with Germany and Italy," Washington, DC, December 11, 1941, American Presidency Project, UC Santa Barbara, https://www.presidency.ucsb.edu/documents/message-congress-requesting-war-declarations-with-germany-and-italy.
62 **Thrilled to bust out:** L. DeCola, unpublished manuscript, n.d.
62 **"I need a map":** L. DeCola, interview by Patrick Golden, "The Lost Boys: WWII Veteran Reunited with Concentration Camp Survivor He Helped Save," *Metro West Daily News*, November 11, 2002.
62 **the WACs, the WAVES:** "History at a Glance: American Women in World War II—On the Home Front and Beyond," National WWII Museum, New Orleans, https://www.nationalww2museum.org/students-teachers/student-resources/research-starters/women-wwii. Nearly 350,000 American women

NOTES

served in uniform in the Women's Army Auxiliary Corps and in the women's organizations of other services.

63 **"a fancy thing"**: "Elmer L. Hovland Collection," Veterans History Project, American Folklife Center, Library of Congress, https://www.loc.gov/item/afc2001001.94051/.

63 **a boy named Hendrickson:** S. Hovland, interview with author, May 20, 2018.

64 **"Arsenal of Democracy"**: "Take a Closer Look: America Goes to War, Dec. 7, 1941," National WWII Museum, New Orleans, https://www.nationalww2mu seum.org/students-teachers/student-resources/research-starters/america-goes-war-take-closer-look.

64 **from making cars to:** Ken Burns, Lynn Novick, "War Production," *The War*, PBS, https://www.pbs.org/kenburns/the-war/war-production.

64 **half a million parts:** Arthur Herman, *Freedom's Forge: How American Business Produced Victory in World War II* (New York: Random House, 2013), 221.

64 **every sixty-three minutes:** A. J. Baime, "How Detroit Factories Retooled During WWII to Defeat Hitler: America's Largest Industry Shifted from Making Cars to Bombers, Tanks and More—at Unparalleled Speed," History.com, March 19, 2020, https://www.history.com/news/wwii-detroit-auto-factories-retooled-homefront.

64 **Artistic Furniture Manufacturing Company:** Charles Davidow, interview with author, July 2024.

64 **even kitchen grease:** Adee Braun, "Turning Bacon into Bombs: The American Fat Salvage Committee," *Atlantic*, April 18, 2014, https://www.theatlantic.com/health/archive/2014/04/reluctantly-turning-bacon-into-bombs-during-world-war-ii/360298/.

65 **"Step right up, son"**: L. DeCola, conversation with author, April 11, 2010.

65 **for basic training:** Elmer Hovland Collection, Veterans History Project, American Folklife Center, Library of Congress.

65 **"learned to kill"**: Bernard Close, *Memories of World War II: New Friends Revive Old Memories* (unpublished manuscript, West Linn, Oregon), 9–29.

65 **"don't volunteer for anything"**: S. Hovland, interview with Elmer Hovland, 2004.

65 **"don't have a choice"**: Elmer Hovland Collection, Veterans History Project; E. Hovland, telephone conversation with author, February 20, 2003.

CHAPTER TEN: THE VINEYARDS

67 **could figure out:** Eddie Willner, conversations with author.

68 **a stone church:** The name of the church was L'Église Sainte-Eugénie, Ortaffa, France.

68 **would conceal the family:** Eddie Willner, interviewed by Ellen Epstein, Oral History Interview with Eddie Willner, United States Holocaust Memorial Museum, May 25, 1989.

68 **stomped barefoot, macerating:** Eddie Willner, interviewed by Ellen Epstein, May 25, 1989.

69 **bound for Paris:** Eddie Willner, interviewed by Esther Finder, Jewish Survivor, USC Shoah Foundation, Falls Church, Virginia, June 22, 1997; Serge Klarsfeld, *French Children of the Holocaust: A Memorial* (New York: Holocaust

NOTES

Publications, 1996), 57; Eddie Willner, interviewed by Neal Goldenberg, Oral History Interview, Jewish Community Council of Greater Washington, United States Holocaust Memorial Museum, March 15, 1987; and Erckens, "Juden in Mönchengladbach," Band 2, 389.

69 **police were gathering Jews:** Laurence Schram, "The Deportation of the Jews from the Nazi Transit Camps Drancy (France) and Malines (Belgium)," European Holocaust Remembrance Infrastructure (EHRI) Online Course in Holocaust Studies, https://training.ehri-project.eu/deportation-jews-nazi-transit-camps-drancy-france-and-malines-belgium.

CHAPTER ELEVEN: NEW YORK HARBOR

70 **Of the twenty-one male graduates:** Ken Burns and Lynn Novick, "War Production," *The War*, PBS, https://www.pbs.org/kenburns/the-war/war-production.
70 **New York harbor, tens of thousands:** L. DeCola, unpublished manuscript, n.d.
70 **Cunard Line's RMS *Aquitania*:** Roland W. Charles, *Troopships of World War II* (Washington, DC: Army Transportation Association, 1947), 310.
70 **goodbye to Pa:** L. DeCola, unpublished manuscript, n.d.

CHAPTER TWELVE: TRANSPORT 31

72 **tens of thousands of European Jews:** "Drancy," *Holocaust Encyclopedia*, United States Holocaust Memorial Museum, https://encyclopedia.ushmm.org/content/en/article/drancy.
72 **living or hiding out:** Eddie Willner, conversations with author.
72 **resettled and to work:** Eddie Willner, conversations with author; Eddie Willner, interviewed by Esther Finder, Jewish Survivor, USC Shoah Foundation, Falls Church, Virginia, June 22, 1997.
72 **rail company, SNCF:** "France Agrees Holocaust SNCF Rail Payout with US," BBC, December 5, 2014, https://www.bbc.com/news/world-europe-30351196.
72 **September 11, 1942:** Danuta Czech, *Auschwitz Chronicle: 1939–1945* (New York: Henry Holt, 1997), 237.
73 **into Transport 31:** Serge Klarsfeld, *Memorial to the Jews Deported from France, 1942–1944* (New York: B. Klarsfeld, 1983), 260–61; Serge Klarsfeld, *French Children of the Holocaust: A Memorial* (New York: New York University Press, 1996), 268–73.
73 **Telex XXVb-162 was sent:** Klarsfeld, *Memorial to the Jews Deported from France*, 261.
73 **was no ventilation:** Eddie Willner, interviewed by Ellen Epstein, Oral History Interview with Eddie Willner, United States Holocaust Memorial Museum, May 25, 1989.
73 **"Don't cry. I am here":** "Robert Clary Speaks as a Holocaust Survivor," YouTube, posted March 15, 2016, https://www.youtube.com/watch?v=Kn1r_9AJiF8.
73 **"when all this is over":** Eddie Willner, conversation with author.
73 **three agonizing days:** Czech, *Auschwitz Chronicle*, 237.
74 **not Germany but Kosel:** Eddie Willner, interviewed by Neal Goldenberg, Oral History Interview, Jewish Community Council of Greater Washington, United States Holocaust Memorial Museum, March 15, 1987.

NOTES

74 **SS guards shouted:** Edward Gastfriend, *My Father's Testament: Memoir of a Jewish Teenager, 1938–1945* (Philadelphia: Temple University Press, 1999), 90.
74 **"All males between the ages":** Eddie Willner, interviewed by Esther Finder, Jewish Survivor, USC Shoah Foundation, Falls Church, Virginia, June 22, 1997; Paul D. Holocaust Testimony (HVT-620), Fortunoff Video Archive for Holocaust Testimonies, Yale University, https://fortunoff.aviaryplatform.com/collections/5/collection_resources/689?u=t&keywords[]=Paul&keywords[]=P.
74 **men and boys spilled out:** Boleslaw Brodecki, interviewed by Linda G. Kuzmack, Oral History Interview with Boleslaw Brodecki, United States Holocaust Memorial Museum, September 18, 1989, https://collections.ushmm.org/search/catalog/irn504542.
74 **"*Raus! Schnell!*":** Eddie Willner, conversation with author.
75 **a boy soldier:** Eddie Willner, interviewed by Esther Finder, June 22, 1997.
75 **three hundred men and boys:** Czech, *Auschwitz Chronicle*, 237. Transport 31: "300 men chosen for Schmelt operations on September 12, 1942."
75 **carrying their loved ones:** Eddie Willner, interviewed by Esther Finder, June 22, 1997.
75 **led down the tracks:** "Extermination Procedure in the Gas Chambers," Auschwitz-Birkenau Memorial and Museum, https://www.auschwitz.org/en/history/auschwitz-and-shoah/the-extermination-procedure-in-the-gas-chambers/.
76 **seventy-eight women were selected:** Czech, *Auschwitz Chronicle*, 237.
76 **"We *want* you to work":** "Robert Clary Speaks."
76 **clothing on hooks:** "Robert Clary Speaks."
77 **Zyklon B, a powerful cyanide:** "Zyklon B," Jewish Virtual Library, https://www.jewishvirtuallibrary.org/zyklon-b.
77 **a poisonous gas:** Yisrael Gutman and Michael Berenbaum, eds., *Anatomy of the Auschwitz Death Camp* (Bloomington: Indiana University Press, 1998), 157–82.
77 **Hitler's Final Solution:** "The Wannsee Conference," Yad Vashem: The World Holocaust Remembrance Center, https://www.yadvashem.org/holocaust/about/final-solution-beginning/wannsee-conference.html.

CHAPTER THIRTEEN: SHIP TO ENGLAND

81 **stacked five high:** Belton Cooper, *Death Traps: The Survival of an American Armored Division in World War II* (Novato, CA: Presidio Press, 2003), 4.
82 **"I worry night and day":** William L. Anderson, letter, April 25, 1942, William L. Anderson Papers, Minnesota Historical Society, http://www2.mnhs.org/library/dindaids/00638.xml.
82 **time playing pinochle:** L. DeCola, unpublished manuscript, n.d.
83 **"can be a big brother":** L. DeCola, interview with author, July 13, 2013.
83 **"Zat your real name?":** L. DeCola, interview with author, July 13, 2013.
83 **nicknaming each other:** L. DeCola, interview with author, July 13, 2013.
84 **unusually long eyelashes:** Stuart Thayer's notes.
84 **Atlantic without incident:** Frank Woolner, *Spearhead in the West: The Third Armored Division, 1941–45* (Nashville, TN: Battery Press, 1980), 56.
85 **cabin of his ship:** S. Hovland, interview with author, April 21, 2019.

NOTES

85 **"Lord, we pray thee":** Elmer Hovland, conversation with author, April 9, 2004; Episcopal Church, Army and Navy Commission, *A Prayer Book for Soldiers and Sailors* (Frederick, MD: HardPress, 2024).

86 **Scabbard and Blade:** Special Collections & College Archives, Gettysburg College Musselman Library, Gettysburg, PA.

CHAPTER FOURTEEN: ŁAZY

87 **even the disabled:** "Euthanasia Program and Aktion T4," *Holocaust Encyclopedia*, United States Holocaust Memorial Museum, https://encyclopedia.ushmm.org/content/en/article/euthanasia-program.

87 **student Sophie Scholl:** "Sophie Scholl and the White Rose," National World War II Museum, New Orleans, February 22, 2020, https://www.nationalww2museum.org/war/articles/sophie-scholl-and-white-rose.

87 **"I ask you":** "The White Rose Project—Pamphlets," University of Oxford, http://whiteroseproject.seh.ox.ac.uk.

88 **In her defense:** John Simkin, "Biography of Sophie Scholl," Spartacus Educational, September 1997 (updated January 2020), https://spartacus-educational.com/GERschollS.htm.

88 **guillotined for the crime:** Simkin, "Biography of Sophie Scholl," Sophie Scholl and her brother were guillotined by Nazis, February 22, 1943.

88 **the Schmelt organization:** Robert Clary, interviewed by Hugh Earnhart, "Holocaust," Youngstown State University, Department of History, Oral History Program, https://jupiter.ysu.edu/search/d?SEARCH=Clary%2C+Robert%2C++1926.

88 **soldiers and some local auxiliary:** Czesław Karolczyk, Nowo Foundation and Instytut Pamięci Narodowej (Institute of National Remembrance), conversation with author, April 13, 2019.

88 **several hundred Jewish prisoners:** Czesław Karolczyk, conversation with author, April 13, 2019.

89 **repairing railroad tracks:** Eddie Willner, interviewed by Ellen Epstein, Oral History Interview with Eddie Willner, United States Holocaust Memorial Museum, May 25, 1989.

89 **expand the main highway:** Wolf Gruner, *Jewish Forced Labor Under the Nazis: Economic Needs and Racial Aims, 1938–1944* (Cambridge, UK: Cambridge University Press, 2006).

89 **heavy manual labor:** Eddie Willner, interviewed by Ellen Epstein, May 25, 1989.

89 **arrived in the camp:** Mike Swaab interview, "Personal Wartime History," *Lone Star Wing Newsletter* 11 (November 2000): 6–7.

89 **ten-minute walk:** Mike and Anne Frank may have gone to the same grade school. Mia Swaab, conversation with author, May 30, 2018.

89 **traumatized and terrified:** Mike Swaab, conversation with author, August 2, 1980.

89 **turnips and potatoes:** Eddie Willner, interviewed by Neal Goldenberg, Oral History Interview, Jewish Community Council of Greater Washington, United States Holocaust Memorial Museum, March 15, 1987.

90 **the salivating inmates:** M. Swaab, conversation with author, August 2, 1980.

90 **kept him focused:** M. Swaab interview, *Lone Star Wing Newsletter*.

NOTES

90 **Lessons came fast:** Mike Swaab, conversation with author, June 11, 1977.
90 **Certain guards were prone:** M. Swaab, conversation with author, June 11, 1977.
91 **worked on construction projects:** M. Swaab interview, *Lone Star Wing Newsletter*.
91 **they could improve their chances:** Eddie Willner, interviewed by Neal Goldenberg, Oral History Interview, Jewish Community Council of Greater Washington, United States Holocaust Memorial Museum, March 15, 1987.
91 **threatened with a beating:** Mike Swaab, conversation with author, June 11, 1977.
91 **quota of two hundred heels:** "Robert Clary Speaks as a Holocaust Survivor," YouTube, https://www.youtube.com/watch?v=Kn1r_9AJiF8.
91 **took full advantage:** Geoffrey P. Megargee, *The United States Holocaust Memorial Museum Encyclopedia of Camps and Ghettos, 1933–1945*, vol. 1 (Bloomington: Indiana University Press, 2009).
91 **Daimler-Benz, Porsche/Volkswagen, BMW:** David de Jong, *Nazi Billionaires: The Dark History of Germany's Wealthiest Dynasties* (New York: Mariner Books, 2022), 156, 166–67, 172–73, 176; "1933–1945: National Socialism and the War Economy," Siemens company website, https://www.siemens.com/global/en/company/about/history/company/1933-1945.html; "1937 to 1945— Founding of the Company and Integration into the War Economy," Volkswagen Group company website, https://www.volkswagen-group.com/en/volkswagen-chronicle-17351/1937-to-1945-founding-of-the-company-and-integration-into-the-war-economy-17354#; "Bayer, Key Facts," *Holocaust Encyclopedia*, U.S. Holocaust Memorial and Museum, https://encyclopedia.ushmm.org/content/en/article/bayer; "BMW during the Era National Socialist," BMW company website, https://www.bmwgroup.com/en/company/history/BMW-during-the-era-of-national-socialism.html; Herbert Mitgang, "Books of the Times, Mercedes Benz and Its Nazi Past," *New York Times*, August 23, 1990; "Our History. Our Responsibility," Mercedes Benz company website, https://group.mercedes-benz.com/company/tradition/company-history/75th-anniversary-of-the-end-of-world-war-ii.html; "History," Claims Conference: Conference on Jewish Material Claims Against Germany, https://www.claimscon.org/about/history/; Neil Gregor, *Daimler-Benz in the Third Reich* (New Haven, CT: Yale University Press, 1998), 276.
91 **IBM's German affiliate:** Edwin Black, *IBM and the Holocaust: The Strategic Alliance Between Nazi Germany and America's Most Powerful Corporation* (New York: Crown, 2001); David Turner, "Arming the Enemy: US Industry, Hitler and the Holocaust," *Jerusalem Post*, February 15, 2012, https://www.jpost.com/blogs/the-jewish-problem---from-anti-judaism-to-anti-semitism/arming-the-enemy-us-industry-hitler-and-the-holocaust-366097#google_vignette; Jack Beatty, "Hitler's Willing Business Partners," *Atlantic*, April 2001, https://www.theatlantic.com/magazine/archive/2001/04/hitlers-willing-business-partners/303146/.
92 **encouraged the boys:** Eddie Willner, conversations with author.
92 **188 names were read off:** Czech, *Auschwitz Chronicle*, 632.

NOTES

CHAPTER FIFTEEN: COMING ASHORE

94 **some 50,000 German troops:** David Roos, "D-Day: Facts on the Epic 1944 Invasion That Changed the Course of WWII," History.com, March 13, 2024, https://www.history.com/news/d-day-normandy-wwii-facts.

94 **156,000 Allied troops:** Roos, "D-Day: Facts."

94 **23,000 paratroopers dropped:** "D-Day: The Beaches," *US European Command,* https://dod.defense.gov/Portals/1/features/2016/0516_dday/docs/d-day-fact-sheet-the-beaches.pdf.

94 **some 9,000 Allied troops:** Katie Lang, "Five Things You Many Not Know about D-Day," Department of Defense, June 3, 2022, https://www.defense.gov/News/Feature-Stories/story/Article/3052217/5-things-you-may-not-know-about-d-day/.

95 **prepared to enter northern France:** L. DeCola, unpublished manuscript, n.d.

95 **they were scared:** Frank Woolner, *Spearhead in the West: The Third Armored Division, 1941–45* (Nashville, TN: Battery Press, 1980), 61.

95 **a lot of silent reflection:** L. DeCola, unpublished manuscript, n.d.

95 ***I wonder how many:*** Woolner, *Spearhead in the West,* 61.

96 **3rd Armored Division tanks spilled:** Cooper, *Death Traps,* xxii.

96 **"Look out, Hitler":** Stuart Thayer's notes.

CHAPTER SIXTEEN: AUSCHWITZ

97 **signs with black skulls:** Ed Haduch, Blechhammer 44 Association, interview with author, December 20, 2022.

98 ***"Arbeit Macht Frei":*** E. Haduch interview; Marcin Kopytko, Blechhammer 44 historian, interview with author, February 10, 2020; Mel Mermelstein, interviewed by Dr. Richard J. Prystowsky, Oral History Interview, United States Holocaust Memorial Museum, January 10, 1993, https://collections.ushmm.org/search/catalog/irn512013; Gastfriend, *My Father's Testament,* 114.

98 **a concrete wall:** Mike Swaab interview, "Personal Wartime History," *Lone Star Wing Newsletter* 11 (November 2000).

98 **conceal from the outside:** Eddie Willner, interviewed by Neal Goldenberg, Oral History Interview, Jewish Community Council of Greater Washington, United States Holocaust Memorial Museum, March 15, 1987.

98 **ensuring no one escaped:** Gastfriend, *My Father's Testament,* 113.

98 **gave the boys confidence:** Eddie Willner, conversations with author.

98 **"drop your things":** Simon Michalowicz, interviewed by R. Banczewska, Oral History Interview, United States Holocaust Memorial Museum, November 22, 1995, https://collections.ushmm.org/search/catalog/irn507198.

98 **Jewish camp elder:** M. Karl Demerer testimony, Yad Vashem Archives, O313655, February 15, 1973.

99 **protect the prisoners:** Robert Clary, *From the Holocaust to Hogan's Heroes: The Autobiography of Robert Clary* (Lanham, MD: Taylor Trade, 2007), 86.

99 ***"Lav moes. Leave most":*** Hebrew translation courtesy of Dr. Lily Kahn, University College, London, March 2014.

99 **confiscate the valuables:** Mel Mermelstein, interviewed by Dr. Richard J. Prystowsky, Oral History Interview, United States Holocaust Memorial Museum, January 10, 1993; M. Karl Demerer testimony, Yad Vashem Archives, O313655, February 15, 1973.

NOTES

99 **when needed to barter:** M. Karl Demerer testimony, Yad Vashem Archives, O313655, February 15, 1973.
100 **(prisoner) registration cards:** Ernst Koenig, conversation with author, July 12, 1982.
100 **simply wrote, *Schüler*, student:** M. Swaab, conversation with author, June 11, 1977.
100 **rumors of the shower gassings:** Eddie Willner, interviewed by Esther Finder, Jewish Survivor, USC Shoah Foundation, June 22, 1997.
100 **weren't coming out alive:** Eddie Willner, interviewed by Neal Goldenberg, Oral History Interview, Jewish Community Council of Greater Washington, United States Holocaust Memorial Museum, March 15, 1987.
101 **started spraying water:** Eddie Willner, interviewed by Esther Finder, June 22, 1997.
101 **slave laborers at Auschwitz III:** Czech, *Auschwitz Chronicle*, 188.
101 **largest Jewish forced-labor:** "Blechhammer," Auschwtiz-Birkenau Memorial and Museum, https://www.auschwitz.org/en/history/auschwitz-sub-camps/blechhammer/.
101 **prison barbers roughly plowing:** Louis de Wijze, *Only My Life: A Survivor's Story*, 2nd ed. (Catawba, 2007), 13–14.
101 **full head of hair:** Eddie Willner, conversations with author.
101 **pushed their heads down:** Clary, *From the Holocaust to* Hogan's Heroes, 83.
101 **finally ordered out:** Eddie Willner, interviewed by Esther Finder, Jewish Survivor, USC Shoah Foundation, June 22, 1997.
101 **uniform that didn't fit:** Paul D. Holocaust Testimony (HVT-620), Fortunoff Video Archive for Holocaust Testimonies, Yale University.
101 **cross-intersected to form:** Dr. Teresa Wontor-Cichy, Centrum Badań/Research Center, Państwowe Muzeum Auschwitz-Birkenau, conversation with author, April 12, 2019.
102 **"Left arm out!":** Eddie Willner, conversations with author.
102 **metal stamp with needles:** Israel J. Rosengarten, *Survival: The Story of a Sixteen-Year-Old Jewish Boy* (Syracuse, NY: Syracuse University Press, 1999), 133–35.
102 **tattoo marked a new beginning:** Eddie Willner, conversations with author.
102 **Romanian Jew Elie Wiesel:** Wiesel was the 1986 Nobel Prize winner and author of *Night*.
102 **Where up to 90 percent:** "Auschwitz 1940–45, The Killing Evolution," PBS, https://www.pbs.org/auschwitz/40-45/killing/.
103 **melting pot of Jews:** Clary, *From the Holocaust to* Hogan's Heroes, 83; Records of the Central Office of the Judicial Authorities of the Federal States for the Investigation of National Socialist Crimes (*Zentrale Stelle der Landesjustizverwaltungen zur Aufklärung Nationalsozialistischer Verbrechen*), Bundesarchiv B 162 / 8863.
103 **three-tiered wooden bunks:** Clary, *From the Holocaust to* Hogan's Heroes.
103 **one could lie:** Paul D. Holocaust Testimony (HVT-620), Fortunoff Video Archive for Holocaust Testimonies, Yale University.
103 **the single light bulb:** M. Swaab interview, *Lone Star Wing Newsletter*.
103 **SS rules, shouted, "Silence!":** Jack Mandelbaum audio testimony, Midwest Center for Holocaust Education, Overland Park, KS, https://mchekc.org/testimonial/jack-mandelbaum/.

NOTES

103 **by a piercing whistle:** Gastfriend, *My Father's Testament*, 116; Simon Michalowicz, interviewed by R. Banczewska, Oral History Interview, United States Holocaust Memorial Museum, November 22, 1995.

103 ***kapo* shouting, "*Alles raus!*":** Paul D. Holocaust Testimony (HVT-620), Fortunoff Video Archive for Holocaust Testimonies, Yale University.

104 **mad dash to the "bathhouse":** "Robert Clary, Hogan's Heroes Actor and Holocaust Survivor and Educator," USC Shoah Foundation, https://sfi.usc.edu/video/robert-clary.

104 **bread distribution lineup:** Gastfriend, *My Father's Testament*, 116.

104 **chaotic double time:** Paul D. Holocaust Testimony (HVT-620), Fortunoff Video Archive for Holocaust Testimonies, Yale University.

104 **square of coarse bread:** Zentrale Stelle, Bundesarchiv B 162 / 8863; Gastfriend, *My Father's Testament*, 117–18.

104 **tasted like sawdust:** Gastfriend, *My Father's Testament*, 117–18.

104 ***Appellplatz,* the roll call square:** Simon Michalowicz, interviewed by R. Banczewska, Oral History Interview, United States Holocaust Memorial Museum, November 22, 1995.

105 **a highly militarized supermax prison:** Eddie Willner, interviewed by Ellen Epstein, Oral History Interview with Eddie Willner, United States Holocaust Memorial Museum, May 25, 1989.

105 **Hitler's elite SS:** Zentrale Stelle, Bundesarchiv B 162 / 8863.

105 **two hundred handpicked guards:** "Companies and Prisoner Labour," Sub Camps of Auschwitz Project, https://subcamps-auschwitz.org/companies/.

105 **largely true believers:** "Robert Clary Speaks as a Holocaust Survivor," YouTube, 58:35, https://www.youtube.com/watch?v=Kn1r_9AJiF8.

105 **hardened their hearts:** Israel Gutman, ed., *Encyclopedia of the Holocaust*, vol. 3 (New York: Macmillan, 1990).

105 **(Captain) Otto Brossmann:** Zentrale Stelle, Bundesarchiv B 162 / 18175; Dachau Detachment, Identification Document of Prisoner Otto Broszmann, February 4, 1947.

105 **avowed Nazi patriot:** "Companies and Prisoner Labour," Sub Camps of Auschwitz Project, https://subcamps-auschwitz.org/companies/; Franciszek Piper, *Auschwitz Prisoner Labor* (Auschwitz-Birkenau State Museum, 2001), 84–87.

105 **Klipp, carried a leather whip:** SS Private Franz Ludwig, Seventh Totenkopf Wach Battalion (Blechhammer) testimony, Declassified U.S. Army Investigation on Nazi War Crimes in Poland, Karta Informacyjnac, Instytut Pamięci Narodowej, Warsaw (IPN GK 184/ 262).

105 **Silesian coal miner:** *Law Reports of the Trials of War Criminals*, United Nations War Crimes Commission, vol. 2, *The Belsen Trial* (London: His Majesty's Stationary Office, 1947); "30 Germans Guilty of Camp Murders," Associated Press, November 16, 1945, *New York Times* report, http://www.bergenbelsen.co.uk/Pages/Staff/StaffPhotographs.asp?CampStaffID=58&index=21.

105 **butcher shop employee:** *Law Reports of the Trials of War Criminals*; "30 Germans Guilty," Associated Press.

106 **nickname "the Goons":** Ernst Koenig, conversation with author, July 12, 1982.

106 **"Don't let your eyes":** E. Koenig conversation.

NOTES

106 **walked up and down:** Mike Swaab conversation with author, July 2, 1978.
106 **removed his cap:** Willy Berler, *Durch die Hölle: Monowitz, Auschwitz, Groß-Rosen, Buchenwald* (Oelbaum Verlag, 2003), 60.
106 **did not make eye contact:** Paul D. Holocaust Testimony (HVT-620), Fortunoff Video Archive for Holocaust Testimonies, Yale University.
106 **With a flick:** Myron B. Holocaust Testimony (HVT-1507), Gross Center for Holocaust and Genocide Studies, Fortunoff Video Archive for Holocaust Testimonies, Yale University Library, June 20, 1990, https://fortunoff.aviaryplatform.com/collections/5/collection_resources/1571?u=t&keywords[]=myron.
106 **Rules were made clear:** Stanislav Zamecnik, *Das War Dachau* (Luxembourg: Stiftung Comité International de Dachau, 2002), 406–11; "Lagerordnung," Disciplinary and Penal Code IMG XXVI, Dok. 775-PS, 291–96.
107 **ten of his friends:** Ernst Koenig, interview with author, July 12, 1982.

CHAPTER SEVENTEEN: BAPTISM

108 **come ashore in their tanks:** Frank Woolner, *Spearhead in the West: The Third Armored Division, 1941–45* (Nashville, TN: Battery Press, 1980), 18.
108 **They felt confident:** Stuart Thayer's notes; Cooper, *Death Traps*, xii.
108 **bocage hedgerows of Villiers-Fossard:** University of Illinois Archives, https://archives.library.illinois.edu/about-us/program-areas/association-archives/3rd armor/32nd-armored-regiment/; Cooper, *Death Traps*, 8–9, 11–12.
108 **suffered their first casualties:** D Company saw their first casualties on June 29 and 30. "32nd Armored Regiment, Call Sign: 'Oriole,'" University of Illinois Archives, https://archives.library.illinois.edu/about-us/program-areas/association-archives/3rdarmor/32nd-armored-regiment/.
109 **"when it all fell apart":** S. Thayer.
109 **veritable death traps:** Cooper, *Death Traps*, 15.
109 **further traumatized upon hearing:** S. Thayer.
109 **seared through the Sherman:** Correspondence between Haynes Dugan and WWII tanker Walter Stitt.
110 **first in their company:** S. Thayer; "War Diary, Co. 'D,' 32d Armored Regiment."
110 **seated front row center:** Company D, 32 Regiment, 3rd Armored Division group photo, Fred Headrick's archives.
110 **The Panzers were superior:** Zaloga, *Panzerfaust vs. Sherman: European Theater, 1944–45* (London: Osprey, 2019).
110 **bounced off the Panzers:** S. Thayer.
110 **the "mechanized coffin":** "A Poor Defense: Sherman Tanks in WWII," University of Illinois Archives, https://archives.library.illinois.edu/blog/poor-defense-sherman-tanks-ww2/#_edn4.
110 **hit it on the side:** Cooper, *Death Traps*, 336.
110 **two thousand yards from any angle:** Cooper, *Death Traps*, 337.
110 **when their loader froze:** S. Thayer.
111 **"club the Krauts":** S. Thayer.
111 **lost a staggering eighty-three tanks:** Cooper, *Death Traps*, xii.
111 **heavy wooden door:** Photo, University of Illinois Archives, Box 13, Folder 23, 2620076_B13_German 88 #2, July 1944.

NOTES

111 **sergeant named Culin:** "Eisenhower Hails G.I. for Tank Idea; D-Day Paratrooper's Drop on Steeple Also Recalled," *New York Times*, June 6, 1944, https://www.nytimes.com/1964/06/06/archives/eisenhower-hails-gl-for-tank-idea-dday-paratroopers-drop-on-steeple.html.

111 **chewing through roots:** Cooper, *Death Traps*, 50–52; Steven Ossad and Don Marsh, *Major General Maurice Rose: World War II's Greatest Forgotten Commander* (Lanham, MD: Taylor Trade, 2006), 167.

111 **ability to improvise:** Cooper, *Death Traps*, 57.

111 **"that cowboy mentality":** Pam Jones, "Local Resident Belton Cooper—a WWII Tank Expert," *Birmingham Post-Herald* (Alabama), March 8, 2005.

112 **armor was thinner:** "A Poor Defense: Sherman Tanks in WWII"; Steven J. Zaloga, *US Battle Tanks, 1917–1945* (Oxford, UK: Osprey, 2024), 41.

112 **able to hand-crank:** S. Thayer.

112 **more than ten thousand Americans:** "Battle of Saint-Lô 75th Anniversary Commemoration at the WWII Memorial," Friends of the National WWII Memorial, https://wwiimemorialfriends.networkforgood.com/events/13773-battle-of-saint-l-75th-anniversary-commemoration-at-the-wwii-memorial.

112 **the only platoon leader left standing:** McDowell is a name change. His name has been changed out of respect for his family.

113 **towed back for repair:** Elmer Hovland, interview with author, June 9, 2001.

113 **tank mechanics miracle workers:** Clarence Smoyer, "My Combat Story," E Co, 32nd AR, 3rd Armored Division, as told to Vic Damon and Dan Fong, 3AD.com.

113 **take his place:** Elmer L. Hovland Collection, Veterans History Project, American Folklife Center, Library of Congress, https://www.loc.gov/item/afc2001001.94051/.

113 **slow to act:** S. Thayer.

113 **Major General Maurice Rose:** Ossad and Marsh, *Major General Maurice Rose*, 38–51.

114 **half a showcase mile:** S. Thayer.

114 **Elmer leaned forward:** Fred Headrick, conversation with author, March 16, 2005.

114 **saw the war through his periscope:** Fred Jackson Headrick Sr. Collection (AFC/2001/001/5954), Veterans History Project, American Folklife Center, Library of Congress.

114 **inside a cramped cabin:** Steve Zaloga, *U.S. Army Tank Crewman, 1941–45: European Theater of Operations, 1944–45*, 18, 27.

114 **feel like a steel boiler:** S. Thayer.

115 **wine, champagne, and cognac:** Bertrand Close, "Memories of World War II: New Friends Revive Old Memories," unpublished memoirs, n.d.

115 **smiled, and waved:** S. Thayer.

116 **At Mons, the division:** "War Diary, Co. 'D,' 32d Armored Regiment."

116 **cut off the Germans:** 32nd Armored Regiment, 3rd Armored Spearhead Division, published by Ravensteins Geographische Verlangsanstalt u. Drükerei, Frankfurt-Main; Woolner, *Spearhead in the West*, 86–87.

116 **more than ten thousand prisoners:** "War Diary, Co. 'D,' 32d Armored Regiment."

NOTES

116 **fresh bread, steaming meatloaf:** L. DeCola, conversation with author, August 18, 2007.
117 **"also feed the soul":** L. DeCola, conversation with author, August 18, 2007.
117 **"carry the spatula!":** L. DeCola, conversation with author, August 18, 2007.
117 **"He had more energy":** Fred Headrick, conversation with author, March 16, 2005.
118 **firing off the first shot:** Stuart Thayer's notes.
118 **"something might be out there":** Fred Jackson Headrick Sr. Collection, Veterans History Project.
118 **with a lit cigarette:** Cooper, *Death Traps*, 56.
119 **"a lot of work to do":** Elmer Hovland, conversation with author, June 9, 2001.

CHAPTER EIGHTEEN: NORTH PLANT

120 **arrived at "the worksite":** Marcin Kopytko, Blechhammer 44 Association historian, interview with author, February 10, 2020; "Blechhammer," *Holocaust Encyclopedia*, United States Holocaust Memorial Museum, https://encyclopedia.ushmm.org/content/en/article/blechhammer.
121 **synthetic oil factory:** Declassified Secret 15th U.S. Air Force Targeting Information Sheet, Blechhammer Synthetic Oil Manufacturing Plant," April 4, 1944.
121 **known as Blechhammer North:** U.S. Air Force Targeting Information Sheet, Blechhammer; Declassified Secret 15th U.S. Air Force Supplementary Briefing Note on Synthetic Oil Plants; "Arbeitslager Blechhammer," Sub Camps of Auschwitz, https://subcamps-auschwitz.org/auschwitz-subcamps/arbeitslager-blechhammer/.
121 **200,000 tons a year:** "Oil as a Factor in the German War Effort, 1933–1945," Chiefs of Staff Committee, UK Ministry of Defense, March 8, 1946, 183.
121 **out of range of Allied bombers:** "Front Line Is Nearing Synthetics Oil Plants," *Windsor Star* (Windsor, Ontario), January 22, 1945.
121 **renowned civilian firms:** Ed Haduch, Blechhammer 44 Association historian, conversation with author, March 25, 2022.
121 **sixty thousand forced workers:** E. Haduch conversation.
122 **majority of "unskilled labor":** Sigmund W. Holocaust Testimony (HVT-55), interviewed by Laurel Vlock, Dori Laub, and Eva Kantor, May 12, 1982, Oral History Collection, United States Holocaust Memorial Museum, https://collections.ushmm.org/search/catalog/hvt616892.
122 **"Form up work details!":** Oral History Interview with Max Drimmer and Herman Shine, interviewed by Anne Feibelman, Jane Goldman, Judy Wellisch, and Lorene Wilk, November 15, 1989, April 1990, January 15, 1996, Bay Area Holocaust Oral History Project, United States Holocaust Memorial Museum, https://collections.ushmm.org/search/catalog/irn511712.
122 **for the same *Arbeitskommando*:** Eddie Willner, conversations with author.
122 **prodding or beating:** Gastfriend, *My Father's Testament*, 131.
122 **wore double holstered pistols:** Gastfriend, *My Father's Testament*, 131–32; Zentrale Stelle, Bundesarchiv B 162 / 8867.
122 **rode around the North plant:** Robert Clary, interviewed by Merle Goldberg, Jewish Survivor, Visual History Archive, USC Shoah Foundation, September 12, 1994.

NOTES

122 **on a bicycle:** M. Swaab, conversation with author, June 11, 1977.
122 **most sadistic of all:** "Robert Clary Speaks as a Holocaust Survivor," YouTube, https://www.youtube.com/watch?v=Kn1r_9AJiF8.
123 **a volcanic temper:** Ernst Koenig, conversation with author, July 12, 1982.
123 **in his mid-thirties:** *Zentrale Stelle,* Bundesarchiv B 162 / 18175; Rosengarten, *Survival,* 159.
123 **"cold, mean face":** Gastfriend, *My Father's Testament,* 132.
123 **striking like a viper:** *Zentrale Stelle,* Bundesarchiv B 162 / 18175.
123 **he whipped out:** "Ghetto Fighter's House," Peter Sturm testimony, Yad Vashem.
123 **both his revolvers and fired:** Eddie Willner, interviewed by Ellen Epstein, Oral History Interview with Eddie Willner, United States Holocaust Memorial Museum, May 25, 1989.
123 **fell over dead:** *Zentrale Stelle,* Bundesarchiv B 162 / 8867.
123 **"over Hitler's dead body!":** "Tom Mix," *Pennsylvania Heritage,* Fall 2003, http://paheritage.wpengine.com/article/tom-mix-1880-1940/.
124 **look more fit:** Paul D. Holocaust Testimony (HVT-620), Fortunoff Video Archive for Holocaust Testimonies, Yale University.
124 **POWs came through:** Eddie Willner, conversations with author.
124 **calling the SS "Boches!":** Ernst Koenig, *Im Vorhof der Vernichtung: Als Zwangsarbeiter in den Außenlagern von Auschwitz* (Fischer Taschenbuch, 2000).
124 **British POWs of Stalag VIIIB:** Koenig, *Auschwitz;* Eddie Willner, conversations with author; Eddie Willner, interviewed by Esther Finder, Jewish Survivor, USC Shoah Foundation, June 22, 1997.
124 **To speak to another:** Sigmund W. Holocaust Testimony (HVT-55), Fortunoff Video Archive for Holocaust Testimonies, Yale University Library.
125 **inmates called it "water soup":** *Zentrale Stelle,* Bundesarchiv B 162 / 18175.
125 **beatings, even shootings:** Mike Swaab, conversation with author, July 2, 1978.
125 **in Mike's case, about food:** M. Swaab conversation with author, July 2, 1978.
125 **"God, why have you forsaken":** Ernst Koenig, conversation with author, July 12, 1982.
125 **cramped triple bunks:** Richard Blatt, *Memoir of Richard Blatt During Hitler's Regime,* interview, 1975, transcribed by Claudia Weiss Greve, Internet Archive, https://archive.org/details/bib262050_001_001/mode/2up.
125 **pinched them in half:** "Robert Clary Speaks as a Holocaust Survivor"; *Zentrale Stelle,* Bundesarchiv B 162 / 8863.
125 **with a shower:** Henryk Symchowicz, Collection of Reminiscences, vol. 62, Auschwitz-Birkenau Archives (APMAB), 3-4 Auschwitz.
125 **wide-eyed stare:** Ernst Koenig, conversation with author, July 12, 1982.
126 **got diarrhea in this camp:** Eddie Willner, interviewed by Esther Finder, June 22, 1997.
126 **Chewing on a piece of wood:** Eddie Willner, interviewed by Ellen Epstein, Oral History Interview with Eddie Willner, United States Holocaust Memorial Museum, May 25, 1989.
126 **against becoming dehumanized:** Eddie Willner, United States Holocaust Memorial Museum.

NOTES

127   **through illicit "dealings":** M. Karl Demerer testimony, Yad Vashem Archives, O313655, February 15, 1973.
127   **trade for two bags:** Alex H. Holocaust Testimony (HVT-210), Fortunoff Video Archive for Holocaust Testimonies, Yale University Library.
127   **save prisoners' lives:** M. Karl Demerer testimony, Yad Vashem Archives, O313655, February 15, 1973: Gastfriend, *My Father's Testament*, 116, 120.
128   **warned the boys:** Eddie Willner, conversations with author.
128   **There was an infirmary:** M. Karl Demerer testimony, Yad Vashem Archives, O313655, February 15, 1973.
128   **no medical aid:** *Zentrale Stelle,* Bundesarchiv B 162 / 8863 / 8866.
128   **it was a death ward:** "Conditions in the Hospital," Auschwitz-Birkenau Former German Nazi Concentration and Extermination Camp, Memorial and Museum, https://www.auschwitz.org/en/history/camp-hospitals/conditions-in-the-hospital/.
128   **but to aid and abet:** Dokumentationsarchiv des osterreichischen Widerstandes, Jahrbuch 1996, Siegwald Ganglmair, 56–59.
128   **the end of you:** Simon Michalowicz, interviewed by R. Banczewska, Oral History Interview, United States Holocaust Memorial Museum, November 22, 1995.
128   **box the man's ears:** Rosengarten, *The Story of a Sixteen-Year-Old Jewish Boy,* 97.
128   **punch him in the face:** Ernst Koenig and Eddie Willner conversation with author, July 12, 1982; Eddie Willner, interviewed by Ellen Epstein, May 25, 1989.

CHAPTER NINETEEN: "KOM GOED THUIS"

130   **nearly five hundred American bombers:** Mediterranean Allied Strategic Air Force (MASAF), INTOPS (Intelligence Operations) Summary 351/ 7 July 1944, D/JR-W/fl; Marcin Kopytko, Blechhammer 44 Association historian, interview with author, August 4, 2024.
130   **around three hundred fighters:** MASAF, INTOPS; M. Kopytko interview.
130   **in a simultaneous attack:** Peter Kassak, "First Raid to Blechhammer, Escaping and Evading in Southwest Slovakia," *Flight Journal,* April 2020, https://membership.flightjournal.com/first-raid-blechhammer-escaping-evading-southwest-slovakia/.
130   **highly flammable fuel depots:** Gastfriend, *My Father's Testament,* 124.
131   **wire hung down:** Robert Clary, *From the Holocaust to Hogan's Heroes: The Autobiography of Robert Clary* (Lanham, MD: Taylor Trade, 2007), 88.
131   **one hundred Jewish prisoners:** *Zentrale Stelle,* Bundesarchiv B 162 / 8863.
131   **destruction of Blechhammer:** "Oil as a Factor in the German War Effort, 1933–1945," Chiefs of Staff Committee, Officers of the Cabinet and Minister of Defence, W.W. 1. March 8, 1946.
131   **number one target:** "Oil as a Factor," Chiefs of Staff Committee report, 1946; Marcin Kopytko, Blechhammer 44 Association historian, interview with author, October 5, 2024.
131   **If they disabled:** Jack R. Myers, *Shot at and Missed: Recollections of a World War II Bombardier* (Norman: University of Oklahoma Press, 2004), 101.

NOTES

131 **Loaded down with eight:** Ed Haduch, Blechhammer 44 Association historian, conversation with author, April 22, 2022.

132 **help was on the way:** Testimony of Kurt Baum, Jewish Survivor, USC Shoah Foundation Institute, United States Holocaust Memorial Museum, May 15, 1997, https://collections.ushmm.org/search/catalog/vha29790.

132 **bombing raised the prisoners' spirits:** Sigmund W. Holocaust Testimony (HVT-55), interviewed by Laurel Vlock, Dori Laub, and Eva Kantor, May 12, 1982, Fortunoff Collection, Yale University Library, United States Holocaust Memorial Museum.

132 **in a violent rage:** Israel J. Rosengarten, *Survival: The Story of a Sixteen-Year-Old Jewish Boy* (Syracuse, NY: Syracuse University Press, 2000), 161.

132 **"Jump! Bounce! Leap!":** Simon Michalowicz, interviewed by R. Banczewska, Oral History Interview, United States Holocaust Memorial Museum, November 22, 1995.

132 **"Up, down, jump higher!":** Robert Clary, interviewed by Merle Goldberg, Jewish Survivor, Visual History Archive, September 12, 1994, USC Shoah Foundation.

132 **could not get back up:** Gastfriend, *My Father's Testament*, 136; Simon Michalowicz, interviewed by R. Banczewska, Oral History Interview, United States Holocaust Memorial Museum, November 22, 1995; Henryk Symchowicz APMAB, Collection of Reminiscences, vol. 62, Auschwitz, 1940–1945.

132 **flown by the famed Tuskegee Airmen:** Marcin Kopytko, Blechhammer 44 Association historian, interview with author, August 4, 2024; "Tuskegee Airmen, Photo of the Red Tails of the 332nd Fighter Group Take Off to Escort Heavy Bombers Sent to Bomb Enemy Oil Fields at Blechhammer, Germany, on Aug. 7, 1944," National Museum of the United States Air Force, https://www.nationalmuseum.af.mil/Upcoming/Photos/igphoto/2000981891/.

132 **crawled into a metal pipe:** Mike Swaab, conversation with author, August 2, 1980; "Robert Clary Speaks as a Holocaust Survivor," YouTube, https://www.youtube.com/watch?v=Kn1r_9AJiF8; Richard Blatt, *Memoir of Richard Blatt During Hitler's Regime*, interview, 1975, transcribed by Claudia Weiss Greve, Internet Archive.

133 **"here come your friends":** Simon Michalowicz, interviewed by R. Banczewska, Oral History Interview, United States Holocaust Memorial Museum, November 22, 1995.

133 **launched Messerschmitt fighters:** Peter Kassak, "First Raid to Blechhammer," Everand, February 20, 2020, https://www.everand.com/article/475092898/First-Raid-To-Blechhammer.

133 **four hundred heavy flak guns:** Ed Cornelia, Lindell Crew historian, interview with author, October 17, 2020.

133 **twisted metal rained down:** Gastfriend, *My Father's Testament*, 132–34.

133 **heart of the industrial plant:** Declassified Secret 15th U.S. Air Force Targeting Information Sheet, Blechhammer Synthetic Oil Manufacturing Plant, April 4, 1944.

133 **pilots called it Black Hammer:** Ted Withington, *Flight to Black Hammer: The Letters of a World War II Pilot* (Brunswick, ME: Biddle, 1993).

133 **twenty-two-year-old George McGovern:** Kurt Baum, testimony of a Jewish Survivor, USC Shoah Foundation Institute, United States Holocaust Memorial Museum, May 15, 1997.

NOTES

- 133 **even pilots' faces:** "Robert Clary Speaks as a Holocaust Survivor," YouTube, https://www.youtube.com/watch?v=Kn1r_9AJiF8.
- 133 **"precision of the targeting":** Gastfriend, *My Father's Testament*, 124.
- 134 **"damaged or destroyed":** Kurt Baum, testimony, May 15, 1997.
- 134 **the deadly explosions:** Stephen E. Ambrose, *The Wild Blue: The Men and Boys Who Flew the B-24s over Germany, 1944–45* (New York: Simon & Schuster, 2002), 426.
- 134 **"there was total glee":** Henry S. Holocaust Testimony (HVT-578), Fortunoff Video Archive for for Holocaust and Genocide Studies, Yale University Library, 1996.
- 134 **"We were not afraid":** Elie Wiesel, *Night*, translated by Marion Wiesel, 30th anniversary ed. (New York: Hill and Wang), 60.
- 134 **some risked it:** Charles Baron, "Du Z.A.L. au K.L.: Blechhammer," *Le Monde Juif*, Cairn Info Science Humanais Sociales, https://www.cairn.info/revue-le-monde-juif-1985-4-page-131.html.
- 134 **took advantage of moments:** Sigmund W. Holocaust Testimony (HVT-55), interviewed by Laurel Vlock, Dori Laub, and Eva Kantor, May 12, 1982, Fortunoff Collection, Yale University Library, United States Holocaust Memorial Museum, https://collections.ushmm.org/search/catalog/hvt616892; Charles Baron, "Du Z.A.L. au K.L.: Blechhammer."
- 134 **smashing valuable precision equipment:** Dokumentationsarchiv des osterreichischen Widerstandes, Jahrbuch 1996, 23; John Steiner, *Reflections on Experiences in Nazi Death Camps* (Claims Conference Holocaust Survivor Memoir Collection, United States Holocaust Memorial Museum, 2001).
- 135 **decree to halt it:** "Night and Fog Decree," *Holocaust Encyclopedia*, United States Holocaust Memorial Museum, https://encyclopedia.ushmm.org/content/en/article/night-and-fog-decree.
- 135 **into an unoccupied *Einmannbunker*:** Eddie Willner, interviewed by Esther Finder, Jewish Survivor, USC Shoah Foundation, June 22, 1997; Eddie Willner, interviewed by Neal Goldenberg, Oral History Interview, Jewish Community Council of Greater Washington, United States Holocaust Memorial Museum, March 15, 1987.
- 136 **production was back in action:** Clary, *From the Holocaust to Hogan's Heroes*, 87.
- 136 **greeted by Tom Mix:** M. Karl Demerer testimony, Yad Vashem Archives, O313655, February 15, 1973.
- 136 **suspected the worst:** Eddie Willner, conversations with author.
- 137 **shirk barracks cleanup:** Eddie Willner, conversations with author; Eddie Willner, interviewed by Ellen Epstein, Oral History Interview with Eddie Willner, United States Holocaust Memorial Museum, May 25, 1989.
- 137 **easily result in the death:** Alter W. Holocaust Testimony (HVT-1729), Fortunoff Video Archive for Holocaust Testimonies, Yale University Library.
- 137 **unable to sit:** Eddie Willner, conversations with author.
- 138 **he was not hurt:** "Hitler's Radio Proclamation About the Assassination Attempt on 20 July 1944," Traces of War, https://www.tracesofwar.com/articles/5311/Hitlers-radio-proclamation-about-the-assassination-attempt-on-20-July

NOTES

-1944.htm. Although the July 20, 1944, assasination plot was not the first attempt on Hitler's life, it appears to have been the best planned and most ambitious.

138 **for the "dud commando":** Steiner, *Reflections,* 3.
138 **killing the entire team:** Clary, *From the Holocaust to* Hogan's Heroes, 87–88.
138 **did not live to tell:** Steiner, *Reflections,* 21.
138 **not worth the risk:** Steiner, *Reflections,* 21.
139 **boys had volunteered:** Eddie Willner, interviewed by Esther Finder, June 22, 1997.
139 **messages scrawled by GIs:** "Writing Funny Stuff on Ammo Is over 2000 Years Old," We Are the Mighty, https://www.wearethemighty.com/mighty-trending/writing-funny-messages-bomb-ammo/.
139 **heard for miles:** Rosengarten, *Survival,* 154–55.
139 **"Speed it up!":** Eddie Willner, interviewed by Esther Finder, June 22, 1997.
140 **canvassing back and forth:** Eddie Willner, interviewed by Ellen Epstein, May 25, 1989; Eddie Willner, interviewed by Neal Goldenberg, Oral History Interview, Jewish Community Council of Greater Washington, United States Holocaust Memorial Museum, March 15, 1987; Eddie Willner, conversations with author.
140 **a lot of blood:** Eddie Willner, interviewed by Esther Finder, June 22, 1997.
140 **managed to sew:** Eddie Willner, interviewed by Esther Finder, June 22, 1997; Eddie Willner, interviewed by Neal Goldenberg, March 15, 1987; Eddie Willner, conversations with author. Note: "The doctor in the barracks saved my life."
141 **"I'm fine. I'm ready to work!":** Eddie Willner and Mike Swaab, conversations with author.
141 **armed with machine guns:** Eddie Willner, interviewed by Neal Goldenberg, March 15, 1987; M. Swaab interview, *Lone Star Wing Newsletter.*
141 **Gallows had been set up:** Sam Silberberg, *From Hell to the Promised Land: A Boy's Daring Escape from a Nazi Concentration Camp* (CreateSpace, 2011), 78–79.
141 **tie up his pants:** Clary, *From the Holocaust to* Hogan's Heroes, 88; "Robert Clary Speaks as a Holocaust Survivor"; Steiner, *Reflections,* 4–6.
141 **accused the teen:** "Robert Clary Speaks as a Holocaust Survivor."
142 **witnessed the Dutch boy:** *Zentrale Stelle,* Bundesarchiv B 162 / 8863.
142 **all three were in:** *Zentrale Stelle,* Bundesarchiv B 162 / 8864.
142 **"Eyes front!":** Eddie Willner, conversations with author; *Zentrale Stelle,* Bundesarchiv B 162 / 8864 / 8865.
142 **climb the scaffold:** Ernest Koenig, *Im Vorhof der Vernichtung, Als Zwangsarbeiter in den Aussenlagern von Auschwitz* (Tischer Taschenbuch, 2000), 470–72; Silberberg, *From Hell to the Promised Land,* 78–79; *Zentrale Stelle,* Bundesarchiv B 162 / 8864.
142 **placed the nooses:** *Zentrale Stelle,* Bundesarchiv B 162 / 8864.
142 **like a lawful proceeding:** Rosengarten, *Survival,* 152–54.
142 **delivered his proclamation:** *Zentrale Stelle,* Bundesarchiv B 162 / 8864.
142 **"By order of the":** Eddie Willner, interviewed by Esther Finder, June 22, 1997.

NOTES

142 **kicked the stools:** Steiner, *Reflections*, 5; *Zentrale Stelle*, Bundesarchiv B 162 / 8864.

142 **God has spoken:** Mark Jarzombek, "From Bedzin to Blechhammer to Buchenwald: The Survival Story of Henry and Mathias Jarzombek," Internet Archive, 2019, https://archive.org/details/bib273278_001_001/page/n55/mode/2up.

143 **halt the procedure:** M. Karl Demerer testimony, Yad Vashem Archives, O313655, February 15, 1973.

143 **there was a law:** *Zentrale Stelle*, Bundesarchiv B 162 / 8864.

143 **"Hang him again!":** M. Karl Demerer testimony, February 15, 1973; *Zentrale Stelle*, Bundesarchiv B 162 / 18175; Eddie Willner, interviewed by Neal Goldenberg, March 15, 1987.

143 **fired shots into the air:** Jarzombek, "From Bedzin to Blechhammer to Buchenwald."

143 **ordered another rope:** *Zentrale Stelle*, Bundesarchiv B 162 / 8864.

143 **Demerer continued to plead:** Silberberg, *From Hell to the Promised Land*, 79.

143 **"Come home well":** Steiner, *Reflections*; Rosengarten, *Survival*, 153.

143 **Tom Mix shouted:** *Zentrale Stelle*, Bundesarchiv B 162 / 8867.

143 **he called out to his fellow:** Rosengarten, *Survival*, 153; Eddie Willner, conversations with author.

144 **tears in his eyes:** Eddie Willner, conversations with author.

144 **Tom Mix screamed again:** Rosengarten, *Survival*, 153.

144 **hung for three days:** Eddie Willner, conversations with author; Simon Michalowicz, interviewed by R. Banczewska, Oral History Interview, United States Holocaust Memorial Museum, November 22, 1995, https://collections.ushmm.org/search/catalog/irn507198; Jarzombek, "From Bedzin to Blechhammer to Buchenwald."

144 **"Keep your heads up!":** Steiner, *Reflections*, 5–6, 23; Dokumentationsarchiv des osterreichischen Widerstandes, Jahrbuch 1996.

144 **Some stopped believing:** Ofer Aderet, "Newly Unearthed Version of Elie Wiesel's Seminal Work Is a Scathing Indictment of God, Jewish World," *Haaretz*, May 1, 2016, https://www.haaretz.com/jewish/2016-05-01/ty-article/.premium/harsher-version-of-night-found-in-elie-wiesel-archive/0000017f-f663-d318-afff-f7636c560000; Eddie Willner, conversations with author.

145 **"Shame!" "Swine!" "Bahstads!":** Ernst Koenig, conversation with author, July 12, 1982; E. Koenig, *Im Vorhof der Vernichtung, Als Zwangsarbeiter in den Aussenlagern von Auschwitz*.

145 **downward and away:** Simon Michalowicz, interviewed by R. Banczewska, Oral History Interview, United States Holocaust Memorial Museum, November 22, 1995, https://collections.ushmm.org/search/catalog/irn507198.

145 **little square of chocolate:** Eddie Willner, conversations with author; Eddie Willner, interviewed by Esther Finder, June 22, 1997; Eddie Willner, interviewed by Neal Goldenberg, March 15, 1987.

CHAPTER TWENTY: THANKSGIVING

146 **assault at the Siegfried Line:** "War Diary, Co. 'D,' 32d Armored Regiment."

147 **a panic situation:** Stuart Thayer's notes.

NOTES

147 **"like an oversized coat":** S. Thayer.
147 **named him Shaky:** S. Thayer.
147 **go see Pepsi:** L. DeCola, conversation with author, July 13, 2013.
148 **worked until they didn't:** S. Thayer.
148 **captain to "stand down":** S. Thayer.
148 **rumor mill had it:** S. Thayer.
148 **lack of knowledge:** Fred Headrick, conversation with author, March 16, 2005.
149 **a real leader:** F. Headrick, conversation with author, March 16, 2005.
149 **over the next ridge:** S. Thayer.
149 **"Got a challenge up ahead":** F. Headrick, conversation with author, March 16, 2005.
149 **"Let's get on it":** S. Thayer.
150 **never stopped working:** F. Headrick, conversation with author, June 12, 2007.
150 **"He listened, then he led":** S. Thayer.
151 **Myers yelled, "Incoming!":** F. Headrick, conversation with author, June 12, 2007.
151 **"No! Get back in!":** S. Thayer.
152 **"a fountain of strength":** Army and Navy Commission, *A Prayer Book for Soldiers and Sailors* (Frederick, MD: HardPress, 2024).
152 **"keep movin' forward":** F. Headrick, conversation with author, June 12, 2007.
153 **temporary camp in Stolberg:** "War Diary."
153 **Elmer and Myers were promoted:** "War Diary."
153 **fit right in:** S. Thayer.
154 **told a joke:** L. DeCola, conversation with author, July 13, 2013.
154 **with birthday wishes:** Fred Headrick, Bernie Clow, conversation with Jeff Holachek, September 7, 2000.
154 **demoted for talking back:** "War Diary, Co. 'D,' 32d Armored Regiment."
154 **bedded or pretended to have:** S. Thayer.
154 **let their brothers down:** S. Thayer.
155 **"not leaving these goddam Krauts":** S. Thayer.
155 **with red wine:** F. Headrick, conversation with author, March 16, 2005.
155 **there was Private Bizjack:** S. Thayer.
155 **and played cards:** S. Thayer.
155 **his officer's alcohol rations:** S. Thayer.
156 **flood of letters:** Elmer Hovland letter and postcards sent to Harriet Hovland, C. Hovland personal papers.
156 **"I'm proud of you":** L. DeCola, conversation with author, June 4, 2011.
156 **Fred Jr., would remember:** Fred Jackson Headrick Sr. Collection, Veterans History Project, American Folklife Center, Library of Congress (AFC/2001/001/5954), https://www.loc.gov/item/afc2001001.05954/.
157 **photograph of "Blue Eyes":** L. DeCola, conversation with author, June 4, 2011.
157 **with the largest contingent:** S. Hovland, taped interview with Elmer Hovland, 2004, Hovland Family Records, Luverne, Minnesota.
157 **would have made Pa proud:** L. DeCola, conversation with author, June 4, 2011.

NOTES

CHAPTER TWENTY-ONE: SIEGFRIED'S PROPHECY

159 **Why had God not answered:** Ernst Koenig, conversation with author, July 12, 1982.

160 **names of the twenty-six members:** Eddie Willner, conversations with author.

160 **Eddie went to find him:** Eddie Willner, interviewed by Esther Finder, Jewish Survivor, USC Shoah Foundation, June 22, 1997.

161 **"sending me for a rest":** Eddie Willner, interviewed by Ellen Epstein, Oral History Interview with Eddie Willner, United States Holocaust Memorial Museum, May 25, 1989.

161 **guard ordered him away:** Eddie Willner, conversations with author; Eddie Willner, interviewed by Esther Finder, June 22, 1997; Eddie Willner, interviewed by Ellen Epstein, Oral History Interview with Eddie Willner, United States Holocaust Memorial Museum, May 25, 1989.

161 **murdered at the hands:** Eddie Willner, interviewed by Esther Finder, June 22, 1997.

161 **turned to a Goethe poem:** Eddie Willner, conversations with author.

162 **sure Fritz would do it:** Eddie Willner, interviewed by Ellen Epstein, May 25, 1989.

162 **make a break for freedom:** Eddie Willner, conversations with author.

CHAPTER TWENTY-TWO: CHRISTMAS EVE

167 **sixty-mile retreat:** "War Diary, Co. 'D,' 32d Armored Regiment."

167 **relentless Allied pounding:** "WWII Allied 'Oil Plan' Devastates German POL Production," Air University History Office, Maxwell Air Force Base, June 26, 2019, https://www.maxwell.af.mil/News/Display/Article/1887774/wwii-allied-oil-plan-devastates-german-pol-production/.

167 **saw chaos everywhere:** Frank Woolner, *Spearhead in the West: The Third Armored Division, 1941–45* (Nashville, TN: Battery Press, 1980), 107.

168 **"You cannot imagine":** Michael E. Ruane, "On Christmas Eve in 1944, the Snow Turned Red with Blood," *Washington Post*, December 23, 2019, https://www.washingtonpost.com/history/2019/12/23/christmas-eve-snow-turned-red-with-blood/.

168 **all the chaos, near Lamormenil:** "War Diary, Co. 'D,' 32d Armored Regiment."

168 **small village called Malmedy:** Alex Kershaw, *The Longest Winter: The Battle of the Bulge and the Epic Story of WWII's Most Decorated Platoon* (Cambridge, MA: Da Capo Press, 2005), 132–35; Anthony Beevor, *Ardennes 1944: The Battle of the Bulge* (New York: Penguin Books, 2015), 144–47.

168 **News of that atrocity:** Beevor, *Ardennes 1944*, 162, 222; Ken White, "Malmedy Survivor Recalls Massacre," Baugnez, Belgium, IMCOM-Europe Public Affairs Office, U.S. Army, December 21, 2007, https://www.army.mil/article/6726/malmedy_survivor_recalls_massacre.

169 **"obvious to the Germans":** Gerald Astor, *A Blood-Dimmed Tide: The Battle of the Bulge by the Men Who Fought It* (New York: Donald I. Fine, 1992), 283.

NOTES

169   **bottle under each arm:** Astor, *Blood-Dimmed Tide*, 312–13.
169   **"We're floatin' out here alone":** S. Hovland, taped interview with Elmer Hovland, 2004, Hovland Family Records, Luverne, Minnesota; Elmer Hovland, conversation with author, February 20, 2003.
169   **"We'll fight our way out":** E. Hovland, conversation with author.
170   **"watch over my men":** S. Hovland, taped interview with Elmer Hovland, 2004; Elmer Hovland, conversation with author, April 9, 2004.
170   **"Stay tight. Have faith":** E. Hovland conversation.
170   **"Turn 'em over":** E. Hovland conversation.
171   **prayers had been answered:** E. Hovland conversation.
171   **Belgian village of Freyneux:** Astor, *Blood-Dimmed Tide*, 310.
171   **just ten tanks:** George Winter, *Freineux and Lamormenil: The Ardennes* (Winnipeg: J. J. Federowicz, 1994), 13.
172   **"the hottest spot":** Astor, *Blood-Dimmed Tide*, 279, 292.
172   **hamlet of 42 homes:** Winter, *Freineux*, 30.
172   **Myers positioned his tank:** Winter, *Freineux*, 30.
172   **St. Isidore Church:** Eddy Monfort, Battle of the Bulge historian, conversation with author, April 24, 2019.
172   **In freezing conditions:** Winter, *Freineux*, 32; Fred Headrick, conversation with author, March 16, 2005.
172   **"I'm dreamin' of a white":** F. Headrick conversation.
172   **cleared the top:** Winter, *Freineux*, 32; Eddy Monfort, conversation with author, April 24, 2019.
173   **the man in charge:** Winter, *Freineux*, 34.
173   **infantry soldier excitedly ran up:** Winter, *Freineux*, 34.
173   **2nd SS "Das Reich":** Woolner, *Spearhead of the West*, 114.
173   **war crimes including the executions:** "Oradour-sur-Glane," *Holocaust Encyclopedia*, United States Holocaust Memorial Museum, https://encyclopedia.ushmm.org/content/en/article/oradour-sur-glane.
173   **vulnerable sides exposed:** Winter, *Freineux*, 34–35.
174   **(Lieutenant) Fritz Langanke:** Winter, *Freineux*, 33–36.
174   **another direct hit:** Winter, *Freineux*, 35–36.
174   **fire on Vance's tank:** Winter, *Freineux*, 35–36.
174   **Elmer scaled the church steeple:** Elmer Hovland, conversation with author, February 20, 2003.
175   **"best gunner in the company":** Stuart Thayer's notes; L. DeCola, conversation with author, August 18, 2007.

CHAPTER TWENTY-THREE: *BUTCH*

176   **ornament that bore:** John Locket, "Violent Night: How Adolf Hitler Hijacked Christmas and Rewrote Silent Night to Make It All about Celebrating Nazi Bloodshed," *The Sun*, December 19, 2018, https://www.thesun.co.uk/news/8009200/hitler-hijacked-christmas-bloodshed-nazis/.
177   **"stays on guard":** Locket, "Violent Night"; "How the Nazis Stole Christmas," *Independent*, December 21, 2009, https://www.independent.co.uk/news/world/europe/how-the-nazis-stole-christmas-1846365.html.

NOTES

177 **"the Savior Führer":** Locket, "Violent Night"; "How the Nazis Stole Christmas," *Independent.*
177 **holiday glitterati parties:** Locket, "Violent Night."
177 **sixteen U.S. air raids:** Ed Haduch, Blechhammer 44 Association historian, interview with author, June 21, 2021; Kevin A. Mahoney, *Fifteenth Air Force Against the Axis* (Lanham, MD: Scarecrow Press, 2013), 300.
177 **First Lieutenant Arthur Lindell:** Ed Cornelia, Lindell Crew historian, interview with author, October 23, 2023.
178 **outside the chapel:** Ed Cornelia interview, October 23, 2023.
178 **attended a targeting briefing:** Ed Cornelia interview, October 23, 2023.
178 **risking their lives on every mission:** Sgt. Sheila Holifield, "World War II Veteran Passes on History," First Army Public Affairs, U.S. Army, May 18, 2013, http://www.army.mil/article/103618/world_war_ii_veteran_passes_on_history.
178 **"Godspeed and a safe return":** Harold Kempffer, "Life at the Venosa Airfield During WWII," http://www.storiedelsud.altervista.org/Venosa%20PSP/PSP%20RED%20ENGLL.htm
178 **built a snowman:** Photograph, courtesy 485th Bomb Group Association.
178 **a mammoth armada:** Michael J. Neufeld and Michael Berenbaum, eds., *The Bombing of Auschwitz: Should the Allies Have Attempted It?* (Lawrence: University Press of Kansas, 2003); Alfred Konieczny, *Śląsk a wojna powietrzna lat 1940–1944* (Wrocław, Poland: Wydawnictwo Uniwersytetu Wrocławskiego, 1998), 207–8.
178 **five hundred American B-24:** U.S. Strategic Bombing Survey summarizing 15th Air Force bombing attacks in 1944.
179 **fifty degrees below zero:** Stephen Ambrose, "World War II Military Pilots," presentation on World War II U.S. military pilots who flew B-24s over Germany, C-SPAN, September 8, 2001, https://www.c-span.org/program/book-tv/world-war-ii-military-pilots/122694.
179 **freezing to their faces:** Ambrose, "World War II Military Pilots."
179 **650 miles for over four hours:** Ed Cornelia, interview, October 23, 2023.
179 **one minute later:** "Witness Statement, Sgt. John McKamey (nose gunner)," Debriefed on 29 December 1944, 828th Bombardment Squadron; Ed Cornelia, Lindell crew historian, interview with author, October 17, 2022.
179 **The plane exploded:** Ed Cornelia interview, October 17, 2022.
179 **slammed into the electricity power:** German report: *Angaben uber Erboutung eines Feindflugzeuges*, Anlage 3 dem.D (Luft) 2706/07 Dep 11/VIII, December 29, 1944; Ed Cornelia interview, October 17, 2022.
179 **ground to a final halt:** Stephen E. Ambrose, *The Wild Blue* (New York: Simon & Schuster, 2002), 122.
179 **33,000 bombs on the Silesian:** Marcin Kopytko, Blechhammer 44 Association historian, interview with author, August 4, 2024; Jan Mahr, *Vzpomínky na neznámé letce. Havárie spojeneckých letadel na Moravě a ve Slezsku v období 2. světové války* (Kovářská, Czech Republic: Muzeum letecké bitvy nad Krušnohořím, 2011), 15; Alfred Konieczny, *Śląsk a wojna powietrzna lat 1940-1944* (Wrocław, Poland: Wydawnictwo Uniwersytetu Wrocławskiego, 1998), 201.

NOTES

179 **seventeen air-raid missions:** U.S. air-raid missions on Blechhammer (1944): July 7; August 7, 22, 27; September 13; October 13, 14, 17; November 12 ("Lone Wolf" night raid), 17, 20; December 2, 12, 17, 18, 19, 26. Marcin Kopytko, Blechhammer 44 Association historian, interview with author, February 10, 2020.

179 **loss of 137 U.S. airmen:** Ed Haduch, Blechhammer 44 Association historian, conversation with author, June 21, 2021.

179 **fraction of their intended goal:** Arnold Krammer, "Technology Transfer as War Booty: The U.S. Technical Oil Mission to Europe, 1945," *Technology and Culture* 22, no. 1 (January 1981): 68–103.

180 **synthetic plants by 97 percent:** "WWII Allied 'Oil Plan' Devastates German POL Production," Air University History Office, Maxwell Air Force Base, June 26, 2019, https://www.maxwell.af.mil/News/Display/Article/1887774/wwii-allied-oil-plan-devastates-german-pol-production/.

180 **seriousness of the situation:** A. Krammer, "Technology Transfer as War Booty," 68–91.

CHAPTER TWENTY-FOUR: THE LONG MARCH

181 **exodus of tens of thousands of prisoners:** Ed Haduch, Blechhammer 44 Association historian, interview with author, December 20, 2022.

181 **nearly four thousand Jews:** Franciszek Piper, "Nebenlager Blechhammer," *Hefte von Auschwitz* 10 (1967): 19–39.

181 **Klipp was promoted:** *Zentrale Stelle*, Bundesarchiv B 162 / 18175.

182 **warmly cloaked in heavy woolen:** Staatarchiv Ludwigsburg: St Al EL 48–21 BA 2242_0004; *Zentrale Stelle*, Bundesarchiv B 162 / 8864.

182 **in threadbare prison uniforms:** Eddie Willner, conversations with author.

182 **legions of shivering prisoners:** John Steiner, *Reflections on Experiences in Nazi Death Camps* (Claims Conference Holocaust Survivor Memoir Collection, United States Holocaust Memorial Museum, 2001), 16–17.

182 **loaf of bread:** Edward Gastfriend, *My Father's Testament: Memoir of a Jewish Teenager, 1938–1945* (Philadelphia: Temple University Press, 1999), 148–49.

182 **Soviet artillery fire:** Sigmund W. Holocaust Testimony (HVT-55), interviewed by Laurel Vlock, Dori Laub, and Eva Kantor, Fortunoff Video Archive for Holocaust Testimonies, Yale University Library, United States Holocaust Memorial Museum, May 12, 1982.

182 **direction of the Russians:** Eddie Willner, interviewed by Neal Goldenberg, Oral History Interview, Jewish Community Council of Greater Washington, United States Holocaust Memorial Museum, March 15, 1987.

182 **guards whipping those:** Steiner, *Reflections*, 20–22; Gastfriend, *My Father's Testament*, 142–46.

182 **"dreckliche Juden":** Eddie Willner and Mike Swaab, conversations with author.

183 **"Don't despair," she assured:** John M. Steiner, interviewed by Sandra Bendayan and Carol Horwitz, written transcript by Dawn S. Scruggs, San Francisco, CA, Holocaust Oral History Project, United States Holocaust Memorial Museum, August 22, 1991, https://collections.ushmm.org/oh_find

NOTES

ingaids/RG-50.477.0497_01_trs_en.pdf; Steiner, *Reflections on Experiences in Nazi Death Camps*, 19–20.

183 **laid out a pail:** Eddie Willner, conversations with author.
183 **kicking over buckets:** Eddie Willner, conversations with author.
183 **Tom Mix had no pity:** *Zentrale Stelle*, Bundesarchiv B 162 / 8865.
183 **forbade any prisoner:** *Zentrale Stelle*, Bundesarchiv B 162 / 8864.
183 **who could not keep up:** *Zentrale Stelle*, Bundesarchiv B 162 / 8864 / 8865; Felix Gutmacher testimony, Trial of Adolf Eichmann Session 34, https://www.nizkor.org/session-034-06-eichmann-adolf/.
183 **watched for those who faltered:** *Zentrale Stelle*, Bundesarchiv B 162 / 8864 / 8865.
183 **shot them dead:** John M. Steiner, interviewed by Sandra Bendayan and Carol Horwitz, August 22, 1991; Steiner, *Reflections*; Eddie Willner, conversations with author.
183 **they slogged onward:** Gastfriend, *My Father's Testament*, 142–44.
183 **unable to keep up:** *Zentrale Stelle*, Bundesarchiv B 162 / 8864 / 8865.
183 **not wanting to risk:** *Zentrale Stelle*, Bundesarchiv B 162 / 8864 / 8865.
183 **walked in bare feet:** Eddie Willner, conversations with author; *Zentrale Stelle*, Bundesarchiv B 162 / 8863 / 8864; Felix Gutmacher testimony, Trial of Adolf Eichmann Session 34 (part 6 of 8).
184 **"going to make it":** Mike Swaab, conversation with author, July 2, 1978.
184 **lobbing back and forth:** Gastfriend, *My Father's Testament*, 145.
184 **"strengthen the heart":** Adolf Hitler, Broadcast on the 12th Anniversary of the National Socialist Regime, January 30, 1945.
184 **passed an SS casino:** Aleksandra Kobielec, interview with author, Research Division, Gross-Rosen Museum, February 23, 2023.
185 **camp reported in to:** Franciszek Piper, "Nebenlager Blechhammer," H*efte von Auschwitz* 10 (1967): 19–39.
185 **eight hundred had perished:** M. Karl Demerer testimony, Yad Vashem, February 15, 1973.
185 **surviving the long march:** *Zentrale Stelle*, Bundesarchiv B 162 / 8865; Piper, "Nebenlager Blechhammer," 37–39.
185 **torrential shower pummeled:** Sigmund W. Holocaust Testimony (HVT-55), interviewed by Laurel Vlock, Dori Laub, and Eva Kantor, Fortunoff Video Archive for Holocaust Testimonies, Yale University Library, United States Holocaust Memorial Museum, May 12, 1982; Eddie Willner conversations with author.
185 **slush and mud:** Eddie Willner, conversations with author; M. Karl Demerer testimony, February 15, 1973.
185 **sank into the bogs:** Eddie Willner, interviewed by Neal Goldenberg, Oral History Interview, Jewish Community Council of Greater Washington, United States Holocaust Memorial Museum, March 15, 1987; Eddie Willner, interviewed by Ellen Epstein, Oral History Interview with Eddie Willner, United States Holocaust Memorial Museum, May 25, 1989; Sigmund W. Holocaust Testimony (HVT-55), interviewed by Laurel Vlock, Dori Laub, and Eva Kantor.
185 **with different patches:** Eddie Willner, interviewed by Ellen Epstein, May 25, 1989.

NOTES

185 **Eddie snapped to attention:** Mike Swaab conversation with author, July 2, 1978.

CHAPTER TWENTY-FIVE: THE TALISMAN

187 **"Can we get in there?":** Fred Jackson Headrick Sr. Collection, Veterans History Project, American Folklife Center, Library of Congress.
188 **"sending an entire Nazi":** Fred Jackson Headrick Sr. Collection, Veterans History Project.
188 **handed him a telegram:** Steve Hovland, taped interview with Elmer Hovland, 2005, Hovland Family Records, Luverne, Minnesota.
188 **pull a wounded crewman:** Fred Jackson Headrick Sr. Collection, Veterans History Project.
188 **carried the bleeding man:** Elmer L. Hovland Collection (AFC/2001/001/94051), Veterans History Project, American Folklife Center, Library of Congress, https://www.loc.gov/item/afc2001001.94051/; Elmer Hovland, conversation with author, February 20, 2003.
188 **mess trucks were hit:** L. DeCola, unpublished manuscript, n.d.
189 **only to be wounded:** S. Hovland, taped interview with Elmer Hovland, 2005, Hovland Family Records, Luverne, Minnesota.
189 **"only followin' Hovland":** Elmer Hovland, conversation with author, February 20, 2003; Stuart Thayer's notes.
189 **like a mutiny:** S. Thayer.
190 **"here to do a job":** S. Thayer.
190 **"followed that man anywhere":** S. Thayer.
191 **hand move to rest:** Fred Headrick, conversation with author, March 16, 2005; Bernie Clow, conversation with Jeff Holachek, September 7, 2000.
191 **some 75,000 casualties:** "Battle of the Bulge," Monuments and Memorials, Arlington National Cemetery, https://www.arlingtoncemetery.mil/Explore/Monuments-and-Memorials/Battle-of-the-Bulge#:~:text=Battle%20of%20the%20Bulge%20Memorial,-The%20Battle%20of&text=Soldiers%20fought%20in%20brutal%20winter,single%20World%20War%20II%20battle.
191 **awarded the Silver Star:** S. Hovland, taped interview with Elmer Hovland, 2004; "Former and Current Members Who Have Distinguished Themselves in Battle: Hovland, Elmer L., "For Gallantry in Action, January 16, 1945," NARA files no. 7350.
192 **"I was hell-bent":** Fred Headrick, conversation with author, March 16, 2005.
192 **told of feeling empty:** S. Thayer.
192 **"I got *nothin'* left!":** L. DeCola, conversation with author, July 13, 2013.
192 **"make the boys happy":** L. DeCola, audio interview, 2015, Willner Family Archives.
193 **discarded weapons they found:** Stuart Thayer, "D Company Tales," *3rd Armored Division Association Newsletter*, September 1991.
193 **siphoning the tiny vial:** L. DeCola, conversation with author, July 13, 2013.
194 **everyone was going to get sick:** L. DeCola, conversation with author, July 13, 2013.

NOTES

194 **"Best hotcakes I ever ate"**: Fred Headrick, conversation with author, March 16, 2005; Fred Jackson Headrick Sr. Collection, Veterans History Project.

CHAPTER TWENTY-SIX: THE TUNNELS

196 **house underground factories**: Declassified Confidential Extract, Headquarters Eighth Air Force, Office of the Director of Intelligence, Annex to Daily Intelligence Summary No. 31, Special Intelligence, 8 June 1945.

196 **Germany's new fleet**: "Junkers Jumo 004 Turbojet," National Museum of the U.S. Air Force, Wright-Patterson Air Force Base, Dayton, Ohio, https://www.nationalmuseum.af.mil/Visit/Museum-Exhibits/Fact-Sheets/Display/Article/196238/junkers-jumo-004-turbojet/#:~:text=The%20Jumo%20004%20powered%20the,5%2C000%20engines%20had%20been%20produced; "Messerschmitt Me 262A Schwalbe," National Museum of the U.S. Air Force, Wright-Patterson Air Force Base, Dayton, Ohio, https://www.nationalmuseum.af.mil/Visit/Museum-Exhibits/Fact-Sheets/Display/Article/196266/messerschmitt-me-262a-schwalbe/; "Jumo 004 B," Flugwerft Schleissheim, Deutsches Museum, https://www.deutsches-museum.de/en/flugwerft-schleissheim/ausstellung/flugantriebe-und-raketen/jumo-004.

196 **new kind of airplane engine**: *Underground Factories in Germany*, declassified Secret, Combined Intelligence Objectives Sub-Committee, Item Nos. 21, 22, 31, File No. XXXIII-38, 21.

196 **shafts and galleys**: *Underground Factories*, 22–24.

196 **produce parts for**: Dr. Nicolas Bertrand, Director of Langenstein Concentration Camp Memorial and Museum, conversation with author, November 18, 2019, citing Bertrand's conversation with Ewald Bremm, German apprentice engineer, 1944–45, Langenstein concentration camp.

196 **ambitious and dangerous operation**: Eddie Willner, interviewed by Neal Goldenberg, Oral History Interview, Jewish Community Council of Greater Washington, United States Holocaust Memorial Museum, March 15, 1987; Eddie Willner, interviewed by Ellen Epstein, Oral History Interview with Eddie Willner, United States Holocaust Memorial Museum, May 25, 1989.

196 **("extermination through labor")**: Eddie Willner and Mike Swaab, conversations with author.

196 **getting maximum productivity out of**: Eddie Willner and Mike Swaab, conversations with author.

196 **steady stream of replacement**: Eddie Willner and Mike Swaab, conversations with author.

197 **"*Schlagt sie nur*"**: Willi Sonnenberg (tunnels foreman), witness testimony quoting Wilhelm Lübeck, Protokoll Josef Vik, Sammlung Gedenkstätte, Langenstein-Zwieberge, Signaturnnummer 65.

197 **crematorium in the nearby town**: Alberto Berti, "Recollections of Langenstein Concentration Camp, as translated by Johanna Willner," n.d.; Peter Filkins, *H. G. Adler: A Life in Many Worlds* (Oxford, UK: Oxford University Press, 2019), https://books.google.com.tr/books?id=KOCGDwAAQBAJ&pg=PT285&lpg=PT285&dq=Oberscharf%C3%BChrer+Paul+Tscheu&source=bl&ots=r3-62fhb1Y&sig=ACfU3U1jB-JDjt3Su8elQq0Mnq6hyUqGmA&hl

NOTES

=en&sa=X&ved=2ahUKEwisoo6BmJPiAhVtwcQBHZicBW8Q6AEwB3oEC AgQAQ#v=onepage&q=Oberscharf%C3%BChrer%20Paul%20Tscheu&f =false.

197 **five hundred Death's Head SS:** Gedenkstätte für die Opfer des KZ Langenstein-Zwieberge, n.d.

197 **men from twenty-three different countries:** Eddie Willner, interviewed by Neal Goldenberg, March 15, 1987; Eddie Willner, interviewed by Ellen Epstein, May 25, 1989.

197 **Jews were separated out:** Bernard Klieger, "Zwieberge" testimony, as translated by Johanna Willner, n.d.

197 **targeted with typical extreme hate:** Jean Soulas, French partisan, witness, and Langenstein survivor, conversation with author, April, 2009: "Jews were treated the worst."

197 **only barracks with no bunks:** Herb Mandel, 8th Armored Division, conversation with French Langenstein prisoner: "Jews treated twice as bad as everyone else"; "Conversation with Herbert Mandel, Stuart Lesorgen, and Noel March," United States Holocaust Memorial Museum, May 2021, https://collections.ushmm.org/search/catalog/irn724181.

198 **twelve-hour shifts:** *Underground Factories*, 38.

198 **at a blistering pace:** Abraham S. Holocaust Testimony (HVT-2499), Fortunoff Video Archive for Holocaust Testimonies, Yale University.

198 **In just eleven months:** Dr. Nicolas Bertrand, conversation with author, April 17, 2019; *Gedenkstätte für die Opfer des KZ Langenstein-Zwieberge*.

198 **had already carved out:** Headquarters Eighth Air Force, Office of the Director of Intelligence Annex to Daily Intelligence Summery No. 31, Special Intelligence, 8 June 1945.

198 **metal filament lamps:** *Underground Factories*, 28.

198 **sea of backbreaking slave labor:** Benjamin Kawer, interviewed by Geoffrey D. Reynolds, West Bloomfield, MI, USC Shoah Foundation, YouTube, August 28, 1996, https://www.youtube.com/watch?v=VUh5TEuV6xg.

198 **cycle of blasting:** A. D. I. (K) Report No. 625/1944. Testimony of German Army POW 1944 who worked in Langenstein as a toolmaker for Junkers, Langenstein Memorial and Museum; Eddie Willner and Mike Swaab, conversations with author.

198 **the fine dust:** Edward Gastfriend, *My Father's Testament: Memoir of a Jewish Teenager, 1938–1945* (Philadelphia: Temple University Press, 1999), 156.

198 **sledgehammers and pickaxes:** Bernard Klieger, *Der Weg, den Wir Gingen* (Brüssel: Verlag Codac Juifs, 1960).

198 **Roof collapses due to the friable:** *Underground Factories*, 80.

199 **had been electrocuted:** Eddie Willner, conversations with author.

199 **not allowed to evacuate:** Eddie Willner, interviewed by Ellen Epstein; Eddie Willner and Mike Swaab, conversations with author.

199 **blasting teams carving out:** Gastfriend, *My Father's Testament*, 156; Bernard Klieger, "Zwieberge" testimony, as translated by Johanna Willner, n.d.; Eddie Willner and Mike Swaab, conversations with author.

199 **five feet every eight hours:** *Underground Factories*, 24.

199 **dynamiting and drilling:** *Underground Factories in Central Germany, Declassified Secret,* Combined Intelligence Objective Sub-Committee, Item Nos.

NOTES

        4, 5, 25, 30, File No. XXXII-17; Eddie Willner and Mike Swaab, conversations with author.
199   **Some couldn't even swallow:** Alex H. (HVT-210) and Sigmund W. (HVT-55) Holocaust Testimony, Fortunoff Video Archive for Holocaust Testimonies, Yale University Library.
199   **just dropped dead:** Eddie Willner, conversations with author; Gastfriend, *My Father's Testament*, 163–65.
199   **finally did so at Langenstein:** Eddie Willner, conversations with author.
199   **end of their endurance:** "Gedenkstätte für die Opfer des KZ Langenstein-Zwieberge," Langenstein Concentration Camp Memorial and Museum, Langenstein, Germany.
199   **knowing they were going to die:** Sigmund W. (HVT-55) Holocaust Testimony, Fortunoff Video Archive for Holocaust Testimonies, Yale University Library.
199   **end of their suffering:** Berti, "Recollections of Langenstein Concentration Camp."
199   **prayed to die:** Alex H. (HVT-210) Holocaust Testimony, Fortunoff Video Archive for Holocaust Testimonies, Yale University Library.
200   **throw in *Muselmänner*:** Eddie Willner, interviewed by Ellen Epstein, May 25, 1989; Eddie Willner, conversations with author.
200   **greatest fight of their lives:** Eddie Willner, interviewed by Ellen Epstein, May 25, 1989.

CHAPTER TWENTY-SEVEN: THE PRAYER

201   **"Dick to all dick stations":** Stuart Thayer's notes.
201   **a gentleman wearing an ascot:** S. Thayer.
202   **"borrowed" a blowtorch:** Fred Jackson Headrick Sr. Collection, Veterans History Project, American Folklife Center, Library of Congress.
202   **warning to his soldiers:** John Nichol, *The Last Escape: The Untold Story of Allied Prisoners of War in Europe, 1944–45* (New York: Viking, 2003), 35.
202   **"I expect every able-bodied German":** Adolf Hitler, Broadcast on the 12th Anniversary of the National Socialist Regime, January 30, 1945.
203   **the M26 Pershing:** Zebra Mission Report, D/32nd Armored Regiment received one T26E3 Pershing heavy tank Serial No. 36, NARA (courtesy of Steve Zaloga).
203   **"helmet right off his head":** S. Thayer.
203   **"two months quicker":** Stuart Thayer, conversation with Reese Graham, D Company Pershing tank 90mm gunner, Stuart Thayer's notes.
203   **more to using the Panzerfaust:** Peter Chamberlain and Terry Gander, *Anti-Tank Weapons* (World War 2 Fact Files) (New York: Arco Publishing, 1974).
203   **Launched by a single soldier:** Steven J. Zaloga, *US Battle Tanks, 1917–1945* (Oxford, UK: Osprey, 2024), 41.
203   **Like a ton of dynamite:** Fred Headrick, conversation with author, March 16, 2005.
203   **turning the inside:** S. Thayer.
204   **take up arms and defend:** Adolf Hitler, "Broadcast on the 12th Anniversary of the National Socialist Regime," January 30, 1945.

NOTES

204 *give me a sign*: Elmer Hovland, conversation with author, June 7, 2001.
204 **drop back down:** S. Hovland, taped interview with Elmer Hovland, 2004, Hovland Family Records, Luverne, Minnesota.
204 **feather of sharp steel:** Elmer Hovland, conversation with author, June 7, 2001; Elmer L. Hovland Collection (AFC/2001/001/94051), Veterans History Project.
204 **company was shaken:** Elmer Hovland, conversation with author, June 7, 2001.
204 **"If I didn't listen":** Elmer Hovland, conversation with author, June 7, 2001.
204 **"Hovland, you all right?":** S. Hovland, taped interview with Elmer Hovland, 2004.
205 **"built a brotherhood":** Elmer Hovland, conversation with author, February 20, 2003.
205 **Myers scouted forward:** Fred Jackson Headrick Sr. Collection, Veterans History Project.
205 **sliding like a boxer:** S. Thayer.
206 **blast of an 88mm gun:** Fred Jackson Headrick Sr. Collection, Veterans History Project.
206 **side of Myers's tank:** S. Thayer.
206 **knocking out a tank destroyer:** S. Thayer; Fred Headrick, conversation with author, March 16, 2005.
206 **ball of flames:** S. Thayer.
206 **watched from the ditch:** S. Thayer.
207 **inventoried Myers's belongings:** Inventory form AG ETO, form no. 26, "Inventory of Personal Effects, First Lieutenant Charles E. Myers, May 8, 1945, signed, Lieutenant Elmer Hovland. (Courtesy of Myers-Keeley family records.)
207 **"one of our finest":** Chaplain (Captain) James S. Timberlake letter to Mr. and Mrs. Martin L. Myers, May 17, 1945. (Courtesy of Myers-Keeley family records.)
207 **silver ID bracelet:** S. Thayer.
208 **Vance brought food to him:** S. Thayer; Fred Headrick, conversation with author, March 16, 2005.

CHAPTER TWENTY-EIGHT: BREAKOUT

209 **Dora V-2 production:** "Liberation of Dora-Mittelbau, April 11, 1945," *Holocaust Encyclopedia*, United States Holocaust Memorial Museum, https://encyclopedia.ushmm.org/content/en/timeline-event/holocaust/1942-1945/liberation-of-dora-mittelbau, https://encyclopedia.ushmm.org/content/en/timeline-event/holocaust/1942-1945/liberation-of-dora-mittelbau.
209 **"No prisoners shall be allowed":** Anjan Basu, "Abandon Hope All Ye Who Enter Here: The Hell-Gates of Dachau," The Wire, March 22, 2019, https://thewire.in/history/holocaust-nazis-dachau-world-war; Letter to SS Oberstürmbahnfuhrer Eduard Weiter, Commandant of Dachau, April 1945, Subject: Liberating Dachau 1945.
209 **town of Gardelegen:** "Gardelegen," *Holocaust Encyclopedia*, United States Holocaust Memorial Museum, https://encyclopedia.ushmm.org/content/en/article/gardelegen.

NOTES

209 **camp to be evacuated:** Jean-Pierre Valantin and Nicolas Bertrand, *Der Todesmarsch der Häftlinge des Konzentrationslagers Langenstein-Zwieberge* (Saxony-Anhalt, Germany: Mitteldeutscher Verlag, 2018), 16–25.

210 **making plans to escape:** Eddie Willner, conversations with author.

210 **now or never:** Eddie Willner, interviewed by Ellen Epstein, Oral History Interview with Eddie Willner, United States Holocaust Memorial Museum, May 25, 1989; Edward Gastfriend, *My Father's Testament: Memoir of a Jewish Teenager, 1938–1945* (Philadelphia: Temple University Press, 1999), 165.

210 **heavily armed with machine guns:** Eddie Willner, interviewed by Ellen Epstein, May 25, 1989.

210 **march them out:** Eddie Willner, interviewed by Ellen Epstein, May 25, 1989

211 **marching them into the tunnels:** Valantin and Bertrand, *Der Todesmarsch*, 17.

211 **sealed and dynamited:** U.S. Army Interrogation of Langenstein Concentration Camp SS Guard Unterscharführer Machold, Declassified Executive Order 11356, NARA Archive, NND775032.

211 **killing them all:** Berti, "Recollections of Langenstein Concentration Camp"; Peter Filkins, *H. G. Adler: A Life in Many Worlds* (Oxford, UK: Oxford University Press, 2019).

211 **"First column, march!":** Valantin and Bertrand, *Der Todesmarsch*, 29–30.

211 **abruptly changed plans:** Eddie Willner, interviewed by Neal Goldenberg, Oral History Interview, Jewish Community Council of Greater Washington, United States Holocaust Memorial Museum, March 15, 1987.

211 **"I carry the Hosts":** Valantin and Bertrand, *Der Todesmarsch*, 45.

212 **"Criminals coming through!":** "Conversation with Herbert Mandel, Stuart Lesorgen, and Noel March," United States Holocaust Memorial Museum, May 2021.

212 **"last stages of life":** Paul Scherf, witness, Von Sven Gückel, "Kriegsende im Kreis Wittenberg: Martyrium hat sich ins Gedächtnis gebrannt," *Mitteldeutsche Zeitung,* April 17, 2015.

212 **coal window to see:** "Conversation with Herbert Mandel, Stuart Lesorgen, and Noel March," United States Holocaust Memorial Museum, May 2021.

212 **they ate weeds:** Recollections Familie Tenhumberg, http://www.tenhumbergreinhard.de/1933-1945-lager-1/1933-1945-lager-h/halberstadt-langenstein-zwieberge.html.

212 **"sacrifice our life":** Valantin and Bertrand, *Der Todesmarsch*, 29–30.

213 **lay among "hundreds":** Valantin and Bertrand, *Der Todesmarsch*, 44.

213 **handful of dandelion:** Valantin and Bertrand, *Der Todesmarsch*, 44; Paul Le Goupil, *From Normandy to Auschwitz* (Barnsley, South Yorkshire, UK: Pen & Sword Military, 2018), 45.

213 **a woman appeared:** Author interview with Volker Geppert, Welbsleben, April 2015; Recollections Familie Tenhumberg.

213 **drove them like hares:** Recollections Familie Tenhumberg.

214 **the leader yelled, "Go!":** Eddie Willner, interviewed by Ellen Epstein, May 25, 1989; Eddie Willner, conversations with author.

NOTES

214 **groaned, "I'm done":** Eddie Willner, conversations with author; Eddie Willner, interviewed by Neal Goldenberg, March 15, 1987.
214 **strangled the dog:** Eddie Willner, interviewed by Neal Goldenberg, March 15, 1987; Eddie Willner, interviewed by Ellen Epstein, May 25, 1989; Eddie Willner, conversations with author.
214 **thrashing and clawing:** Eddie Willner, interviewed by Neal Goldenberg, March 15, 1987.

CHAPTER TWENTY-NINE: ANGELS
216 **home guard Volkssturm militias:** Louis de Wijze, as told to Kees van Cadsand, *Only My Life: A Survivor's Story* (New York: St. Martin's Press, 1997); Jean-Pierre Valantin and Nicolas Bertrand, *Der Todesmarsch der Häftlinge des Konzentrationslagers Langenstein-Zwieberge* (Saxony-Anhalt, Germany: Mitteldeutscher Verlag, 2018), 37–39.
216 **had shown no mercy:** Valantin and Bertrand, *Der Todesmarsch*, 37–39.
216 **five years in captivity:** Eddie Willner, conversation with author. (Five years in captivity includes internment and labor concentration camps.)
217 **would kill him:** Eddie Willner, interviewed by Neal Goldenberg, Oral History Interview, Jewish Community Council of Greater Washington, United States Holocaust Memorial Museum, March 15, 1987; Eddie Willner, interviewed by Ellen Epstein, Oral History Interview with Eddie Willner, United States Holocaust Memorial Museum, May 25, 1989.
217 **shadow to shadow:** Eddie Willner, interviewed by Neal Goldenberg, March 15, 1987.
217 **picked the bullet out:** Eddie Willner, conversations with author.
217 **steer clear of any sign:** Eddie Willner, interviewed by Arwen Donahue and Gail Schwartz, Oral History Interview, United States Holocaust Memorial Museum, July 12, 2000.
218 **wandered right smack:** Eddie Willner, interviewed by Neal Goldenberg, March 15, 1987.
218 **two boys sneaked past:** Eddie Willner, interviewed by Ellen Epstein, May 25, 1989.
218 **Bernburg and Köthen:** Eddie Willner, conversations with author.
220 **face-to-face:** Fred Jackson Headrick Sr. Collection, Veterans History Project; Fred Headrick, conversation with author, June 12, 2007.
220 **"They were shaking":** Elmer Hovland interview, *Beacon News* (Luverne, MS), June 6, 2001.
220 **"We stared at them":** Fred Headrick, conversation with author, June 12, 2007.
220 **"younger than me":** F. Headrick conversation with author, June 12, 2007.
220 **"had seen evil":** F. Headrick conversation with author, June 12, 2007.
221 **"I am also a Jew":** Eddie Willner, interviewed by Neal Goldenberg, March 15, 1987; Eddie Willner, conversations with author.

CHAPTER THIRTY: "THEY'RE WITH US NOW"
222 **Eddie was speaking excitedly:** Eddie Willner, conversations with author.
222 **loose blue-and-white-striped uniforms:** Lori Ehde, "Jewish Prison Escapee Thanks U.S. Veterans, Interview with Elmer Hovland," *Rock County Star*

NOTES

Herald, interview, 2002; Elmer Hovland, conversation with author, April 9, 2004.
223 **first minutes of being rescued:** Eddie Willner, interviewed by Ellen Epstein, Oral History Interview with Eddie Willner, May 25, 1989, United States Holocaust Memorial Museum; Eddie Willner, conversations with author.
223 **relinquishing their weapons:** Eddie Willner, interviewed by Ellen Epstein, May 25, 1989.
224 **"They're with us now":** Elmer Hovland, conversation with author, June 8, 2001.
224 **weighed in at seventy-five pounds:** Eddie Willner, interviewed by Ellen Epstein, May 25, 1989.
224 **to a nearby farmhouse:** Eddie Willner, interviewed by Ellen Epstein, May 25, 1989.
224 **Elmer replied: "Eat":** Elmer Hovland, conversation with author, June 8, 2001.
225 **"found two boys":** Elmer Hovland, conversation with author, June 8, 2001.
225 **"kept smiling at us":** L. DeCola, conversation with author, July 13, 2013.
225 **unwrapping C-rat crackers:** L. DeCola, conversation with author, June 13, 2013.
226 **everything was indeed going to be okay:** Eddie Willner, conversations with author.
226 **"whaddya wan' me to fix ya?":** L. DeCola, conversation with author, July 13, 2013; Mike Swaab, conversation with author, July 2, 1978.
227 **"it was touch 'n' go":** L. DeCola, conversation with author, July 13, 2013.
227 **"all we needed to know":** Louis DeCola, interview by Patrick Golden, *Metro West Daily News* (Waltham, MA), November 11, 2002; L. DeCola, conversation with author, April 10, 2010.
227 **happily helped him:** Eddie Willner, conversations with author.

CHAPTER THIRTY-ONE: BIG BROTHERS

229 **"snipers and bazookamen":** 1st Battalion and D Company Daily Activity Logs for April 14–15, 1945, NARA Declassification Authority NND735017, National Archives and Records Administration.
229 **German troops assaulted:** Frank Woolner, *Spearhead in the West: The Third Armored Division, 1941–45* (Nashville, TN: Battery Press, 1980), 250.
229 **"They were like sponges":** L. DeCola, conversation with author, July 13, 2013.
229 **"Tell him we need":** L. DeCola, conversation with author, July 13, 2013.
230 **part of the team:** Eddie Willner, conversations with author.
230 **soldiers lit up:** L. DeCola, conversation with author, July 13, 2013.
231 **"I'm from Chatt'nooga, see":** Fred Headrick, conversation with author, March 16, 2005.
232 **place they wanted to be:** Eddie Willner, conversations with author.

NOTES

232 **Overwhelmed with emotion:** Eddie Willner, conversations with author.
232 **boys on the army payroll:** Eddie Willner, conversations with author.
232 **Elmer had Eddie accompany him:** Eddie Willner, conversations with author.
233 **his right-hand man:** Elmer Hovland, conversation with author, June 8, 2001.

CHAPTER THIRTY-TWO: UNBREAKABLE BOND

234 **the Mulde River:** Stuart Thayer's notes.
234 **had been killed:** "Third Armored Division," US Center of Military History, US Army, https://history.army.mil/documents/eto-ob/3ad-eto.htm.
234 **100 percent of its tanks:** Belton Y. Cooper, *Death Traps: The Survival of an American Armored Division in World War II*, xxii.
235 **"No more firing the tank":** S. Thayer.
235 **2 million German women:** Eric Westervelt, "Silence Broken on Red Army Rapes in Germany," NPR, July 17, 2009, https://www.npr.org/templates/story/story.php?storyId=106687768.
235 **draw up new mandates:** Letters to local German authorities following armistice issuing directives (in German), May–August 1945, 3rd Armored Division letterhead, signed by 1LT Elmer Hovland or 1LT Lewis Lively.
235 **commanded immediate compliance:** Eddie Willner, conversations with author.
236 **"Eddie Willner, Company Assistant":** Letters to the Mayor of Wenigumstadt issuing directives (in German), June 4, 1945, signed by 1LT Lewis Lively and Eddie Willner.
236 **quite the education:** Eddie Willner, conversations with author.
236 **absorbed it all:** L. DeCola, conversation with author, July 13, 2013.
237 **hit a baseball:** Fred Headrick, conversation with author, March 16, 2005.
237 **dote on the boys:** L. DeCola, conversation with author, July 13, 2013.
237 **"like our little brothers":** L. DeCola, conversation with author, July 13, 2013

CHAPTER THIRTY-THREE: LIBERATION

240 **"We'll never give up":** Volker Ullrich, *Hitler: Ascent, 1889–1939*, 317.
240 **addressed the world:** "Proclamation of President Truman—May 8, 1945," Avalon Project, Lillian Goldman Law Library, Yale University, https://avalon.law.yale.edu/wwii/gs8.asp#:~:text=The%20Allied%20armies%2C%20through%20sacrifice,millions%20of%20free%2Dborn%20men.
241 **83rd Infantry Division:** Medical Report of Concentration Camp Thekenburg near Langenstein, 8th Armored Division, Langenstein Concentration Camp Museum.
241 **medical team led by:** Kenneth Z. testimony (HVT-1485), Fortunoff Video Archive for Holocaust Testimonies, Yale University Library, https://fortunoff.aviaryplatform.com/collections/5/collection_resources/1548?u=t&keywords[]=Zierler.
241 **accompanied by American war correspondent:** Kenneth Z., Fortunoff Video Archive.

NOTES

241 **rickety legs or lying:** Conversation with Herbert Mandel, Stuart Lesorgen, and Noel March, May 2021, United States Holocaust Memorial Museum.
241 **"surrounded by human wreckage":** Dr. Kenneth Zierler to Mr. Dieter Bohl, letter, March 31, 1995.
241 **"You are free!":** "Bittersweet Reunion: A Nazi Camp Survivor Finds a U.S. Soldier Who Helped Free Him," *Sun Sentinel, Boca Raton News*, no. 22, January 22, 2004.
241 **"kissed my shoes":** Kenneth Z., Fortunoff Video Archive.
241 **"lifted him back up":** Dr. Kenneth Zierler to Mr. Dieter Bohl, letter, March 31, 1995.
241 **prisoners stared blankly back:** "USC Shoah Foundation Institute Testimony of Bernard Metrick," September 14, 1977, https://collections.ushmm.org/search/catalog/vha34321.
242 **fell down dead:** "USC Shoah Foundation Testimony of Bernard Metrick."
242 **twenty and twenty-five freed:** "Gedenkstätte für die Opfer des KZ Langenstein-Zwieberge," Concentration Camp Memorial and Museum, Langenstein, Germany.
242 **demanded to speak:** Dr. Kenneth Zierler to Mr. Dieter Bohl, letter, March 31, 1995, "Gedenkstätte für die Opfer des KZ Langenstein- Zwieberge," Concentration Camp Memorial and Museum, Langenstein, German.
243 **Patton and Bradley:** "Eisenhower Asks Congress and Press to Witness Nazi Horrors," History Unfolded: U.S. Newspapers and the Holocaust, U.S. Holocaust Memorial Museum, https://newspapers.ushmm.org/events/eisenhower-asks-congress-and-press-to-witness-nazi-horrors; "What We Fought Against: Ohrdruf," April 4, 2020, National World War II Museum, New Orleans, https://www.nationalww2museum.org/war/articles/ohrdruf-concentration-camp.
243 **"things I saw beggar description":** "What We Fought Against: Ohrdruf," April 4, 2020, National World War II Museum.
243 **"We are told":** "What We Fought Against: Ohrdruf."
243 **Eisenhower ordered local Germans:** "Holocaust and the Concentration Camp Trials: Prosecution of Nazi War Crimes," Gale, https://www.gale.com/c/holocaust-and-the-concentration-camp-trials-prosecution-of-nazi-war-crimes.
243 **"I visited every nook":** "Eisenhower's Foresight: Protecting the Truth of the Holocaust," United States Holocaust Memorial Museum, https://www.ushmm.org/online-calendar/event/VEFBSTAYCONEISEN0121.
244 **"The wrongs which we seek":** "The Nuremberg Trials (1945)," *British Pathe Gazette*, YouTube, https://www.youtube.com/watch?v=szhpgDz5iC8.861.
244 **"I did not see anything":** Karta Informacyjna, Instytut Pamięci Narodowej, Warsaw (IPN GK 184/ 262).
244 **"did not see anyone being killed":** Karta Informacyjna.
245 **"against the atrocities":** Karta Informacyjna.
245 **presided over many killings:** Karta Informacyjna.

NOTES

245 **sentenced to death:** *Zentrale Stelle*, Bundesarchiv B 162/ 8866; see also Elżbieta Kobierska-Motar, *Ekstradycja przestępców wojennych do Polski z czterech stref okupacyjnych Niemiec, 1946–1950* (Warsaw, 1992).

245 **died a free man:** Interrogation Report 12, August 1947, Josef Szylingow, Polish Military Mission for War Crimes.

245 **"splendid work in exterminating":** Karta Informacyjna.

245 **Kurt Klipp, commandant of Blechhammer:** Karta Informacyjna.

245 **died of typhus:** *Zentrale Stelle*, Bundesarchiv B 162/ 8863.

245 **the cowboy monster:** Steiner testimony; *Zentrale Stelle*, Bundesarchiv B 162: survivor testimonies of witnesses Arno Lustiger, Peter Sturm (Ghetto Fighters testimony); Siegwald Ganglmair and other witnesses.

245 **listed as a "war death":** Hermann Leinkenjost, Recollections Familie Tenhumberg, http://www.tenhumbergreinhard.de/1933-1945-taeter-und-mitlaeufer/1933-1945-biografien-l/leinkenjost-hermann.html

245 **convicted and sentenced to death:** "The Pichen and Francioh Tribunals," Bergen Trials, Imperial War Museum (IWM), https://www.iwm.org.uk/search/global?query=Bergen+trials, http://www.bergenbelsen.co.uk/pages/trial/trial/trialdefencecase/Trial_046_Pichen.html; http://www.bergenbelsen.co.uk/pages/Trial/Trial/TrialDefenceCase/Trial_041_Francioh.html.

246 **released and went on:** Willi Sonnenberg (tunnels foreman), witness testimony quoting Wilhelm Lübeck, Protokoll Josef Vik, Sammlung Gedenkstätte, Langenstein-Zwieberge, Signaturnnummer 65.

246 **1,600 Nazi scientists:** Clair E. Aubin, "The History of Nazi Immigration to the U.S. Has Been Forgotten," *Time*, October 12, 2023, https://time.com/6322156/history-of-nazi-immigration/.

246 **Wernher von Braun:** Michael Neufeld, "Project Paperclip and American Rocketry After World War II," March 31, 2023, National Air and Space Museum, Smithsonian, https://airandspace.si.edu/stories/editorial/project-paperclip-and-american-rocketry-after-world-war-ii.

246 **cost of tens of thousands:** Alejandro de la Garza, "How Historians Are Reckoning with the Former Nazi Who Launched America's Space Program," *Time*, July 18, 2019, https://time.com/5627637/nasa-nazi-von-braun/.

CHAPTER THIRTY-FOUR: THE FINAL GOODBYE

248 **last possible moment:** L. DeCola, conversation with author, July 14, 2013.

248 **a lucky hand:** Eddie Willner, conversations with author.

249 **"you boys are gonna be all right":** Elmer Hovland, conversation with author, April 9, 2004.

249 **fighting back emotions:** Fred Headrick, conversation with author, March 16, 2005.

249 **"painful to separate":** L. DeCola, conversation with author, July 14, 2013.

NOTES

CHAPTER THIRTY-FIVE: "I WANT THOSE DAYS BACK"

253 **"It was a privilege"**: Stuart Thayer's notes.
254 **he was the best leader**: S. Thayer.
255 **disembarked in New York Harbor**: Steve Hovland, interview with author, May 20, 2018.
255 **craftsmanship and his dedication**: S. Hovland, interview with author, May 20, 2018.
255 **giving to charities**: Jon Hovland, interview with author, April 29, 2018.
255 **power of faith**: Elmer Hovland to Eddie Willner, letter, June 8, 1995, Willner Family Archives.
255 **"good citizens, good neighbors"**: *Rock County Star Herald* (Luverne, MN) editorials written by Elmer Hovland, Hovland Family Records.
256 **two more diners**: L. DeCola, conversation with author, April 10, 2010.
256 **Bradley Full Fashion Hosiery Mill**: Fred Jackson Headrick Sr. Collection, Veterans History Project (AFC/2001/001/5954), American Folklife Center, Library of Congress, https://www.loc.gov/item/afc2001001.05954/.
257 **never fully let go**: S. Thayer.
257 **volunteered at the Medal of Honor**: Fred Jackson Headrick Sr. Collection, Veterans History Project.
257 **"it made you appreciate"**: Fred Jackson Headrick Sr., Veterans History Project.
257 **"he wasn't given a Silver Star"**: Fred Jackson Headrick Sr. Collection, Veterans History Project.
257 **three Panzers in Freyneux**: "James William Vance Obituary," https://www.asturner.com/obituaries/james-william-vance.
258 **Myers's remains stayed on**: "Charles E. Myers World War II Gold Star Veteran from Pennsylvania," HonorStates, https://www.honorstates.org/profiles/327451/.
259 **their coming of age**: S. Thayer.
259 **"That's why I'm here"**: S. Thayer.
260 **"went to the moon"**: S. Thayer.
261 **"good and skilled men"**: Elmer Hovland, conversation with author, June 8, 2001.
261 **"My Christian faith"**: Steve Hovland, interview with author, April 21, 2019.
261 **"face death in battle"**: *Rock County Star Herald* editorial written by Elmer Hovland, Hovland Family Records.
261 **"Is prayer still important"**: *Rock County Star Herald*, Elmer Hovland letter to the editor, Hovland Family Records.
261 **"As an individual"**: Elmer L. Hovland Collection, Veterans History Project (AFC/2001/001/94051), American Folklife Center, Library of Congress, https://www.loc.gov/item/afc2001001.94051/.
262 **"War was H-E-double-L"**: Fred Headrick, conversation with author, June 12, 2007; Fred Jackson Headrick Sr. Collection, Veterans History Project.
262 **"They were kids"**: L. DeCola, conversation with author, April 10, 2010.
262 **"needed all the compassion"**: Lori Ehde, "Interview with Elmer Hoveland," *Rock County Star Herald*, 1998.

NOTES

262 **"wanted to eat"**: L. DeCola, conversation with author, April 10, 2010.
262 **"Oh, they were in rough shape"**: L. DeCola, conversation with author, April 10, 2010.
262 **"step away from death"**: Patrick Golden, "Interview with Louis 'Pepsi' DeCola," *Metro West Daily News* (Waltham, MA), November 11, 2002.
262 **"we saved 'em"**: Fred Headrick, conversation with author, June 12, 2007; Fred Jackson Headrick Sr. Collection, Veterans History Project.
263 **"I look at this bunch"**: S. Thayer.

CHAPTER THIRTY-SIX: THE CALL

265 **a letter arrived**: 3rd Armored Division Veterans Association Letter to Johanna Willner, Willner Family Archives, 1999.
266 **his whole life**: Johanna Willner, conversation with author, February 2, 2022.
267 **sailed separately to the United States**: Eddie Willner, interviewed by Esther Finder, Jewish Survivor, USC Shoah Foundation, June 22, 1997.
268 **military police criminal investigator**: Eddie Willner, interviewed by Ellen Epstein, Oral History Interview with Eddie Willner, United States Holocaust Memorial Museum, May 25, 1989.
268 **newly formed *Bundesnachrichtendienst***: Eddie Willner, conversations with author.
269 **attributed his survival**: Eddie Willner, interviewed by Neal Goldenberg, Oral History Interview, Jewish Community Council of Greater Washington, United States Holocaust Memorial Museum, March 15, 1987.
269 **for over twenty years**: Johanna Willner, conversation with Elmer Hovland, February 7, 2000.
270 **"call gave me goosebumps"**: Patrick Golden, "Interview with Louis 'Pepsi' DeCola," *Metro West Daily News* (Waltham, MA), November 11, 2002; L. DeCola, conversation with author, April 11, 2010.
270 **"want to see you guys again"**: Eddie Willner, conversations with author.

CHAPTER THIRTY-SEVEN: THE REUNION

271 ***Washington Post* sent a reporter**: Tamara Jones, "Thanking 'the Boys' Who Gave Him Life," *Washington Post*, September 16, 2002.
275 **"saving our father"**: Fred Jackson Headrick Sr. Collection (AFC/2001/001/5954), Veterans History Project, American Folklife Center, Library of Congress, https://www.loc.gov/item/afc2001001.05954/.
277 **to be personally thanked**: Lori Ehde, "Jewish Prison Escapee Thanks U.S. Veterans, Interview with Elmer Hoveland," *Rock County Star Herald* (Luverne, MN), 2002.

CHAPTER THIRTY-EIGHT: POSTCRIPT

278 **begin with "Here lived"**: Gunter Demnig "Stolperseine" (Stumbling Blocks) Project to Remember the Victims of the Holocaust, https://www.stolpersteine.eu/en/home; Suzanne Cords, "Stolperstein Holocaust Memorial Gets New App," Deutsche Welle, November 9, 2022, https://www.dw.com/en/stolperstein-holocaust-memorial-gets-new-app/a-41107926.

NOTES

279 **"thanked God many times":** Letters between Eddie Willner and Elmer Hovland, 2002–2006.
279 **"you are a hero":** Fred Headrick to Eddie Willner, letter, undated.
279 **"I will never forget":** Eddie Willner to Brady Laird, letter, 2003.

EPILOGUE

284 **Total U.S. losses topped:** "U.S. Department of Defense Casualty Analysis System," https://dcas.dmdc.osd.mil/dcas/app/summaryData/casualties/principalWars.
284 **UK would also lose:** "The Fallen," UK Parliament, https://www.parliament.uk/business/publications/research/olympic-britain/crime-and-defence/the-fallen/#:~:text=In%20WWII%20there%20were%20384%2C000,half%20of%20them%20in%20London.
284 **French partisans played:** "Remembering D-Day: Key Facts and Figures About Epochal World War II Invasion," Associated Press, June 5, 2023, https://apnews.com/article/d-day-invasion-normandy-france-nazis-07094640dd7bb938a23e144cc23f348c.
285 **"forgotten" Fifteenth Air Force:** "The United States Strategic Bombing Survey," U.S. Air Force Air University, U.S. Government Printing Office, September 30, 1945 (7th printing, March 2001), https://www.airuniversity.af.edu/Portals/10/AUPress/Books/B_0020_SPANGRUD_STRATEGIC_BOMBING_SURVEYS.pdf
286 **1,460-mile drive across Europe:** "Third Armored Division Accomplishments," https://3ad.com/.
287 **known to have survived:** Benjamin Rosendahl, "Moenchengladbach," Destroyed German Synagogues and Communities, http://germansynagogues.com/index.php/synagogues-and-communities?pid=63&sid=905:moenchengladbach.
288 **Transport 31 that deported:** Serge Klarsfeld, *Memorial to the Jews Deported from France, 1942–1944: Documentation of the Deportation of the Victims of the Final Solution in France* (Klarsfeld Foundation, 1983), 261.
288 **only around 2,000 survived:** Katherine Shaver, "U.S. Begins Paying Out Reparations from France to Holocaust Survivors and Their Heirs," *Washington Post*, September 15, 2016, https://www.jewishvirtuallibrary.org/france-compensates-americans-deported-on-french-trains.
288 **frigid death march from Blechhammer:** Danuta Czech, *Auschwitz Chronicle*; Franciszek Piper, "Nebenlager Blechhammer," *Hefte von Auschwitz* 10 (1967): 37–39.
288 **500 survived the march:** "Halberstadt (Langenstein-Zwieberge)," Recollections Familie Tenhumberg, http://www.tenhumbergreinhard.de/1933-1945-lager-1/1933-1945-lager-h/halberstadt-langenstein-zwieberge.html; Peter Filkins, *H. G. Adler: A Life in Many Worlds* (New York: Oxford University Press, 2019).
288 **More than 56,500 Dutch Jews:** "The Netherlands," *Holocaust Encyclopedia*, U.S. Holocaust Memorial Museum, https://encyclopedia.ushmm.org/content/en/article/the-netherlands.
288 **more than seven thousand captives:** Dr. Gero Fedtke, Gedenkstätte für die Opfer des KZ Langenstein-Zwieberge.

NOTES

288 **Bertrand, a French resistance fighter:** "French Resistance Veteran Buried Near German Camp," *Times of Israel*, April 12, 2014, https://www.timesofisrael.com/french-resistance-veteran-buried-near-german-camp/#:~:text=Bertrand's%20ashes%20were%20interred%20on,forces%20on%20April%2011%2C%201945.

SELECTED BIBLIOGRAPHY

Ambrose, Stephen E. *Band of Brothers: E Company, 506th Regiment, 101st Airborne from Normandy to Hitler's Eagle's Nest*. New York: Simon & Schuster, 2001.
———. *Citizen Soldiers*. New York: Simon & Schuster, 1998.
———. *The Wild Blue*. New York: Simon & Schuster, 2001.
Astor, Gerald. *A Blood-Dimmed Tide: The Battle of the Bulge by the Men Who Fought It*. New York: Dutton, 1992.
Atkinson, Rick. *The Guns at Last Light: The War in Western Europe, 1944–1945*, vol. 3 of the Liberation Trilogy. New York: Henry Holt, 2013.
Beevor, Antony. *Ardennes 1944: The Battle of the Bulge*. New York: Viking, 2015.
Brokaw, Tom. *The Greatest Generation*. New York: Random House, 2000.
Clary, Robert. *From the Holocaust to Hogan's Heroes: The Autobiography of Robert Clary*. Boulder, CO: Taylor Trade, 2007.
Cooper, Belton Y. *Death Traps: The Survival of an American Armored Division in World War II*. New York: Presidio Press, 2003.
Czech, Danuta. *Auschwitz Chronicle: 1939–1945*. New York: Henry Holt, 1997.
De Wijze, Louis. *Only My Life: A Survivor's Story*. New York: St. Martin's Press, 1997.
Ercken, Günter. *Juden in Mönchengladbach, Band 1-3*. Mönchengladbach: Stadtarchiv Mönchengladbach, 1988–1990.
Filkins, Peter. *H. G. Adler: A Life in Many Worlds*. New York: Oxford University Press, 2019.
Frank, Werner. *The Curse of Gurs: Way Station to Auschwitz*. Charleston, SC: CreateSpace, 2012.
Gastfriend, Edward. *My Father's Testament: Memoir of a Jewish Teenager, 1938–1945*. Philadelphia: Temple University Press, 1999.
Hayes, Peter. *Why?: Explaining the Holocaust*. New York: W. W. Norton, 2017.
Junger, Sebastian. *Tribe: On Homecoming and Belonging*. New York: Twelve, 2016.
Kershaw, Alex. *The Liberator: One World War II Soldier's 500-Day Odyssey from the Beaches of Sicily to the Gates of Dachau*. New York: Crown, 2013.

SELECTED BIBLIOGRAPHY

———. *The Longest Winter: The Battle of the Bulge and the Epic Story of WWII's Most Decorated Platoon*. New York: Da Capo Press, 2005.

Klarsfeld, Serge. *Le Mémorial de la Deportation des Juif de France, Memorial to the Jews Deported from France, 1942–1944: Documentation of the Deportation of the Victims of the Final Solution in France*. New York: B. Klarsfeld Foundation, 1983.

Ossad, Steven L., and Don R. Marsh. *Major General Maurice Rose: World War II's Greatest Forgotten Commander*. Boulder, CO: Taylor Trade, 2006.

Rather, Dan, and Elliot Kirschner. *What Unites Us: Reflections on Patriotism*. Chapel Hill, NC: Algonquin Books, 2019.

Rosengarten, Israel J. *Survival: The Story of a Sixteen-Year-Old Jewish Boy*. Syracuse, NY: Syracuse University Press, 2000.

Rossel, Seymour. *The Holocaust: The World and the Jews, 1933–1945*. Millburn, NJ: Behrman House, 1992.

Silberberg, Sam. *From Hell to the Promised Land: A Boy's Daring Escape from a Nazi Concentration Camp*. Charleston, SC: CreateSpace, 2011.

Ullrich, Volker. *Hitler: Ascent, 1889–1939*. New York: Vintage, 2017.

Valantin, Jean-Pierre, and Nicolas Bertrand. *Der Todesmarsch der Häftlinge des Konzentrationslagers Langenstein-Zwieberge / La marche de la mort des détenus du camp de concentration de Langenstein-Zwieberge: Kartografie und Zeitzeugenberichte*. Saxony-Anhalt: Mitteldeutscher Verlag, 2018.

Weber, Louis. *The Holocaust Chronicle: A History in Words and Pictures*. Morton Grove, IL: Publications International, 2000.

Wiesel, Elie. *Night*. New York: Hill and Wang, 2006.

Wilson, George. *If You Survive: From Normandy to the Battle of the Bulge to the End of World War II, One American Officer's Riveting True Story*. New York: Ballantine Books, 1987.

Winter, George. *Freineux and Lamormenil, The Ardennes*. Winnipeg, Canada: J. J. Fedorowicz, 1994.

Woolner, Frank. *Spearhead in the West: The Third Armored Division, 1941–1945*. Nashville, TN: Battery Press, 1980.

Zaloga, Steven J. *Armored Thunderbolt: The U.S. Sherman in World War II*. Mechanicsburg, PA: Stackpole Books, 2008.

———. *Panther vs. Sherman, Battle of the Bulge, 1944*. Oxford, UK: Osprey, 2008.

———. *US Army Tank Crewman, 1941–45: European Theater of Operations, 1944–45*. Oxford, UK: Osprey, 2004.

INDEX

Note: Italicized page numbers indicate material in photographs or illustrations.

Abernathy, Private, 287
Adler, H. G., 209
Adolf Hitler Canal, 120
airborne forces, 284
air raids, 112, 121, 130–39, 141, 145, 159, 177–80, 285
alcohol, 155
Alpha Tau Omega, 86
Altenkirchen, Germany, *xii–xiii*, 205
Altersheim, 58
ambushes, 191, 203–4, 218, 222–23
"America First" movement, 50
American dream, 10
American Fat Salvage Committee, 64
American Legion, 50, 256–57
Amsterdam, Netherlands, 89
anti-aircraft, 133
antisemitism
    and Aryanization of Jewish businesses, 56–57
    and Hitler's rise to power, 23–28, 29–36
    and Hitler Youth, 182–83
    and Kristallnacht, 41–45
    in Nazi-occupied Poland, 120
    and rise of Nazism in Germany, 23–24
Antwerp, Belgium, 173
Appellplatz (roll call)
    at Blechhammer, 104–7, 128, 132, 141
    at Langenstein-Zwieberge, 198–99, 210–11
    prisoners marched from Poland to Germany, 181–82, 185
Ardennes Forest, 158, 167–75
Argentina, 246
Arlington National Cemetery, 289–90
Armstrong, Louis "Satchmo," 48
Arsenal of Democracy, 64
artillery, 174, 182, 184, 188, 217
Artistic Furniture Manufacturing Company, 64
Aryanism, 32–33, 56, 87
Auschwitz-Birkenau concentration camp, *xii–xiii*, 73, 77, 92, 97–107, 134, 138, 181, 278. *See also* Blechhammer camp
Australia, 94, 284
Austria, 47

INDEX

B-24 Liberators
  bombing raids on Blechhammer, 130–34, 159, 177–78
  Butch crew, 176, 178–79, 258
  and U.S. wartime manufacturing, 64
baseball, 10, 12, 39, 48–49, 84, 237, 249
basic training, 64–66
Bata shoe factory, 91
Battle of Stalingrad, 137
Battle of the Bulge, 167–75, 191, 285
Battle of the Bulge Association, 257
Battle of Vilnius, 16
Belgium, 56–59, 115–16, 137, 158, 167, 187, 266
Bergen-Belsen concentration camp, 245
Berlin, Germany, 39–40, 239–40
Bernburg, Germany, *xii–xiii,* 218
Bertrand, Jean-Louis, 289
Bertrand, Louis, 289
Bizjack, Private, 155
Black Americans, 50, 63, 254
Blechhammer camp
  Allied bombing raids on, 121, 130–34, 136–37, 141, 159, 177–80, 285
  and bomb disposal, 138–39
  executions of prisoners, 140–44
  information sources on, 289
  Langenstein compared to, 199
  living conditions at, 120–29, 159–61
  location, *xii–xiii*
  prisoners marched from Poland to Germany, *xii–xiii,* 181–85, 288
  and remains of Allied servicemen, 258
  sabotage by prisoners, 134–36
  and Siegfried's death, 161
  slave labor system at, 101–7
  survivor's return to, 278
  and war crimes trials, 244–45
Blechhammer North, 121, 124, 130, 141, 145, 181
Blechhammer South, 121, 130, 134, 181
Bleimeister, Conrad, 259
Blitz, 137, 284
Blue Mound Lutheran Church, 255
Blume, Corporal, 234

BMW, 91
Bolshevism, 24
bombing raids, 112, 121, 130–39, 141, 145, 159, 177–80, 285
Boston Braves, 39
Boston Red Sox, 10
boycotts, 32
Bradley, Omar, 243
Bradley Full Fashion Hosiery Mill, 256
Brandenburg Gate, 240
Brazil, 246
Britain and the United Kingdom
  and Allied liberation of concentration camps, 243
  British POWs, 124, 127, 145, 181
  casualties of war, 284
  and D-Day invasion, 94, 284
  and German Blitz, 137
Brooklyn, 84, 220, 231, 259
Brossmann, Otto, 105, 142, 143, 181, 245
Brussels, Belgium, *xii–xiii,* 56, 266
Buchenwald concentration camp, 185, 196–97, 243, 278. *See also* Langenstein-Zwieberge concentration camp
Bund Mädel League, 32–33
Butch (B-24 Liberator), 176, 178–79, 258

Canada, 94, 284
Canton de la Plaine d'Illibéris, 67
care packages, 145
Casillas, Arturo, 205–7, 276
casualties of war
  and air forces, 285
  and Allied assault at Cologne, 206, 207
  and Battle of the Bulge, 191
  D Company, 286–87
  and D-Day invasion, 284–85
  General Rose, 207–8
  German losses, 146
  military and civilian losses, 284
  and scale of Holocaust, 283, 287–89
  3rd Armored Division, 234, 286
Cathedral Square, 204
censorship, 27

350

INDEX

Chile, 246
Christianity, 31
Christmas celebrations, 176–78
Chrysler, 64
Church, Tom, 82, 191
Churchill, Winston, 61, 138
Clary, Robert (Widerman), 102
clergy targeted by Nazis, 287
Clow, Bernie, 220, 273
Cologne, Germany, xii–xiii, 203–5, 286
combat stress, 147–48, 230, 260
Combined Chiefs of Staff, 93
conspiracy theories, 22–23
contraband in prison camps, 127
Copland, Aaron, 48
Cradle of Liberty, 9
C-rations, 192–93, 223, 225
crematoriums, 105, 128, 140, 184, 197, 200
crimes against humanity, 243
Cuba, 44
Culin, Sergeant, 111
curfews, 34–35, 235
cyanide, 77, 240. *See also* Zyklon B
Czechoslovakia, 47

Daimler-Benz, 91
Daughters of the American Revolution, 49–50
"Dawn of a New Day" (1939 World's Fair), 47
D Company
   adoption of camp escapees, 222–31, 279–80
   Allied assault at Cologne, 203, 205–6
   Allied assault on the Siegfried Line, 146–52
   Battle of the Bulge, 167–75
   bonds between soldiers, 201–2
   casualties, 153, 258, 286
   D-Day invasion, 94–96
   demobilization after war, 247–48
   disbanding of, 253–54, 258
   discovery of camp escapees, 220–21
   downtime between battles, 153–58
   first combat actions, 108–19
   and Hovland's leadership, 187, 189–93
   letters from home, 155–56
   Myers's death, 206–8
   nicknames, 83–84
   offensive after Ardennes, 187–88
   and postwar occupation of Germany, 234–38
   progress through Europe, xii–xiii
   reunions, 258–63, 271–77
   transport to England, 71, 81–84
   and war crimes trials, 243
   and Willner's burial place, 290
   Willner's postwar search for, 264–70
D-Day invasion, xii–xiii, 93–96, 284–85
DeCola, Nicassio ("Pa")
   and Battle of the Bulge, 172
   correspondence with son, 156
   family background, 10–11
   and family's restaurant business, 39, 53–54, 116–17
   and son's military service, 70–71, 157
   and son's return from Europe, 255–56
DeCola, Sammy ("Pepsi")
   and advance into Belgium, 115–16
   and American cultural values, 48
   artillery strikes on food service unit, 188
   basic training, 65–66
   and Battle of the Bulge, 168
   and "Blue Eyes," 156–57
   burial place, 289
   connection with Willner family, 1, 279–82
   and D Company reunions, 259–60, 264, 270, 272, 275
   and D Company's adoption of camp escapees, 224–32, 237, 262–63
   and D-Day invasion, 95
   departure for Europe, 70–71, 82–83
   and disbanding of D Company, 248–49
   enlistment, 55, 62
   family background, 9–12, 38–39

INDEX

DeCola, Sammy ("Pepsi") (cont.)
  and family's restaurant business, 53–55
  and Great Depression, 46
  military food service, 86, 113, 116–17, 192, 193–94
  and nicknames of D Company members, 83–84, 264–65
  and postwar occupation of Germany, 235
  return home, 254–56
  and unit morale, 147–48, 153–55
Demerer, Karl, 98–100, 106, 127, 138, 143
Der Giftpilz (Streicher), 32
Der Stürmer (The Attacker), 27–28
Dessau, Germany, xii–xiii, 234, 288
Devecka, Laddie, 82, 189, 204, 259
DiMaggio, Joe, 84
Disabled American Veterans, 257
displaced persons camps, 223, 248–49
Dora-Mittelbau concentration camp, 196, 209
Downey, Jack, 112
Dragon's Teeth, xii–xiii, 146, 149, 152–53
Drancy, France, xii–xiii, 72, 288
Dr. Oetker food company, 91
"dud commandos," 138–39
Dutch Jews, 288

Earhart, Amelia, 37
École Moyenne de l'État, 58
Ehrenkreuz für Frontkämpfer (Iron Cross), 16, 57
Eichmann, Adolf, 73
8th Armored Division, 241
Eighth U.S. Air Force, 285
88mm guns, 133, 206, 232
82nd Airborne Division (U.S.), 284
83rd Infantry Division, 241
Eine River, 215
Einmannbunker, 135
Eisenhower, Dwight D., 93, 216, 243
Elbe River, 234
England. *See* Britain and the United Kingdom

enlistments, 61–62
executions, 88, 142–44, 168, 182–83, 242–43, 245
"The Eyes of the World Are Upon You" (Eisenhower), 93

Falatovich, Pete ("Fats"), 84, 220, 259, 273
Fascism, 27, 47–48
Federal Bureau of Investigation (FBI), 38
Fifteenth U.S. Air Force, 131, 179, 285
fighter bombers, 174
Final Solution, 77, 128, 240
fireside chats, 50–51
Flaming Guns (film), 122
food scarcity, 182, 192–94, 242
food service crews, 116–17, 188, 226–27, 229–30, 232
forced labor, 146. *See also* slave labor
Ford, Henry, 24
Ford Motor Company, 64
Fort Sill, Oklahoma, 65
"Four Freedoms Speech" (Roosevelt), 46
France, 69, 72, 93–96, 115, 137, 243, 244, 284–85
Francioh, Karl, 105, 245
Frank, Anne, 89, 93
Frank, Hans, 120
Free French commandos, 94
French partisans, 284–85
Freyneux, Belgium, xii–xiii, 171–73, 188, 257–59, 289
Fritz (Willner family's neighbor), 15, 57, 162, 177, 267, 269
Futurama pavilion, 47

Gardelegen, Germany, 209
gas chambers, 100, 106
Gastfriend, Edward, 97
gay people, 87, 287
Gehrig, Lou, 39, 84
General Motors, 47, 64
genocide, 25
"George the Greek," 84, 156–57, 220, 256, 259, 273

INDEX

German American Bund, 50
Germany
    and Aryan ideology, 39
    and Berlin Olympic Games, 39–40
    casualties of war, 284
    Gestapo forces, 27, 42, 57, 232
    and Hitler's rise to power, 21–28, 29–36
    and Kristallnacht, 41–45
    and liberation of concentration camps, 243
    nationalist sentiment, 22–23, 25–26, 41–45
    remilitarization, 31
    surrender of, 239
    U-boats, 81, 84
    and war crimes trials, 244–46
    See also Nazism and Nazi Party; *specific towns, cities, and camps*
Gershwin, George, 48
Gestapo, 27, 42, 57, 232
Gettysburg College, 86
Glenn Miller Orchestra, 48
glider aircraft, 284
Goebbels, Joseph, 177, 240
Goethe, Johann Wolfgang von, 161–62
Gold Beach, 94, 284
Golden Gate International Exposition, 47
Göring, Hermann, 43, 240
Grand Rabbi of Brussels, 59
Great Britain. *See* Britain and the United Kingdom
Great Depression, 5–6, 11, 21, 46
Greenberg, Hank, 39
Gross-Rosen, Poland, *xii–xiii*, 184–85, 288

Haag, Sergeant, 189, 259
Hager (pastor), 212
Halberstadt, Germany, 195, 212, 289
Hamilton (tank driver), 206
Hansen, Sergeant, 220, 222–23
Harris, Whitney, 239
Harz Mountains, 186, 195, 214, 241
hate speech, 24

Havana, Cuba, 44
Hayes, Peter, 26
Headrick, Bobbie, 156, 172
Headrick, Fred ("Redhead Fred"), 83–84, 86, 113, 114–15, 117
hedgerows, 108–9, 111–12, 259
Henri-Chappelle American Cemetery, 258
Herz, Hank ("Heinie Herz"), 84
high-explosive (HE) rounds, 110
Highways and Horizons (World's Fair pavilion), 47
Hilfstruppen guards, 90
Himmler, Heinrich, 142, 181, 209, 240
Hitler, Adolf
    and Allied liberation of concentration camps, 184
    and antisemitism in Germany, 23–28, 29–36, 56
    appointed chancellor, 26
    assassination plot, 138
    and Battle of the Bulge, 173–74
    and bombing raids on oil facilities, 180
    death, 239–40
    declaration of war against U.S., 61–62
    and final days of war, 202
    Final Solution, 77
    and German nationalism, 176–77
    and Nuremberg rally, 243
    rise to power, 21–25, 26–28
    and sabotage in labor camps, 135
    and Tom Mix, 123
    and totalitarian control in Germany, 87–88
    and Volkssturm units, 218
Hitler Youth, 32–33, 41, 62, 182–83, 209, 213
Hogan's Heroes, 102
Holiday, Billie, 48
Hollywood, 48
Holocaust, 76–77, 239, 254, 283
Holocaust awareness projects, 269
Hombourg, Belgium, 258
Horowitz, Anny Yolande, 73, 75–77

INDEX

Höss, Rudolf, 73
Hovland, Elmer LeRoy
  and Allied assault at Cologne,
    204–5, 207
  and Allied assault on the Siegfried
    Line, 147, 153
  and Allied intelligence gathering,
    232–33
  and Allied offensive after Ardennes,
    191–92
  and American cultural values, 48
  and Battle of the Bulge, 169–75
  birth of son, 188
  and bonds between soldiers, 201
  burial place, 289
  correspondence with Willner,
    278–79
  and D Company reunions, 259–62,
    275–77
  and D Company's adoption of camp
    escapees, 222–28
  and D Company's first engagements,
    112–14
  and D Company's transport to
    England, 70, 82
  and D-Day invasion, 95
  death of, 281
  and disbanding of D Company,
    248–49, 254
  discovery of camp escapees, 220
  downtime between battles,
    155–57, 158
  education and school activities, 38,
    51–52
  family background, 5–9, 12
  and Great Depression, 46
  leadership qualities, 38, 149–52,
    169–71, 261
  meeting future wife, 55, 63
  and morale of Company D, 117–19
  officer training, 65–66, 85–86
  and postwar life of Willner, 268
  and postwar occupation of
    Germany, 234–36
  promotions, 153, 189–91
  religious faith, 52, 95, 205, 261, 279
  return home after war, 255
  Silver Star award, 191
  and U.S.'s entry into war, 54–55
  and Willner's postwar search for
    Company D members,
    265–66, 270
Hovland, Harriet
  and Allied assault at Cologne,
    204–5
  birth of son, 188
  correspondence with Elmer, 156
  and D Company reunions, 260
  and D Company's adoption of camp
    escapees, 225
  and Elmer's departure for
    England, 85
  and Elmer's return home, 255
  marriage to Elmer, 70
  meeting Elmer, 55, 63
  and Willner's postwar search for
    Company D members, 265
Hovland, Mary, 5, 7, 38, 51–52, 255
Hovland, Nels, 5–7, 11, 38, 50–52, 255
Hughes, Howard, 37
hydrogenation chambers, 133, 136

IBM, 47, 91
identification patches, 101, 103, 185
I. G. Farben, 91
immigration to U.S.
  and American antisemitism, 50
  and American cultural values, 48
  and concentration camp survivors,
    247–48
  and DeCola family background,
    9–10
  and Great Depression, 46
  and Hovland family background,
    5–6, 8
  military service of immigrants, 82
  Polish immigrants, 113
  postwar life of Willner and Swaab,
    267–69
  and Statue of Liberty, 71

INDEX

improvisation in battle, 111–12
indoctrination of German society, 21
infrastructure projects in Germany, 31
integration of U.S. military, 254
intelligence failures, 171, 285
intelligence gathering, 233
The International Jew (Ford), 24
internet resources, 265
interpreters/translators, 232–33, 235–36
interrogation, 233
Iron Cross awards, 16, 57, 267
Italy, 137

Jackson, Robert H., 244
janteloven, 7
Japan, 55, 61
Japanese Americans, 63
Jehovah's Witnesses, 87, 287
The Jew Named Zuse (film), 31
"Jim Crow" laws, 50
Joint Distribution Committee, 56
Judenältester, 98, 106–7, 127. *See also* Demerer, Karl
Judenlager compound, 139
Jud Süß (film), 31
Juno Beach, 94, 284

kapos, 103–4, 137, 141–42
Kenneth, Minnesota, 5–6, 8, 11, 38, 50–52, 66, 70, 85
Klieger, Bernard, 195
Klipp, Kurt, 105, 107, 122, 141–42, 181–82, 185
Knight's Cross award, 174
Kochstedt, Germany, 229
kos, 7
Kosel, Poland, xii–xiii, 74–75
Köthen, Germany, 218
Kristallnacht, 41–45

Laird, Brady, 259
Lamormenil, Belgium, 168
Langanke, Fritz, 174, 175
Langenstein-Zwieberge concentration camp
   and Allied liberation of concentration camps, 241–42
   and evacuation of labor camps, 209–10
   and labor at Project Malachit, 196–99
   living conditions at, 195
   location of, xii–xiii
   murders of prisoners, 199–200
   and scale of Holocaust, 288–89
   survivor's return to, 278
   underground factories at, 195–96
   and war crimes trials, 245
   Willner and Swaab's escape from, 1–2, 213–21, 240
Languedoc region, France, 67, 68
Latin America, 246
Layton, Joe, 259
Łazy, Poland, xii–xiii, 88–92, 126
Leek family, 58–59, 266
Leinkenjost, Hermann, 245. *See also* "Tom Mix" (Blechhammer guard)
Levi, Primo, 97
Liège, Belgium, 116
Lindbergh, Charles, 50
Lindell, Arthur, 177–78, 258, 285
looting, 155, 202
Lübeck, Wilhelm, 197, 246
Lutheranism, 6
Luverne, Minnesota, 51, 70, 255, 289

M4 Sherman tanks
   and Allied assault at Cologne, 203, 206
   and Allied assault on the Siegfried Line, 148–50
   and Allied offensive after Ardennes, 188
   and American casualty rates, 286
   and Battle of the Bulge, 170–75
   and D Company's first engagements, 109–10, 111–15
   and German Volkssturm units, 218
   maintenance and mechanical issues, 118–19
   mobility advantage, 111–12

INDEX

M4 Sherman tanks (*cont.*)
    and organization of "Spearhead" Division, 66
    shortcomings and weaknesses, 109–10, 148
M26 Pershing tanks, 203
machine gunners, 206
Madison Square Garden, 50
mail service, 155–56
Malmedy, Belgium, 168
Mandel, Ben, 64
maneuver tactics, 111–12
Manhay, Belgium, 171–73
Marashinsky, Julius, 259–60
Marshall, George, 243
mass graves, 200
McDowell, Lieutenant/Captain (pseudonym)
    and Allied assault on the Siegfried Line, 148–50
    and Battle of the Bulge, 168–69
    and D Company's first engagements, 112–14
    downtime between battles, 158
    and food service in D Company, 116
    and Hovland's leadership, 117–18, 153–54, 189
McGovern, George, 133
Medal of Honor Museum, 257
Mein Kampf (Hitler), 25, 27, 30, 34
Messerschmitt fighters, 133, 196
Metrick, Bernard, 241
Military Officer magazine, 265
Military Order of the Purple Heart, 256–57
militias, 204, 218. *See also* Volkssturm units
mines, 65, 118, 147, 191
mobility in battle, 111–12, 147
Monarch Diner, 256
Mönchengladbach, Germany
    and antisemitic propaganda, 31–32, 35
    Aryanization of Jewish businesses, 56
    and Christmas during wartime, 177
    community before Nazism, 13–16
    information sources on, 287–88
    and Kristallnacht, 41–45
    location, *xii–xiii*
    and rise of Nazism in Germany, 29, 35
    Willner's flight from, 1–2
    Willner's return to, after war, 266–67, 269
Monks Gladbach monastery, 13
Mons, Belgium, *xii–xiii*, 116
Mont le Ban, Belgium, 188
Mulde River, 234
Muselmänner, 126, 199–200
Myers, Charles
    and Allied assault at Cologne, 203–6
    and Allied assault on the Siegfried Line, 147, 149–52, 153
    and Battle of the Bulge, 169–70, 171–75
    and bonds between soldiers, 202
    burial place, 258
    and D Company reunions, 259, 276
    and D Company's first engagements, 113–14
    downtime between battles, 155–57
    friendship with Hovland, 151–52
    and Hovland's leadership, 86, 190
    killed in action, 206–8
    and morale of D Company, 117–19
    promotion, 153
    and transfer of D Company members, 192
    and Vance in command, 188

Native Americans, 63
Nazism and Nazi Party
    and architecture of Final Solution, 128
    and Berlin Olympic Games, 39
    and German invasion of Belgium, 59
    and German nationalism, 176–77
    and Hitler's rise to power, 21–28
    pro-Nazi right-wing movement in U.S., 50
    and racism in America, 254
    and scale of Holocaust, 239, 283

INDEX

New Deal, 46–47
New Testament, 25
New York Fair, 47
Night (Wiesel), 133
Nordhausen, Germany, *xii–xiii*, 209
Normandy invasion, 93–96
Norse Glee Club, 255
North Africa, 137
Norway, 51
Norwegian immigrants, 5–7
Norwegian News, 7
Norwegians, 255
Nuremberg Laws, 34, 39
Nuremberg trials, 239, 243–44
Nurse Corps, 62

Ohrdruf subcamp, 243
Olympic Games, 39–40
Omaha Beach, *xii–xiii*, 94–96, 284–85
101st Airborne Division (U.S.), 284
Oppeln, Germany, 182
Ortaffa, France, 67–68, 139, 296
Ottmuth, Poland, 91–92
Our Two Democracies at Work, 207

P-51 fighters, 132
Paderborn, Germany, *xii–xiii*, 207–8
Palestine, 249
Panzerfausts, 203–5, 218, 222–23, 229, 232, 235
Panzer tanks, 110, 112–13, 171, 173–75, 203, 257, 259
Papadopulos, Michael, 176
Paris, France, 112, 115
Parker Brothers, 37
passports, 44
patriotism, 12, 34
Patton, George, 243
Pearl Harbor attack, 55, 61
Pepsi. *See* DeCola, Sammy
Pershing tanks, 203
Pichen, Ansgar, 105, 245
pogroms, 43
The Poisonous Mushroom (Streicher), 32

Poland, 47, 74, 181, 244, 283. *See also specific towns and camps*
Porsche/Volkswagen, 91
prisoners of war (POWs), 116, 123–24, 146, 148, 168, 181, 284, 286
progressivism in Germany, 14, 31
Project Malachit, 196–99, 245–46, 278
propaganda, 27–36, 39–40, 177, 243, 278
Pugliese, Sal, 82, 220, 259, 273
Purple Heart awards, 256–57
Pyrenees Mountains, 59, 67

Quedlinburg, Germany, 200

racism, 24, 62–63, 105, 254
rapes, 235
Red Army, 146, 235
Red Cross, 127, 145
refineries, 121, 130–32, 135–36, 159, 178–80, 285
refugees, 223
Reichstag, 26
religious services, 157
Revolutionary War (U.S.), 9
Rhapsody in Blue (Gershwin), 48
Rhine River, 205
The Rider of Death Valley (film), 122
Rivesaltes internment camp, 59–60
Rock County Star Herald, 255
Rodgers, Jimmie, 48
Roma people, 87, 287
Roosevelt, Eleanor, 50, 55
Roosevelt, Franklin Delano
    and American cultural values, 49, 81
    appointment of Eisenhower as SAC, 93
    death, 240
    declaration of war, 61
    fireside chats, 50–51
    Four Freedoms Speech, 46
    and immigration to U.S., 8
    meeting of Allied leaders, 138
    New Deal, 37, 46–47
    and wartime mobilization, 64
Ros (mayor of Ortaffa), 68

INDEX

Rose, Maurice, 113, 117, 151, 172, 202–3, 207–8, 286
Rothstein, Sylvester, 276, 287
Royal School for Boys, 58
Rundstedt, Gerd von, 180
Russia, 137, 181–84, 234–35
Ruth, Babe, 39, 49, 84

sabotage, 134–37, 142, 285
Saint Lô, France, *xii–xiii*, 112
Salisbury Plain, England, 84
Sandrad of Trier, 13
Scabbard and Blade military society, 86
Scanlon, "Bugle," 83–84
scapegoating of Jews, 24
Scenic Grill Restaurant, 256
Schaefer, Heinrich, 244
Schaerbeek, Belgium, 58
Schmelt organization, 88
Scholl, Sophie, 87
Schutzstaffel (SS) forces
    and Allied intelligence gathering, 232
    and Allied liberation of concentration camps, 241
    and architecture of Final Solution, 128
    and evacuation of labor camps, 209, 211–14
    and executions at Blechhammer, 144
    guards at Auschwitz, 97–103, 105–7
    and labor at Project Malachit, 196–99
    and living conditions at Blechhammer, 127
    prisoners marched from Poland to Germany, *xii–xiii*, 181–85
    2nd SS "Das Reich" Panzer Division, 173
    and *Selektion* at Buchenwald, 186
    and slave labor at Blechhammer, 122, 124
    and sorting of deportees, 74–75, 76
    SS Panzer units, 171
    Waffen SS units, 168, 245
    and war crimes trials, 244, 246
2nd SS "Das Reich" Panzer Division, 173

segregation, 50, 254
Seine River, 115
Selektion (selection of slave laborers), 106–7, 185–86, 198
7th SS *Totenkopf Wach* Death's Head Battalion, 105, 121
"Shaky" (D Company member), 147, 151, 259
Sherman tanks. *See* M4 Sherman tanks
Siegfried Line, 146–53, 286
Siemens, 91
Signal Crest United Methodist Church, 257
Silver Star awards, 255, 263
Sinti people, 287
slave labor, 88–91, 101, 120–22, 146, 186, 195–96, 198
Smieja ("Smeegee"), 84, 259
Smith, Carl ("Big Smith"), 83, 276, 287
Smith, Howard K., 241
Smith, Prescott, 82
Smith, Sam ("Little Smith"), 83
smoke pots, 135
smuggling, 127
SNCF rail company, 72
snipers, 107, 204, 229
Soviet Union
    advance into Germany, 181–84
    and Battle of Stalingrad, 137
    casualties of war, 284
    German attack of, 61
    and liberation of concentration camps, 184
    occupation of Berlin, 239
    and scale of Holocaust, 283
    and war crimes trials, 243–44, 246
Spain, 59
Spearhead in the West (Woolner), 216
Speer, Albert, 180
Spielberg, Steven, 269
SS. *See* Schutzstaffel (SS) forces
Stadelheim Prison, 88
Stalin, Joseph, 61, 138
Stars and Stripes, 265
Steiner, John, 21
"Stille Nacht" ("Silent Night"), 176–77

INDEX

St. Isidore Church, 172–74
MS *St. Louis*, 44
Stockholm Declaration, 239
Stolberg, Germany, *xii–xiii*, 153, 155
Stubbins, Private, 202
"stumbling stones," 278
Sturmabteilung (SA), 24, 41–42, 57
submarine warfare, 81, 84
suicides, 199
Supreme Allied Commander, 93
Swaab, Maurits ("Mike")
   arrival at Auschwitz, 97–98, 100–101
   and bombing raids on Blechhammer, 130–32
   burial place, 289
   and D Company reunions, 261–62, 272, 276–77
   D Company's adoption of, 223–26, 229–33
   and disbanding of D Company, 247–49, 253
   and Eddie's head wound, 139–41
   escape from Germans, 213–21
   escape from Langenstein, 240
   and evacuation of labor camps, 210–11
   and executions at Blechhammer, 143–44
   and labor at Project Malachit, 196–99
   at Łazy, 89–92
   and legacy of war, 280
   life after war, 267–69
   and living conditions at Blechhammer, 127, 159–61
   and murders of Langenstein prisoners, 199–200
   and postwar occupation of Germany, 236–37
   prisoners marched from Poland to Germany, 181–82
   progress through Europe, *xii–xiii*
   and sabotage in labor camps, 135–37
   and scale of the Holocaust, 254, 287–89
   and *Selektion* at Buchenwald, 185–86
   service in U.S. military, 268
   and Siegfried's death, 161–62
   slave labor at Blechhammer, 102–4, 106–7, 120, 123–25
   and SS guards at Blechhammer, 122–23
   and war crimes trials, 243
   and Willner's postwar search for D Company members, 264, 270
swastika symbol, 27, 33
Sword Beach, 94

Tablets of the Missing, 258
tanker training, 65
tattoos, 102
Technicolor motion pictures, 48
Temple, Shirley, 48
"ten-in-one" packaged meals, 116
Thanksgiving celebrations, 157
Thayer, Stuart, 108, 146, 187, 253, 259, 274, 286
Theresienstadt ghetto, 58
3rd Armored Division Veterans Association, 265
3rd Armored "Spearhead" Division
   and Allied assault at Cologne, 203
   and Allied assault on the Siegfried Line, 146, 152
   and American casualty rates, 286
   battle insignia, 273
   and Battle of the Bulge, 168
   casualty rate, 234
   D Company assigned to, 66
   and D Company reunions, 271
   and D Company's adoption of camp escapees, 237
   and D-Day invasion, 94–96
   departure for England, 70
   first combat actions, 108
   and German counterattack in Ardennes, 158
   and liberation of Paris, 115
   and postwar occupation of Germany, 234

INDEX

3rd Armored "Spearhead" Division (*cont.*)
   and prison camp refugees, 223
   transport to England, 81–82
   unit patch, 82
   and Willner's postwar search for D Company members, 265–66
   See also 32nd Armored Regiment, 3rd Armored Division
32nd Armored Regiment, 3rd Armored Division, 66, 81, 237, 253, 265–66, 271, 274. *See also* D Company
"Tom Mix" (Blechhammer guard)
   and Allied bombing raids on Blechhammer, 132, 136–37
   and daily life at Blechhammer, 122–23
   executions of prisoners, 141–44
   prisoners marched from Poland to Germany, 182–83, 185
   sadism of, 128–29
   and slave labor at Blechhammer, 106–7
   and war crimes trials, 245
Transport 31, 73, 76, 288
travel restrictions, 43, 44, 248
trophies of war, 202
Truman, Harry S., 240, 254
Tscheu, Paul, 198, 209–10, 246
Tuskegee Airmen, 132

U-boats, 81, 84
underground factories, 196
United States Holocaust Memorial Museum, 269
University of Munich, 87
Upper Silesia Oberschlesische Hydrierwerke, 121
U.S. Air Force, 285
U.S. Army, 62, 171, 232, 236
U.S. Army Air Corps, 62
U.S. Army Rangers, 285
U.S. Association of War Veterans, 43
U.S. Congress, 61
USC Shoah Foundation, 269
U.S. Holocaust Memorial Museum, 287
U.S. Marine Corps, 62
U.S. Navy, 62
Utah Beach, 94

V-1 and V-2 rockets, 196, 209, 246, 284
Vance, James ("Baby Face")
   and Allied assault at Cologne, 205–8
   and Allied assault on the Siegfried Line, 147, 152–53
   arrival in England, 86
   and Battle of the Bulge, 171–75, 191
   and bonds between soldiers, 201
   burial place, 289
   and D Company reunions, 259–60, 273–74, 276
   and D Company's adoption of camp escapees, 237
   and D Company's first engagements, 113, 114–17
   death of, 281
   and disbanding of D Company, 248
   discovery of camp escapees, 220
   downtime between battles, 155
   nicknames of D Company soldiers, 84
   promotion, 188
   Purple Heart awards, 257
   and Willner's postwar search for D Company members, 265
Venice Film Festival, 31
Venosa Airfield, 177
Vernichtung durch Arbeit ("extermination through labor"), 196
Versailles Treaty, 21, 22
Veterans of Foreign Wars, 257, 265
Veterans of the Battle of the Bulge, 265
Vichy regime, 69, 72
Vienna Convention, 168
Vietnam War, 257
Villiers-Fossard, France, *xii–xiii*, 108–9
Volkssturm units, 204, 209, 213, 216–17, 233
Von Braun, Wernher, 246

Waffen SS units, 168, 245
Walk of Honor Tour (Arlington National Cemetery), 290

INDEX

Wallwitzhafen, Germany, 229
Waltham, Massachusetts, 1, 9, 11, 38, 53, 156, 255–56, 279, 289
war crimes trials, 243–45
Warsaw, Poland, 146
wartime mobilization, 61–64
Washington, George, 50
The Washington Post, 271–72
Wehrmacht, 104–5
Wehrmacht guards, 90
Weiße Rose (White Rose) resistance group, 87–88
Welbsleben, Germany, *xii–xiii*, 213
Westinghouse, 47
West Point (U.S. Military Academy), 85
"We Were Your Neighbors" (Willner), 269
Why? (Hayes), 26
Widerman, Robert, 102
Wiesel, Elie, 72, 102, 133
Willner, Albert, 279
Willner, Auguste
    and Berlin Olympic Games, 40
    family background in Mönchengladbach, 14, 16–17
    and flight of Jews from Germany, 56–59
    and Kristallnacht, 43–45
    murdered by Nazis, 77
    and rise of Nazism in Germany, 23, 32, 35
    on the run in France, 67, 68
    and scale of Holocaust, 288
    and sorting of deportees, 74–76
Willner, Eddie
    and Allied liberation of concentration camps, 184
    arrival at Auschwitz, 97–98, 100–101
    and bombing raids on Blechhammer, 130–32
    burial place, 289–90
    correspondence with Hovland, 278–79
    and D Company reunions, 261–62, 271–77
    D Company's adoption of, 222–26, 229–33
    death of, 281
    deported to slave labor camp, 72–75
    and disbanding of D Company, 247–49, 253
    and escape attempts, 129
    escape from Germany, 2, 57–58
    escape from Langenstein, 213–21, 240
    and evacuation of labor camps, 210–11
    and executions at Blechhammer, 143–44
    family background, 13–15
    and labor camp at Langenstein, 196–99
    at Łazy, 88–92
    and legacy of war, 280
    and living conditions at Blechhammer, 127, 144–45, 159–63
    and living conditions at Langenstein, 195
    and murders of Langenstein prisoners, 199–200
    and postwar occupation of Germany, 235–37
    postwar search for D Company members, 264–70
    prisoners marched from Poland to Germany, 181–82
    progress through Europe, *xii–xiii*
    and rise of German antisemitism, 31–33
    and rise of Nazism in Germany, 23
    on the run in France, 68
    and sabotage in labor camps, 135–37
    and scale of Holocaust, 254, 287–88
    and *Selektion* at Buchenwald, 185–86
    service in U.S. military, 268–69
    shot by prison guard, 139–41
    slave labor at Blechhammer, 101–7, 120–25
    and war crimes trials, 243
Willner, Hanna, 266, 268–70, 276

INDEX

Willner, Josef, 15, 17–18, 32, 42, 58, 162, 266–67
Willner, Michael, 281–82
Willner, Siegfried
   arrival at Auschwitz, 97–98, 100–01
   and Berlin Olympic Games, 40
   and bombing raids on Blechhammer, 130–31
   deported to slave labor camp, 73–75
   and executions at Blechhammer, 138–41, 143–44
   family background, 14–20
   and flight of Jews from Germany, 56–60
   and food scarcity in labor camps, 199
   illness and death, 161–62
   Iron Cross award, 16, 57, 267
   and Kristallnacht, 41, 43–45
   at Łazy, 88–92
   and living conditions at Blechhammer, 144–45, 159–61
   and rise of German antisemitism, 32, 35
   and rise of Nazism in Germany, 23
   on the run in France, 68–69
   and sabotage in labor camps, 135
   and scale of Holocaust, 288
   and service in World War I, 16
   and slave labor at Blechhammer, 103–4, 106–7, 120, 125–28
   and SS guards at Blechhammer, 122–23
Willner family, 160, 177
Women Accepted for Volunteer Emergency Service (WAVES), 62
Women's Airforce Service Pilots (WASPs), 62
Women's Army Corps (WACs), 62
work gangs, 104–5. *See also* slave labor
Works Progress Administration (WPA), 37
World's Fair (1939, Queens, New York), 47
World War I, 16, 21–23, 41, 44

xenophobia, 35

Yiddish, 99, 159
Yom Kippur, 141
Young, Claude, 82, 110, 276

Zierler, Kenneth, 241
Zwieberge. *See* Langenstein-Zwieberge concentration camp
Zyklon B, 77, 91

ABOUT THE AUTHOR

Nina Willner is the author of *Forty Autumns* and *The Boys in the Light*. Prior to her writing career, Nina was a U.S. Army intelligence officer who served in Berlin during the Cold War. Following her career in intelligence, Nina worked in Moscow, Minsk, Prague, Ottawa, and Istanbul promoting human rights, children's causes, and the rule of law for the U.S. government, nonprofits, and a variety of charities. After years of living abroad, she has settled in Washington, DC. Her father, Eddie Willner, survived the Holocaust, and this is his story.